Women, Madness and Medicine

Women, Madness and Medicine

Denise Russell

Polity Press

Copyright © Denise Russell 1995

The right of Denise Russell to be identified as author of this work has been asserted in accordance with the Copyright, Designs and Patents Act 1988.

First published in 1995 by Polity Press
in association with Blackwell Publishers.

Editorial office:
Polity Press
65 Bridge Street
Cambridge CB2 1UR, UK

Marketing and production:
Blackwell Publishers
108 Cowley Road
Oxford OX4 1JF, UK

238 Main Street
Cambridge, MA 02142, USA

ISBN 0 7456 1260 1
ISBN 0 7456 1261 X (pbk)

A CIP catalogue record for this book is available from the British Library and the Library of Congress.

Typeset in 10½ on 12 pt Palatino by Best-set Typesetter Ltd., Hong Kong
Printed in Great Britain by T. J. Press, Padstow, Cornwall

This book is printed on acid-free paper.

*For Judi Chamberlin and Jan Easgate, friends and survivors,
and in memory of Lena Barclay and Margaret Ellis*

Contents

Acknowledgements

I would like to acknowledge with gratitude research support from the Beatrice Bain Research Centre at the University of California, Berkeley, and the University of Sydney Research Grants Scheme. I have also appreciated the assistance of my colleagues in the Department of General Philosophy, University of Sydney, in making it possible for me to take extended leave. My mother, Glad Russell, and my late father, Bern Russell, I thank for their emotional and material nurture. I am indebted to Alex Johnson, Karin Lines and Joanna Castle for invaluable library searches. Danielle Frances, Natalie Pelham and Eleanor McEwan provided excellent clerical assistance. The members of PALA, an ex-psychiatric patients group, and the students in the Department of General Philosophy kept this project alive by their enthusiastic reception and critical feedback. I particularly want to thank the graduate students Louise Gyler, Kerry Sanders, Glynis Johns, Janette Mychalen and Celia Roberts. Several scholars provided encouragement, notably Jane Caputi, Moira Gatens, Leon Kamin and Ralph Hall. An anonymous reader and Rebecca Harkin from Polity provided useful comments on early drafts. Paul Feyerabend's writings nourished my interest in philosophy. My partner, Hal Pratt, his children Wolgan and Halcyon, and my special friends Penny Coleing and San MacColl kept me alive. Tinka, Sally and the wild birds in my garden provided necessary diversions.

Introduction

The focus of this book is on biological psychiatry, which is the loose grouping of theories and practices postulating a distinction between madness, mental illness or disorder on the one side, and sanity or normality on the other. The position is sometimes also referred to as medical psychiatry. Within this perspective there is a guiding assumption that the causes of mental illness or disorder are biological and that the treatments should be in that realm. I do not discuss psychoanalysis except for one important historical episode, Freud's change of mind on hysteria, and the contemporary views of Luce Irigaray, which are goldmines for insights on women. The great diversity of psychological theories and practices are not considered apart from the position of Phyllis Chesler, which is in any case closer to a philosophical account than a psychological one. Biological psychiatry is the dominant form of psychiatry in the Western world. Its influence spreads far beyond actual treatment. It informs our ways of conceptualizing most forms of human distress and eccentricity. It is pervaded with an aura of certainty which makes challenges difficult.

Women are also central to the discussion this book. It is women more than men who directly encounter biological psychiatry in treatment. Also the message of this approach reaches more women than men, for example, through a greater willingness to discuss personal problems with others. Thus the background influence of the psychiatric view of human existence is likely to be stronger than with men. Biological psychiatry has, on balance, produced more harm than good – an audacious statement perhaps, but one I firmly believe. Also given women's greater involvement with the field it is they who have suffered the most. My belief in the harmful nature of psychiatry has motivated the writing of this book. However, the argument is less on explicitly moral grounds and more on the point that psychiatry is on the wrong track. Others have detailed the harms, for example, Peter Breggin's *Toxic Psychiatry*,[1] and the many first-person accounts of psychiatric treatment such as those by Shelagh Supeene[2] and Kate Millett.[3]

My angle of approach is epistemological in that I am concerned to undercover claims to knowledge, grounds for knowledge and methods for acquiring knowledge. My conclusion is that biological psychiatry is a degenerating research programme and that it is time to look in completely new directions if we want to understand mental distress. I consider the writings of Phyllis Chesler, Luce Irigaray, Virginia Woolf and Janet Frame as providing insights to such a direction, though the position I develop cannot be directly attributed to any of these authors. I do not deny the reality of human distress but I do question the usefulness or desirability of categorization. Also I believe that we need to go beyond the individual in seeking explanations of this distress.

To challenge the way of looking at certain phenomena is to invite terminological difficulties. To write about medical psychiatry's view of mental illness seems to imply that mental illness does exist. I want to resist that implication. Of course there are many people who are desperately unhappy, some who hear voices that others don't hear, etc. But is it appropriate or desirable to regard such people as 'ill'? This is one of the central questions of the book. When talking about phenomena that psychiatry claims are mental illnesses, I have made use of broad descriptive terms such as 'madness' or 'mental distress'. They are deliberately vague, not carrying a definite theoretical commitment, as the idea is to throw into question how we should regard extreme unhappiness, socially condemned behaviour and so on. Another related objective is to ask whether there is a division between sanity and madness. I conclude by arguing that there may be advantages in breaking this down.

Not many authors bring together the topics of psychiatry and women, but there are some excellent books which fill out various aspects of the argument below. For example, Yannick Ripa's *Women and Madness: The Incarceration of Women in Nineteenth-Century France*[4] and *For Her Own Good: 150 Years of the Experts' Advice to Women* by Barbara Ehrenreich and Deirdre English[5] detail the historical aspects of the link between women and psychiatry. Elaine Showalter moves the discussion almost up to the present day in *The Female*

Malady: Women, Madness and English Culture, 1830–1980.[6] Phyllis Chesler in *Women and Madness*[7] and Jane Ussher in *Women's Madness*[8] engage with a broad range of contemporary issues relating to women as psychiatric subjects.

1 History of the Relationship between Women and Psychiatry

Before the eighteenth century there were diverse views in Western culture about madness, with only occasional links to medicine. Even when doctors were involved in treatment, this usually had a non-medical character; for example, the Roman doctor Caelius Aurelianus advised that assistance given to the mad should be geared to their particular interests. Thus 'farmers should be engaged in conversation about the soil, sailors about the seas and illiterates about elementary topics. . . . And for intellectuals, disputations of philosophers were highly regarded.' A medieval doctor, Alexander of Trailles, recommended trickery to restore sanity. In one report he made 'a patient wear a leaden hat to "cure" him of the nihilistic delusion that he had no head'.[1] Until the eighteenth century, when psychiatry as a medical specialty looking at problems of the mind began to emerge, there was no consistent, widely accepted set of beliefs and practices within medicine concerning madness.

In the Europe of the Middle Ages and through into the sixteenth century, one collection of beliefs and practices connected madness to religion. The mad were thought to be possessed by the Devil or other evil spirits, and they acquired special knowledge and powers through possession. This was forbidden, evil knowledge, as it emanated from the Devil, and this forbidden element gave madness a certain fascination. Forbidden wisdom and access to 'the other world' were unattainable by the sane; madness was something fantastic yet inhuman and unnatural.[2] The mad were often expelled from villages and towns and left to wander the countryside or sometimes taken on board boats by friendly sailors. Assistance was given by saints or in the names of saints. Walter Scott refers to this in 'Marmion':

> Thence to Saint Fillan's blessed well
> Whose spring can frenzied dreams dispel
> And the crazed brain restore . . .[3]

St Dympna had a special role. She was a seventh-century martyr who fled from Ireland to Gheel in Belgium to escape the incestuous desire of her father – a theme which will recur below. She was pursued by him and he struck off her head in his fury at her rejection. 'According to the legend, several of the "lunatics" who observed these terrible events were shocked into sanity.'[4] She then became the protectress of the mad, and positive changes were attributed to her intercession.[5]

By the end of the fourteenth century a link was forged in European popular imagination between the mad, heretics (those who rejected dominant beliefs, especially dominant religious beliefs), magicians, sorcerers, women who as midwives assisted at the delivery of stillborn infants, alchemists and astrologers. These people were grouped together, as they were all thought to be possessed by evil spirits, and their works were regarded as works of the Devil. This grouping in the imagination was to serve as the basis of widespread persecution in the witch hunts of the fifteenth and sixteenth centuries. These persecutions affected thousands of men, women and children, but women suffered the most. Apparently it was believed that women, among all those possessed, were a greater source of evil.[6] In the seventeenth century, forces opposing the witch hunts from within the law, medicine and religion gained ground. In a certain sense witches ceased to exist, not because they had all been burnt, but because the conception under which some people could be so perceived had changed. If it is not thought possible for the Devil to take control of humans, then there can be no witches.

Another notion of madness gained popularity in the Renaissance and developed alongside the above ideas. This linked madness and folly, divorced it from any religious connotation and applauded the mad as moral satirists. Folly involved a type of immorality but a human weakness not indicating the hand of the Devil. Folly is a moral failing with a positive side. It mocks the constraints of reason and in so doing brings pleasure. According to Erasmus' *The Praise of Folly*, when folly speaks, she declares that 'it is from my influence alone that the whole universe receives her ferment of mirth and jollity.'[7] Under this conception there is no clear distinction between the mad and the sane. There is no imperative for a special form of treatment or social isolation.

This gentler understanding of madness lost out to the influence of the ideas grouping the mad with other social outcasts all accused of serious immorality. During the mid-seventeenth century, economic crises and rising unemployment throughout Europe brought in a new era. In France repressive institutions of detention were set up to curb the consequent dissatisfaction and agitation. The mad were herded into these institutions along with beggars, drunks, vagabonds, other poor people and petty criminals. Foucault argues that similar institutions existed or were set up in England, Holland, Germany, Italy and Spain[8] and that a new conception of madness arose which was linked to this social practice.[9]

The detention centres operated throughout Europe on a massive scale from the mid-seventeenth century to the end of the eighteenth century, a time called the 'Classical Age'. The inmates fell under a general categorization, not as mad or criminal, but as 'unreasonable'. The category has now fallen into disuse, but at the time it served as a description to cover actions, thoughts or states of living that 'went against reason'. Madness was only one such state. Unreasonable ways of life were thought to be freely chosen and immoral, with the failing of sloth figuring prominently.

Towards the end of the eighteenth century in France, economic conditions were such that more people could be absorbed into the workforce. Industry was growing and needed more workers. This led to pressure to release the inmates of the confinement houses such as Salpêtrière and Bicêtre in Paris – at least those who were able and willing to work. Foucault argues that there were changing ideas about poverty. It was no longer regarded as a personal responsibility.[10] In earlier times merely being poor could be a basis for one's detention in a confinement house, but in the late eighteenth century this ceased to serve as a rationale. However, refusal to work still operated as a ground for confinement.[11]

Also during this time there were protests about the detention of the mad with the other prisoners. Some thought that the sane detainees deserved a better fate.[12] This operated as another rationale for the release of many of those who had been confined. According to Foucault,[13] when disease spread through some of the French towns during this period, the confinement houses and their inmates were thought in some vague way to be responsible. Just as the image of disease and contamination had been associated with leprosy and leper houses centuries before, now this image became associated with the confined and the confinement houses.

Foucault claims that the disease image that was associated with the confinement houses provided doctors with an entrance ticket. Yet the doctors did not enter these institutions in a strictly medical capacity, nor was the disease image a strictly medical one. Rather the disease was considered as a type of moral corruption and the doctors acted as moral guardians, not bringing about a medical cure, but working on the source of evil to prevent its spread throughout the city.

Although many people were released from the institutions into the workforce, detention of the mad continued. In the nineteenth century public asylums were set up in Europe and the United States usually under the control of doctors. Why was it doctors who headed these institutions? And why did doctors become the appropriate experts to turn to for help with problems of madness outside the institutions?

The medical interest in madness at this time cannot be explained by some new theoretical breakthrough which made it clear that madness should be regarded as a medical problem, divorced from the earlier associations. Nor were there new empirical discoveries that pointed to this conclusion. Rather doctors started to enter the field in significant numbers and then tried to develop theories and empirical results to justify the move. Several factors seem to have been important in explaining the medical takeover, and their relative weight varied in the different European countries and the United States. The weakening power of the Church and the rise in the importance of science meant that a more scientific and less theological understanding of madness was desired. In the nineteenth century there were moves to improve medical education and put it on a more scientific footing. A further point, stressed by the modern feminist writers Barbara Ehrenreich and Deirdre English, is that the cultural framework of the time was one which equated science with goodness and morality.[14]

Medical practitioners were also concerned about their social status. A nineteenth-century English doctor commented that the clergy and lawyers were regarded as equal to the gentry but that only some doctors had this status.[15] Another consideration was the oversupply of doctors, at least in England[16] and the United States.[17] The conceptualization and treatment of madness would have presented itself as a new area for the evolving medical science. It provided a fertile ground for theorization and experimentation, and in the private sector it secured a good income.

There were moves to develop classification schemes to give a rationale for segregating the mad from the sane and placing the former in asylums. Doctors had had a long history of developing such schemes for physical medicine. So it would have seemed appropriate that they develop classifications for mental medicine also.

Many of the forms of madness isolated in the nineteenth century could loosely be called 'women's complaints', which in previous centuries were commonly dealt with by female healers. However, as an aftermath of the witch hunts, these healers were discredited – another factor opening up the sphere to male doctors.

When doctors entered the field a new conception of madness developed but there was not a complete break with the past. Throughout the Classical Age, madness was regarded as a mixture of error and sin: the mad went against reason and, in addition, breached the moral norms. In European thought from the late eighteenth century on, the mad were no longer held to be responsible for their state of madness and ceased to be viewed as going against reason, as falling into some sort of error. Madness is now understood more as a disturbance of feeling and less as a disturbance of thought. The feelings are inappropriate, abnormal or immoral.

During this time the mad were no longer regarded as responsible for their state of madness, but they were subjected to moral condemnation if they refused to recognize their state or if they did not control the signs of their madness and so disturbed the rest of society.

In the nineteenth-century medical beliefs the unity of body and soul (mind) is broken down. This dualism of body and mind is mirrored in the different treatments advocated. In the Classical Age, cures for madness related to the whole person, even though these may appear to us to be merely physical or merely mental. Thus, for example, the consumption of bitters was thought to purify the soul as well as the body, and a theatrical or musical presentation to a mad person was thought to influence the soul and the body by its effect on the movement of the animal spirits. Under the new line of belief, cures that work solely on the mind were thought to be possible, for example, surveillance and punishment.

The acceptance of a mind/body dualism gave rise to a conceptual mess which still plagues psychiatry. The problem arises if we want an explanation of the cause of mental events. If mental events are caused by physical events and minds and bodies are different substances, then how can there be causal interaction? Similarly, if it is posited that mental events can cause physical events, for example, 'psychosomatic illnesses', how is this possible if the mind is a different sort of stuff from the body?

If it is claimed that mental events cause mental events then the problem about moving between different sorts of substances is evaded, but the relationship between both these sets of mental events and the body is often deemed to be a puzzle. Another problem for nineteenth-century thought would have been the suggestion that the mind is diseased, for if it is diseased then it can die, and this does not fit in well with theological views about an after-life.[18] Finally and probably most importantly, if madness is caused by the mind, then it is not so obviously a medical problem.

Nineteenth-century psychiatrists tried different theoretical paths but most preferred to posit a material cause of madness. The American psychiatrist Benjamin Rush gave a lecture in 1786 entitled 'An enquiry into the influence of physical causes upon the moral faculty'. This was perhaps the first clear statement from a doctor of the acceptance of a body/mind dualism such that physical changes cause mental changes. For Rush, the mind was made up of the moral faculty and the intellectual faculty, but in this lecture he was concerned only with the former. The lecture reads like an announcement that medicine has taken over this new field, that psychiatry is born.[19] It is no surprise, then, that Rush's portrait is on the seal of the American Psychiatric Association. What is surprising is the quagmire he gets into over the mind/body problem. He thought that madness was caused by an irregular action of the arteries of the brain brought on by physical causes, which are listed as climate, diet, alcohol, idleness, solitude, etc.[20] A rather odd grouping of the physical? Furthermore, the eloquence of the pulpit is said to have a curative effect on madness, healing a physical problem by its mechanical effect on morals (the mind).[21]

Henry Maudsley, a very influential nineteenth-century English psychiatrist, posited an inherited predisposition as the most important cause of insanity, and he regarded it as bodily disease.[22] He asserted, without evidence, that 'the fault is a derangement of mental functions owing to their extremely fine, complex, and intricate nervous substrata', and acknowledged as a central problem that it is difficult to get 'a clear and exact idea what mind means'.[23] At odds with his central thesis, he claimed that 'if insanity is increasing among civilised people this is due to pleasures: idleness, luxury and self indulgence not to pains.'[24]

The French psychiatrist Georget stressed the importance of non-physical causes of insanity. 'In his view, 95 per cent of cases of madness were moral in origin.'[25] It was the immorality of leading an intemperate life that was supposed to be the root of the problem. Esquirol, a very influential French psychiatrist, also defended the notion that madness has a psychological basis. Two other key French psychiatrists, Pinel and Charcot, posited an organic base, in line with nineteenth-century developments in German psychiatry. Griesinger was representative of the latter, believing that mental diseases were diseases of the brain. The Germans went a step further than the French organic theorists, actually equating the mind and the brain. Psychiatry was regarded as the same field as neuropathology. This evaded the mind/body problem, but while empirical results were (and are) lacking the justification for the position is rather questionable. Freud was an influential defender of the view that madness has psychological causes, but he wanted to divorce psychiatry (psychoanalysis) from a necessary link with medicine.

Women encounter psychiatry

By the mid-nineteenth century in England there was a predominance of women in public mental hospitals, and by the end of the century there were more women than men in the private mental hospitals also. There were also more women than men in private psychiatric care. Thus, as Showalter notes, 'by the end of the century, women had decisively taken the lead as psychaitric patients, a lead they have retained ever since, and in ever-increasing numbers.'[26] This trend was followed on the Continent[27] and in the United States.[28] Why did such a close relation develop between women and psychiatry? In order to answer this question it is important to look at the evolving ideas in public and private psychiatry, but these should be set against the changing social conditions and the narrowing views on a woman's role.

In early nineteenth-century England there occurred a large growth of industry in the cities and industrial villages. The proportion of town dwellers rose sharply and so did urban poverty. Scull makes the point that this is insufficient to explain the development of psychiatric institutions, however, as in the United States these developed about the same time without the same move to the cities.[29] He contends that a better explanation would highlight 'the effects of the advent of a mature capitalist market economy and the associated ever more thorough-going commercialization of existence'. The market system broke down the urban and rural social structure, and led to 'the abandonment of long-established techniques for coping with the poor and troublesome'.[30] This fits quite well with Ripa's analysis concerning France at the time: population movements to the cities, the collapse of community life and the growing fears by the protectors of bourgeois society about the urban poor lay behind the association of dangerousness and madness. It also prompted the development of the psychiatric institutions.[31]

The United States experienced rapid industrialization during this period, with a broad division developing between the affluent and the working class. The political structure, especially the role of the states, differed from those in Europe, and this led to differences in the welfare system. Some states put more effort into setting up almshouses – lodgings for the indigent and for those incapable of taking care of themselves – than mental hospitals. Guided by the belief which seemed to have been generally abandoned in Europe, that the poor were depraved and responsible for their depravity, these almshouses were quite openly institutions of correction.[32] Even when mental hospitals were set up, they were not clearly separated from almshouses and prisons.[33]

A look at the changing social conditions goes some way towards explaining why psychiatry developed when it did, but the points mentioned above do not explain why women as psychiatric patients became so closely linked with the profession. The exodus from the country to the city was primarily a male exodus, but it still broke up family units, and poor women living alone could fall into a life of vagrancy, a ground for committal in nineteenth-century France,[34] or be single mothers, a ground for committal at that time in England.[35] Showalter comments further on the English scene: poor women may have been labelled insane for the authorities to avoid paying them a dole: 'Poor Law administrators were increasingly reluctant throughout the century to grant outdoor relief ("a weekly subsistence dole upon which they could support themselves") to women deserted by their husbands, wives of prisoners, able-bodied widows with a single child, or mothers of illegitimate children.'[36] Geoffrey Best points out that, as the percentage of Poor Law expenditure for outdoor relief declined, the expenditure for the maintenance of the inmates of asylums increased, especially towards the end of the nineteenth century.[37] Showalter also claims that asylum populations included many women unable to care for themselves because of physical disorders.[38] It would be reasonable to conjecture that disabled men might be more likely to be kept in the home and be cared for by women.

These considerations still do not take us far enough to explain the development of the profession and women's link with it, but another aspect of the social context seems to have been crucially important. I have already mentioned that in this era medicine was taking over from religion as a social force. Religion for centuries had adopted the role of moral arbiter. As the nineteenth century progressed medical discourse attempted to turn many moral categories into medical ones. What in the past had been wrong came to be seen as diseased or unhealthy. In particular, medicine appropriated the social right to pass judgement about sexuality. It was women more than men who were associated with sexuality, embodying it, having too much of it (especially if they were from the lower class), rebelling against it, or disturbing men with it. When female sexuality got out of line, psychiatry could be brought in as a corrective force by either incarceration in an asylum, 'rest cures' in private mental institutions or intimidation in private consultations.

The role that the nineteenth-century Western woman was supposed to play was a very narrow one indeed. Apart from keeping her sexuality in check by getting married and having children (some doctors argued that celibacy led to insanity), she was cautioned not to venture too far into other pursuits for fear that they might affect her reproductive functioning. Maudsley, for instance, argued that intellectual activity in women diverted blood to the brain which would otherwise have succoured the reproductive organs.[39] These views were sexism in the guise of medicine and they had an enormous impact. Women who tried to develop their creativity came in for psychiatric censure. (The story of Charlotte Gilman Perkins will be mentioned in Chapter 7. She was a writer who was encouraged to take a rest cure to dispel her creative urges.) Women who tried to engage in political activity ran the risk of committal to a psychiatric institution,[40] and women who pressed for greater educational opportunities found that doctors were leading the debate against them – claiming that the risk of insanity was too great. At this point it is clear that a link has been made between women and psychiatrists as moral guardians. The latter are needed by the patriarchal culture to keep women within their narrow role boundaries.

Finally, the medical view of women's health regarded her reproductive functions as pathological: menstruation, pregnancy and menopause were all looked upon as diseases.[41] Yet it was the reproductive function that defined woman's nature. As one nineteenth-century doctor remarked, 'It seemed as if the Almighty, in creating the female sex, had taken the uterus and built a woman around it.'[42]

This gives us an explanation of the link between women and sickness. Psychiatrists then conjectured that mental illness was caused by aspects of women's reproductive functioning. This tightened the net. A supposedly scientific rationale had been found for why so many women became mad and why so many women needed the help of psychiatrists.

Psychiatrists and asylums

The moral guardianship role that medicine usurped from religion can be clearly seen in the development of the nineteenth-century asylums. It was the French who led the asylum movement so I will concentrate on the situation in France. Firstly, although the asylums were usually run by doctors and viewed as medical institutions, the basis for committal as defined in law was blatantly moral, centring around the notion of dangerousness or relating to social misfits. Some laws included 'those whose freedom is harmful to society',[43] the young who disobey their parents and refuse to work, single mothers,[44] vagrant women, women of low intelligence, old people,[45] women who led a debauched life, had loose morals or were prone to vice,[46] 'people who fantasized that they were someone else'[47] and 'women who had consciously or unconsciously entered the sphere of politics'.[48] Even 'going dancing, drinking too much ... and promiscuity' were sometimes reasons for committal.[49]

Although the law laid down committal criteria, it was up to doctors to decide who should be detained, released, released into the care of their families, cared for in hospitals, etc. Those released had to exercise extreme caution, as municipal bodies were given a legal right to take care of 'obviating and remedying the disagreeable events that may be occasioned by madmen set at liberty, and by the wandering of vicious and dangerous animals'.[50] Philippe Pinel, regarded as 'the founder of psychiatry in France',[51] gave a lecture to the Society for Natural History in Paris in 1794 revealing the incredible ignorance of the medical profession about madness. Pinel was director of Bicêtre and Salpêtrière, two of the largest asylums in France for different periods in the late eighteenth and early nineteenth centuries. He claimed that there was no accumulated knowledge to draw on either in understanding what was wrong with the mad or in their management. He chose to focus on the latter and claimed that only the English had achieved some success in management, but that 'that haughty and self-righteous nation' would not release their secret.[52]

Pinel was probably referring to the work of William Tuke, a quaker in charge of The Retreat, an asylum near York which was founded two years before Pinel's lecture. Tuke was not a doctor but his views were very influential. In this asylum Tuke used religion as a principle of coercion in treatment. He tried to get the mad to accept religious principles as part of their cure. The patients at The Retreat were not kept in chains and on the surface were given liberty, but in fact a widespead system of constraints was in operation. Tuke stressed the need to work on the mind in attempting to bring about a cure of madness:

> If we adopt the opinion that the disease originates in the mind applications made immediately to it, are obviously the most natural, the most likely to attend with success. If on the contrary, we conceive that mind is incapable of injury or destruction, and that in all cases of apparent mental derangement, some bodily disease, though unseen and unknown, really exists we shall still readily admit, from the reciprocal action of the two parts of our system upon each other, that the greatest attention is necessary, to whatever is calculated to affect the mind.[53]

Note how he hedges his bets on what mental illness is, another indication that there was no developed medical theory at the time. Tuke thought that most of the mad were able to exercise self-control, given some encouragement, and that it was through self-control that cures could be effected. Work and performance of certain rituals were regarded as key ways to build up self-control. For example:

> There were social occasions in the English manner, where everyone was obliged to imitate all the formal requirements of social existence; nothing else circulated except the observation that would spy out any incongruity, any disorder, any awkwardness where madness might betray itself. The directors and staff of the Retreat thus regularly invited several patients to 'tea parties'; the guests 'dress in their best clothes, and vie with each other in politeness and propriety. The best fare is provided, and the visitors are treated with all the attention of strangers. The evening

generally passes with the greatest harmony and enjoyment. It rarely happens that any unpleasant circumstance occurs; the patients control, to a wonderful degree, their different propensities; and the scene is at once curious and affectingly gratifying.'[54]

Pinel laid down his own ideas about the management of the mad in his 1794 lecture. He moved away much more slowly from the old violent imprisonment model than Tuke, perhaps because he was attempting to reform Bicêtre, an old confinement house, rather than start anew. Pinel still saw a use for chains, and suggested only a moderate increase in starvation rations. Also he didn't place the same weight on religion as Tuke: Pinel was more inclined to see it as a source of madness than a cure. However, in other respects there were similarities: both advocated a type of moral management. Pinel stated that 'one of the fundamental principles of the conduct one must adopt toward the insane is an intelligent mixture of affability and firmness. When they are obstinate one must sound totally superior and unshakable so as to convince them to bow to the will of the directors.'[55] It may be necessary to use a 'thundering voice' and threaten with the harshest measures. 'One of the major principles of the psychologic management of the insane is to break their will in a skillfully timed manner without causing wounds or imposing hard labor.'[56]

In 1801 Pinel published *A Treatise on Insanity* which had an enormous influence in France, England and the United States. Castel claims that Pinel's methods were used by US legislators as a basis for reformulating mental health policy in the mid-nineteenth century.[57] In the treatise Pinel dismissed the usefulness of any medical techniques developed up to that time in dealing with the mad. Instead he gave all importance to 'physical and moral regimen'.[58] In the section of the treatise on cures, he gives 'first place to the duties of a humane and enlightened superintendency and the maintenance of order, in the services of hospitals'.[59] He advocates 'intimidation, without severity, . . . oppression, without violence, and . . . triumph, without outrage'.[60]

The cure for madness did not consist in correcting error. He noted in his Memoir: 'Errors of reasoning are much rarer among madmen than is commonly thought'[61] – but rather in the control of certain emotions and feelings that had somehow got off-course. This control was brought about by opposing and balancing the passions. Patients were given liberty within the asylums, as Pinel thought that it was possible to regulate their passions. He had great 'faith in man's powers of emotional self-discipline and control'.[62] Madness appeared to be incurable simply because the mad had been treated the wrong way. With the new moral treatment, hopes for cures ran high.

In the asylums under Pinel, the values of the family and work were dominant, but the work that the mad were given did not have a productive value. The intention was to instil a certain morality. The asylum represented the outside social morality: the values of the family were dominant and the mad were treated like children, the doctors as father-figures. Aspects of the moral treatment of the mad pointed out by Foucault included 1) silence: a refusal to listen to ravings no matter how eloquent; 2) enforced self-reflection: various attempts to get the mad to recognize that they are mad; and 3) perpetual judgement. Some physical measures were used too, for example, harsh showers as punishment for those who would not work. There was an attempt to block rebellion in thought as well as in deed.[63] As Pinel states, 'the madman is made to understand that it is for his sake and reluctantly that we resort to such violent measures; sometimes we add a joke, taking care not to go too far with it.'[64] When self-control takes over, the punishment can stop.

Some of the mad refused to recognize their guilt, so the cures were not entirely effective. There were three major areas where the cures had little effect: where the mad were religious fanatics, where they showed resistance to work and where they indulged in theft. As Foucault notes, these are 'the three great transgressions against bourgeois society, the three major offences against its essential values'.[65] The mad who violated these norms were a great social threat and they were often simply imprisoned, sometimes in dungeons or special confinement houses set up for them, without the 'benefits' of moral treatment.

Although Pinel and Tuke are regarded by some as humanitarian liberators of the insane, and certainly tried to present themselves in that light, many contemporary writers challenge that judgement, claiming that the moral restraints were in fact more confining than the previous physical constraints. Foucault writes that

> Reason's victory over unreason was once assured only by material force, and in a sort of real combat. Now the combat was always decided beforehand, unreason's defeat inscribed in advance in the concrete situation where madman and the man of reason meet. The absence of constraint in the nineteenth-century asylum is not unreason liberated but madness long since mastered.[66]

And Ripa claims that there was an 'astonishing similarity between imprisonment in the Bastille and committal to an asylum'.[67]

There is dispute, then, concerning whether the early psychiatrists were really carrying out reforms. There was another major disagreement at the time and this was over whether the asylum doctors were practising medicine when they engaged in moral management. Some of the asylum doctors insisted that moral management was different from medicine even if it was carried out by doctors. James Monro, a physician to Bethlem, a large asylum in England, commented on the value of medicine in the treatment of the mad to a parliamentary committee in 1815 as follows:

> With respect to the means used, I really do not depend a vast deal upon medicine; I do not think medicine is the sheet-anchor; it is more by management that patients are cured than by medicine, in my opinion. If I am obliged to make that public I must do so.[68]

Similarly, Hill, the resident medical officer at Lincoln Asylum in England in the early nineteenth century, explicity denied that medicine had any part to play in the treatment of the insane unless they were also suffering from a physical disease: 'Moral treatment with a view to induce habits of self-control, is all and everything.'[69]

There were also doctors outside the asylums who did not want to acknowledge that moral management was a medical treatment, and they asserted the value of the medical approach used for non-psychiatric medical complaints, chiefly pharmaceuticals – an approach which did not have acknowledged efficacy in treating the mad, while it seemed that moral management had some success.

The doctors were sometimes successful in revealing transgressions and bringing the mad back to a moral path. This success led patients to believe that the doctors did have a special power to understand and cure madness. The problem seemed to be that it was only by bringing traditional remedies into the field of mental illness that the doctors could be seen as appropriately there. An alternative move could have been to conceptualize moral management as a genuine medical therapy, and this is in fact what happened. Aided by the fact that there were no strong competitors to take over the field at the time, promoters of moral management first began to medicalize the language in speaking about the mad, using terms such as 'patient', 'mental illness' and 'moral treatment'. Then followed a great proliferation of classification schemes, a phenomenon which led the composer Berlioz to comment: 'After their studies have been completed a rhetorician writes a tragedy and a psychiatrist a classification.'[70] Outside the asylums psychiatrists also started to develop theories which purportedly justified bringing the phenomena of madness into the medical domain. Morality was not absent from this theorization, though it was usually more covert than guidelines for moral management – a trend which has stayed with psychiatry to the present day.[71]

Nineteenth-century psychiatric theories of female madness

Psychiatry began at the end of the eighteenth century from within the field of medicine. It was not the same as previous medicine or later physical medicine as it dealt specifically with mental illness. However, psychiatry had strategic reasons for assuming physical causes of mental illnesses, as mentioned above. The psychiarists had no established methods for observing mental illness and no special tools to 'dissect' the mind.[72] Nevertheless, classifications developed rapidly. What is it that these early psychiatrists were classifying? The great variety of schemes suggest that these illnesses were rather illusive. Also there was no agreement of how to classify; for instance, some thought it was best to do it by symptoms, others by causes. There were severe problems with both. If causes were merely assumed, how reliable could such classifications be? Also, if causes were unknown, then arbitrary decisions would, at least to some extent, enter into the make-up of the symptom list. The continuous arguments over classification schemes reflected these problems. Nevertheless, from the late eighteenth century psychiatrists started to refer to specifically female mental problems as if there had been a new medical discovery. It is important to note the moral language used in these descriptions when reflecting on what these psychiatrists were classifying.

It is also clear that they were discussing middle- and upper-class women. It is as if working-class women did not exist, even though the population of poor women in public institutions grew rapidly in the nineteenth century. If we look at some of the writings of the major figures in nineteenth-century psychiatry we begin to get an idea of the nature of early psychiatric thought and practice, which reveals a great deal about the views on women, female sexuality and psychiatric classification.

Benjamin Rush attempted to outline the 'peculiarities of the male and female body and mind' in a lecture of that title given in 1791. Speaking about women's bodies, he said: 'their sedentary lives . . . favour obstructions everywhere'[73] and their minds are by nature inferior to male minds in understanding, memory, judgement and reasoning. They do have quicker perceptions than men, but animal perceptions are even quicker. Rush attributed to women a more acute and sensible moral faculty than men and he thought that they had superior taste, delicacy and modesty.[74] In his 1786 lecture already referred to, Rush talks of hysteria as a vice but says that it cannot be attacked with morality – only with medicine.[75]

The British physician Robert Brudenell Carter defined hysteria as 'a disease which commences with a convulsive paroxysm . . . a short attack of laughing or sobbing . . . [or] energetic involuntary movements, . . . occasionally terminating in coma'.[76] He claimed to differ from the psychiatric fashion in the mid-nineteenth century in that he believed hysteria had an emotional rather than a constitutional origin. He noted that no one had located a constitutional origin at that stage, and his theory about an emotional cause could explain why more women suffered from hysteria than men. He thought that women were more emotional than men and that in particular they had a stronger sexual desire which they had to keep under constraint. It was the sexual emotions in particular that were most important in the production of the disease.[77]

Maudsley claimed that hysteria was a physical disorder which could take many forms. He said that some hysterial women were morally perverted and rather inconsistently accused them of malingering. He wrote about young women believing or pretending that they cannot stand or walk, who lie down, sometimes for months receiving sympathy when their only paralysis is paralysis of the will which an opportune lover could cure.[78] He said that the women acted the way they did for an audience, but he didn't believe they were entirely wilful impostors. Rather, 'the dominating morbid notion in the loose-knit brain, . . . has suspended the remaining thought-tracts . . . she is governed by the disintegrate will . . . when she recovers she has no shame.' The moral tone of this description is backed up by his references to subtle deceit, fraud, and ingenious lying of hysterical patients. Yet this sort of hysteria was supposed to be caused by 'the action of the reproductive organs on an unstable nervous system'.[79] The vacillation between the medical and the moral is capped by his claim that hysteria is sometimes cured by marriage.

Maudsley promoted the view that menstruation, pregnancy, childbirth and menopause were important causes of mental derangement. Menstruation in all women is supposed to give rise to mental instability which may lead on to acute mania. Pregnancy gives rise to melancholia and sometimes moral perversion, perhaps an uncontrollable craving for stimulants. Childbirth may cause mania or melancholia. The problem that arises with menopause is that 'the age of pleasing is past, but not always the desire'. Menopause may result, then, in insane jealousy and a propensity to stimulants.[80]

Andrew Wynter's book *The Borderland of Insanity*, published in 1875, contained a claim which amounted to a further extension of the base for misogynistic thinking within psychiatry. He asserted that insanity is usually inherited from the mother. He pointed out that some physicians insisted that this line of transmission was twice as likely as that from the father.[81] He had no evidence for this position.

There were other influential doctors around this time who were suggesting horrific physical cures for women's disorders. For instance, Gustav Braun recommended amputation of the clitoris for vaginismus, a condition characterized by an irritable vagina. He thought that it could be caused 'by mental and moral impressions. Under the influence of a salacious imagination, which is stimulated by obscene conversations or by reading poorly selected novels, the uterus develops a hyperexcitability which leads to masturbation and its dire consequences.'[82] Young girls, newlyweds who remain abstinent for some time and widows were all at risk of getting this disease. It was thought to be possible to detect who the masturbators were because they were supposed to be prone to excessive blushing.[83] Braun's German article was translated into two languages and cited in texts.[84] The same operations were performed by the English surgeon Baker Brown in an attempt to cure hysteria, which he thought was caused by masturbation.[85]

In an 1880 article James Israel mentioned that removal of the ovaries and amputation of the cervix had been used to attempt to cure hysteria. He reported his study where he only pretended to a patient that he was removing her ovaries and yet she was cured. He urged the medical profession to be sceptical about saying the cause of hysteria was an illness of the sexual organs.[86] The patient later consulted Dr Alfred Hegar, who claimed that she wasn't cured but her problem wasn't hysteria.[87] Hegar was the professor of gynaecology at the University of Freiburg when he began the practice of castration for hysteria, which killed several of his first patients.[88] Nevertheless the operation was enthusiastically supported by Paul Flechsig, who had considerable influence as director of a large, prestigious university department and clinic of psychiatry at the University of Leipzig. In discussing one such operation Flechsig noted that the patient was not told the nature of it. 'We deliberately avoided upsetting her with any discussion of the subject.'[89] Also, when her symptoms didn't disappear after the operation, he con-cluded not that it had been unsuccessful but that her symptoms were deliberate. Flechsig gives a description of an incision of the clitoris as a cure for hysteria and says that one operation proves the success of the method.[90] Note the appalling scientific methodology here. An operation is proved successful no matter what the out-come. Another operation is proved worthwhile on the basis of one trial. Masson argues that these views were 'not just fringe medicine and that they had a destructive, long-lasting influence on European and American attitudes towards women and their sexuality.'[91] He believes that we are slowly emancipating ourselves from these prejudices. Perhaps he has not seen the 1992 article in the *British Medical Journal* entitled 'Are breasts redundant organs?' where Dr James Drife, professor of obstetrics and gynaecology at Leeds, ar-gues for the removal of normal breasts so that breast cancer won't develop. He claims 'our feelings about breasts are far from logical ... rationally, prophylactic mastectomy involves nothing more than excising a redundant gland and a pad of fat'![92]

Returning to other nineteenth-century influences in psychiatry: the emphasis on the external appearance was taken up again in Charcot's views on hysteria. He used the term to describe people who had paralysis with no apparant organic base, or people who had convulsive seizures or extravagant gestures. Showalter de-scribes how Charcot's female patients were surrounded by images of female hysteria. Lithographs and paintings were hung on the wall of his hospital, Salpêtrière, and a great many photographs were taken of the patients.[93] The photographs and their titles suggested a link between hysteria and sexuality, but Charcot wanted to main-tain that, as he crudely put it, 'some female hysterics are ovarian, some not'.[94] He opposed abstractions and claimed that he merely described what he saw. This was most definitely not the case in a lecture he gave in 1888, which is often referred to as his classic lecture on hysteria.[95] Here the patient was brought out in front of a group of doctors and prodded under her breasts until she had what looked like an epileptic fit. The patient called out in fear, 'Mother, I am frightened.' Charcot's response was to address the doctors with: 'Note the emotional outburst', and after a further expression of fear he said: 'Note these screams. You could say it is a lot of noise over nothing. True epilepsy is much more serious and also much more quiet.'[96] This scene tells us a great deal about acceptable doctor–patient relations and it also makes a lie of the claim that Charcot was only a passive observer. It is as if he ordered his assistant to push a button to make the patient move.

Showalter mentions that many at the time claimed that these hysterical displays had been set up, that the patients were merely following suggestions, or that it was straight fraud.[97] Charcot responded to this sort of criticism in the lecture cited above: 'What a marvel this would be if I could, in fact, fabricate illnesses according to my whims or fantasies. But in fact all I am is a photographer. I describe what I see.'[98] He was either a liar or confused, or both, but at least he didn't advocate cutting out sexual organs.

Nor did Freud, but he left a legacy causing a different sort of harm. He was the first psychiatrist to make widely known the extent to which women have been abused as children, and then he developed an elaborate theoretical perspective which I believe has had the effect of silencing women's voices about child abuse. This was such a significant move in the developing ideas about women and madness that it is worthy of detailed consideration: Freud and Breuer published *Studies on Hysteria* in 1895. It is a shift away from the visual representation of madness towards a more developed conceptual account, and the stories, memories and dreams of the patients are recorded. 'Hysteria' is still only vaguely defined as paralysis of various kinds, certain attacks and convulsions, tics, chronic vomiting, anorexia, disturbances of vision and visual hallucinations. In the studies, Freud and Breuer claimed that 'external events determine the pathology of hysteria to an extent far greater than is known and recognized.'[99] These external events have constituted a trauma in the patient's life, usually in childhood. In a letter to his friend and medical colleague Wilhelm Fliess, Freud said in 1895 that 'hysteria is a consequence of a presexual sexual shock . . . "Presexual" means actually before puberty, before the release of sexual substances; the relevant events become effective only as memories.' Or, as he claimed in the studies: 'hysterics mainly suffer from reminiscences.'[100] Freud and Breuer wrote that the traumas are not usually discovered by a simple questioning of the patient. They maintained that the patient may not like to discuss this experience or may be genuinely unable to recollect it. They used hypnosis to uncover the link and claimed that, if the patient could then recall the event with feeling, the hysteria would immediately and permanently disappear.[101] The basic problem, then, is that there has been a sexual trauma but no appropriate reaction to it at the time. 'An injury that has been repaid if only in words is recollected quite differently from one that has had to be accepted.'[102]

Freud developed this position further in a paper the following year called 'The aetiology of hysteria', especially on the nature of the initiating trauma. He concluded: 'Whatever case and whatever symptom we take as our point of departure, in the end we infallibly come to the field of sexual experience.'[103] He claimed that this held true in every instance of hysteria that he had treated and said that perhaps the twentieth century will show that it is only true 80 per cent of the time – but he doesn't think so. The sexual experiences implicated in hysteria are important ones in childhood – sexual experiences affecting the subject's own body such as child abuse, usually by an adult but sometimes by another child. Freud thought that children can become abusers if they have themselves been abused.

Freud dispels doubts about the reality of infantile sexual abuse as the causes of hysteria in seven arguments, including the fact that all his hysterical patients were producing common stories (but they weren't known to one another); the patient's history fits together like a picture puzzle if the initial sexual trauma does exist, and when the trauma is uncovered the patient gets better. There is another factor that isn't noted in the article but could have influenced Freud. He worked for some time in the Paris morgue and saw children who had died of physical abuse.

Given the lengths that Freud went to here to prove the reality of a sexual trauma in hysteria, it is astounding that he later overturned his theory. He said that he came to believe that the patients had been lying to him or that they were describing sexual fantasies. In a letter to Fliess in 1897 Freud listed reasons for changing his mind, including 'the surprise that in all cases, the *father*, not excluding my own, had to be accused of being perverse – the realization of the unexpected frequency of hysteria, with precisely the same conditions prevailing in each, whereas surely such widespread perversions against children are not very probable.'[104] Jeffrey Masson in *The Assault on Truth* points out that Freud had been rejected by the medical community for his ideas on hysteria. In Freud's letters he talks of his isolation. Giving up these views allowed him to participate in the medical community again. His closest friend, Fliess, may have been very unreceptive to Freud's early views because Fliess's son believed his father had sexually molested him (though this did not surface until much later). Of course Freud could simply have decided that he was wrong, but what about all the arguments he gave to establish he was right? He does not answer his own case. Masson's personal position is also of interest. He has had a hostile reception in the psychoanalytic community for making very clear that the change occurred and for his speculations about why. His papers and books are not seriously discussed. He lost his position as curator of the Freud Archives.

This item in the story of the relationship between women and psychiatry is enormously important. Briefly, if Freud's later theories of hysteria are correct, then the social criticism that was in his earlier account is defused. The problem of hysteria is located within the individual patient, not in anything external to her. If hysteria is the result of sexual trauma then the basic fault lies in the aggressor. Of course the victim may need help of one sort or another, but preventative strategies should also be embarked on so that other girls don't suffer from this abuse. I will return to the issue of child abuse in Chapters 2 and 8.

Another influential psychiatrist of the late nineteenth and early twentieth century was Emil Kraepelin. In his authoritative textbook on psychiatry published in 1907 hysteria is defined as a neurosis in which mental states produce manifold physical symptoms with extraordinary ease and facility. He asserts that hysteria develops upon a morbid constitutional base and that there is defective hereditary in 70 to 80 per cent of cases.[105] Neither of these assertions have any empirical backing, as Kraepelin admits on the next page, 'the true nature of the disease is still unknown.' Kraepelin also lists neurasthenia or chronic nervous exhaustion, which is characterized by diminished power of attention, distractibility and tiredness. This is supposed to be more common in women because of their weaker powers of resistance and their greater emotional irritability. It is particularly common in 'overburdened mothers, teachers and nurses'.[106] It would be natural to think that it was the overtaxing work that was the primary problem, and indeed Kraepelin's recommendations for cures are along these lines. He says that they should consist in a changed routine, a trip to the mountains, a sea voyage, removal to a quiet, restful, attractive place or perhaps enforced bed rest with massages and baths, all of which would no doubt sound wonderful to the tired worker. However, the aim of these therapies is 'to get the woman to understand the conditions leading to her breakdown and to inculcate the correct principles of living and working'.[107] The idea is that she has to gain in emotional strength so that she is better able to meet the demands of motherhood or other work. There is no suggestion that perhaps the jobs are too demanding. Also Kraepelin's descriptions of these patients often takes on a tone of moral condemnation. He says that the women sufferers have no appreciation of the burden which they create by becoming ill; they have a keen insight into their condition and tend to exaggerate their symptoms, and they can soon pull themselves together if they are relieved of work or if they have jolly company.[108]

With this brief historical survey of the developing ideas and practices within nineteenth-century psychiatry, we can ask again why did such a close link develop between psychiatry and women? The first point to note is that the categories of mental illness were very poorly defined, and it would have been relatively easy for women consciously to adopt the role of a mentally sick person. Would there be any reason for them to do so? For women working in positions that demanded hard and unpleasant labour the prospect of some chance to rest, perhaps even to have a change of scenery, would have been a great temptation. But most women in such labour would not be offered that sort of cure. They would be risking incarceration in an institution if they were declared insane. The former could have been offered to middle-class women diagnosed as 'hysterics', and perhaps some women did pretend that they had this 'illness' because of the monotony of their enforced idle existence or to get attention. However, even for such women this would have been dangerous as, at the very least, they risked the moral condemnation of the care givers. We have to look elsewhere to find why the link between women and psychiatry arose. Only a small minority would have chosen the role of a mental illness.

There were a number of ideas about the importance of women's reproductive functioning in the causation of madness, but these ideas were unsubtantiated. (In Chapter 3 I will discuss the current views and their scientific standing.) Why would the medical profession in the nineteenth century have been so keen to defend dogmatically a biological base to women's madness? Two clear answers seem to emerge: firstly, to legitimize the entry of medicine into the new field of psychiatry and, secondly, to further the moral guardianship role that medicine had taken on: medicine could act to curtail the protests of women about the constraints of the female role, as those protests were reconceptualized as mental symptoms of underlying physical pathology.

It might be objected that this is far too cynical a view, as medical cures sometimes worked. However, a non-medical explanation is possible. It is easy to understand why 'moral management' might work. It could be very effective in dulling the protest. Similarly the cutting out and cauterizing of sexual organs (or the mere threat of this) could result in changed behaviour, as such procedures could be viewed as straight punishment. This is not to say that women had no problems with their role before the nineteenth century, but it seems that the role did become more restricted at that time. Also before the nineteenth century violations were more likely to be seen as morally reprehensible, even evil, but not so commonly mad.

A large part of the explanation for the link that developed between women and psychiatry can be attributed, then, to the advantages this gave to the developing discipline of psychiatry.

There would of course have been women who were not simply rebels but who were distressed because they had been physically abused, because they found their options too narrow, etc., and the distress might have taken many different forms. Although this is an important area to look into, there was a clear reluctance in nineteenth-century psychiatry to delve into those issues. Nevertheless, such women probably turned to psychiatrists for help in the absence of any other alternative.

Is the present situation a little less bleak?

2 Modern Psychiatric Perspectives on Women

Psychiatric diagnosis and the interests of women

As a first step in understanding modern psychiatric perspectives on women it is important to look at psychiatric diagnosis, as this is the starting point for research and theorization. I will focus on the third revised edition of *Diagnostic and Statistical Manual of Mental Disorders* (1987; DSM-III-R),[1] which is a scheme devised by the American Psychiatric Association and widely used in the Western world. In particular I want to show that the basic concept of psychiatric diagnosis and some of the conceptual distinctions in particular categorizations give rise to problems which will be of particular concern to women.[2]

In this section I highlight the way in which particular behaviour or experience is viewed rather than how it is caused. This is an important distinction, for if there isn't even agreement about how to characterize particular disorders then debates about causes cannot get off the ground. There are three key problems with the DSM-III-R: the first relates to the conceptual foundations, the second the certain subjective features, and the third to the narrowness of focus.

Problems with the conceptual foundations of the DSM-III-R

The DSM-III-R emanates from the American Psychiatric Association and, as such, is firmly embedded in the medical psychiatric tradition. It is therefore very interesting to note that there is an attempt to avoid talking about 'mental illness'. This no longer forms the basic concept of the system of diagnosis. The notion of mental illness is replaced, not entirely consistently,[3] with the notion of 'mental disorder'. This shift is perhaps a reflection of the long-standing failure of psychiatry to answer the conceptual challenge posed by the anti-psychiatrists,[4] or it may amount to a broadening of the conceptual foundation incorporating more phenomena under the domain of psychiatry, possibly to meet the emerging interest in previously 'sub-threshold patients'. The shift in the basic conceptual framework occurred first in the DSM-III, and in that scheme there was an expansion into new areas. For example, the developmental disorders not explainable by mental retardation were expanded into 'developmental reading disorder' and 'developmental language disorder'. The DSM-III-R includes further expansion of these categories. The latter now becomes 'developmental expressive language disorder' or 'developmental receptive language disorder'. While there may be objection to calling such difficulties 'mental illnesses', there may be less resistance to regarding them as 'mental disorders'. The conceptual shift makes it easier to accept the expansion. A similar point applies to the contentious new diagnosis 'late luteal phase dysphoric disorder' (or premenstrual syndrome). Also it is no doubt easier to view a 'sub-threshold' patient as on the verge of a disorder than on the verge of an illness.

For whatever reason, it is the notion of 'mental disorder' which forms the crucial underpinning of the structure of psychiatric diagnosis in the DSM-III-R, and

> [a mental disorder] is conceptualized as a clinically significant behavioral or psychological syndrome or pattern that occurs in a person and that is associated with present distress (a painful symptom) or disability (impairment in one or more important areas of functioning) or with a significantly increased risk of suffering death, pain, disability, or an important loss of freedom.[5]

This definition appears so clear-cut and medical, how could it possibly disadvantage women? The trouble is that beneath its crystal-clear appearance lies a nest of value judgements, and, if one does not happen to share the same values, different decisions will be reached about whether a mental disorder exists or not. I will focus on two aspects of the definition to illustrate this point: distress and disability.

'Distress' is defined as a painful symptom. A 'symptom' is defined in the DSM-III-R as a manifestation of a pathological condition.[6] Yet for most of the DSM-III-R disorders it is acknowledged that the etiology is unknown.[7] If the etiology is unknown, then the pathological condition has not been isolated and is, as yet, a mere conjecture. If there is uncertainty about the pathological conditions which are supposed to give rise to symptoms, then there will be consequent uncertainty about the symptoms. The judgement that something is a symptom must remain tentative until some underlying pathological condition is substantiated. Since in most cases no underlying pathological condition is substantiated, the declaration that aspects of thinking or behaving referred to can be regarded as *symptoms* must be treated with caution. The authors want to avoid the vexing problem of etiology, but they run the risk of conceptual incoherence in their talk of symptoms. It does not make sense to talk of symptoms in the absence of even conjectures about what the symptoms are symptoms of. The authors claim that, when a mental disorder exists, there is an inference that there is a behavioural, psychological or biological dysfunction[8] but no justification is offered for this inference. Rather, it is undercut by the claim that, 'for most of the DSM-III-R disorders . . . the etiology is unknown.'

It could be countered that, for at least some physical disorders, such as AIDS and multiple sclerosis, the etiology is unknown yet the symptoms are real or present. For mental disorders, too, the symptoms may be real and debilitating even though there is no clear-cut agreement on etiology.

This argument does not get over the conceptual problem. The person may be experiencing something abnormal and debilitating without it being appropriate to describe her experiences as symptoms. For that description to hold, there must be agreement that the appropriate way to look at what is going on is in terms of some underlying pathology in the individual. This is not of course the same as saying that the pathology has been located. There is substantial agreement to this approach in physical medicine, and hence talk of the 'symptoms' of AIDS, for instance, is usually regarded as unproblematic, but there is dissension in the psychiatric area. Some theorists reject the individual pathology model,[9] and thus the appropriateness of talk of 'symptoms'. Laing and Esterson provide a long argument for this position in reference to 'schizophrenia'. I agree with the argument but there is not space to present it here. A less controversial example might be the 'adjustment disorder with disturbance of conduct' where 'the predominant manifestation is conduct in which there is violation of the rights of others or of major age-appropriate societal norms and rules. Examples: truancy, vandalism, reckless driving, fighting, defaulting on legal responsibilities.'[10] These manifestations are breaches in morality. There is no need to take the further step and say that immorality is symptomatic of mental disorder.[11]

The vague inference to underlying pathological conditions in the discussion of 'distress' in the DSM-III-R is particularly relevant to women. Numerous psychological studies have pointed out that what in the West is generally regarded as the woman's role happens to coincide with what is regarded as mentally unhealthy. This relationship appears to hold for people unconnected with mental health work and for professional mental health workers. Broverman and others, in a 1970 paper, report on a study done with a group of 79 clinicians: psychologists, psychiatrists and social workers. They found that the clinicians strongly agreed on the behaviours and attributes which characterize a mentally healthy man, a mentally healthy woman or a mentally healthy adult independent of sex.[12] The description of a healthy adult independent of sex closely matched the description of a healthy man but not that of a healthy woman. This confirmed the notion that a double standard of health exists for men and women. The general standard of health is actually applied only to men, while healthy women are perceived as significantly less healthy by adult standards. Clinicians are significantly less likely to attribute traits which characterize healthy adults to a woman than they are to attribute these traits to a healthy man.[13] These differences parallel the sex-role stereotypes in the West and also relate to what is socially valued.

According to the Broverman study, healthy women differ from healthy men by being more submissive, less independent, less adventurous, more easily influenced, less aggressive, less competitive, more excitable in minor crises, having their feelings more easily hurt, being more emotional, more conceited about their appearance and less objective, and disliking maths and science.[14] In general these are traits that are devalued, and hence, the authors argue, the judgements involve a powerful, negative assessment of women.[15]

These results were confirmed in a study reported in 1972 involving 982 subjects, both men and women, married and single, from different age groups and educational and religious backgrounds.[16] Such studies reveal that women are caught in an impossible situation. If a woman breaks out of the female role she may be regarded as mentally unhealthy, as she is not fulfilling her role, but if she stays within the role she may be regarded as mentally unhealthy on an adult standard. Vague talk about psychological and behavioural dysfunction conceals this underlying problem that 'dysfunction' embodies a moral evaluation and that it works strongly against women.

The Broverman studies have been criticized.[17] Stricker has pointed out that there is some arbitrariness in the categorization of certain responses as 'logical' or 'illogical' when the actual scores are not radically apart on a scale. The categorization suggests bipolar opposites but it is more a matter of degree.

This raises a worry about how the studies has been reported but it does not amount to a challenge to the findings. The general direction and tenor of the Broverman studies have been supported in later research.[18] Some authors make particular mention of the 'Catch 22' situation that exists for women:

> The very state of being a woman, it has been argued, contains so many contradictions and so much suffering that what appears as deviant behavior is, in fact, an unwillingness or an inability to fit the oppressive stereotype of health.[19]

And, as Marcia Kaplan suggests, the double bind that exists here could itself drive a woman crazy.[20] Other research has indicated that biases relating to class,[21] skin colour[22] or sexuality[23] may interact with a sex-role bias.

A variety of explanations have been proposed for the existence of different attitudes towards the mental health of women and the mental health of men. Such explanations try to give an answer to the question of why sex roles are the way they are. There is not space to do justice to these issues here. One interesting approach appeals to the early oral dyadic relationship between mother and child, with the need for males to reverse their early helplessness and dependency on a powerful female object.[24] This may be tied in with fantasies about women's destructive power.[25]

In this section I began with what appeared to be an uncontroversial notion: 'distress', which is in this context equated with 'a painful symptom'. This notion suffers from conceptual problems and, at least in the present state of psychiatry, is inextricably bound up with certain value judgements. As these value judgements circumscribe the role of women in an unjustifiable manner, they can be seen to work against their interests, and any diagnosis which relies upon these values should be regarded with a high level of suspicion.

Let us turn now to the notion of disability, another key notion in the DSM-III-R definition of mental disorder and another source of trouble. According to the definition cited above, for a syndrome to be a mental disorder it has to be associated with a painful symptom or *impairment in one or more important areas of functioning (disability)*.[26] Looking into the details of the various classifications, it becomes clear that important areas of functioning concern social, occupational, academic and legal activities. Many references are made to impairment in occupational functioning. Examples are absence from work, loss of job, deterioration in work relations, interference with work efficiency, work inhibition and occupational difficulties relating to authority figures or co-workers.

Impairments in academic functioning cover the difficulties that some children experience in the classroom or with school work or difficulties that students and/or academics have in writing papers. Impairment of functioning in the legal sphere is mentioned in the descriptions of the categories entitled 'alcohol dependence' and 'cannabis abuse'. The phrase 'impairment due to the legal consequences of being apprehended' forms part of the description of the diagnostic categories of kleptomania[27] and pyromania.[28]

'Impairment in social functioning' is the description which occurs most frequently in the DSM classifications. It is supposed to incorporate attributes such as incapacity to develop socialization skills, deterioration in friendships and family relationships, loss of friends, strained social relations, stormy and ungratifying interpersonal relations and so on. This is another point at which the sex-role stereotyping and different attitudes to the mental health of men and women may play a part. Some studies before the DSM-III-R have shown that women who are making a good job of following the feminine role by revealing emotional responsivity, naïveté, dependency and childishness may be subject to the diagnosis of hysteria or hysterical personality.[29] On an adult 'scale', there is impairment in social functioning.

Marcia Kaplan has compared the 'impairment in social functioning' occurring in the DSM-III description of 'histrionic personality disorder' (previously called 'hysterical personality') with the Broverman findings mentioned above. This disorder is far more frequently diagnosed in women than in men. Although the description of this disorder has changed slightly in the DSM-III-R this analogy still holds.

DSM-III descriptions	*Broverman et al. descriptions*
self-dramatization, e.g., exaggerated expression of emotions	being more emotional

overreaction to minor events	more excitable in minor crises
irrational, angry outbursts or tantrums	more excitable, more emotional, less objective
vain and demanding	more conceited about their appearance
dependant, helpless, constantly seeking reassurance	more submissive, less independent, less adventurous, more easily influenced

Kaplan concludes, 'via assumptions about sex roles made by clinicians, a healthy woman automatically earns the diagnosis of histrionic personality disorder.'[30]A sex-bias in judgements about social functioning has been unearthed in another area: left-of-centre political deviance was regarded as more indicative of maladjustment when the purported patient was female than male.[31]

Thus when one looks into the details of what is meant by 'disability' – 'impairment of functioning' – it becomes clear that it amounts to a breach in a certain way of behaving or experiencing. This 'standard' way of behaving or experiencing is not one which emerges from medical theory; rather it is based upon certain judgements, which perhaps enjoy the agreement of many, but by no means all, folk in Western societies. The basic values embodied in this notion of disability centre around the desirability of having stable and peaceful relationships with one's family, friends, employer and the law. There is little room to express dissatisfaction with one's lot without being regarded as impaired. Values may exist which override those which simply support the status quo, but this type of conceptual debate concerning key notions in the DSM-III-R cannot even get off the ground if the dominant values are disguised as medical phenomena. Yet if these 'medical phenomena' do amount to values and if it is the case, as I believe it to be, that there is no uniformity in these values across all sections of Western society, then any discrepancies in the values underlying decisions about what counts as a disability or an impairment will lead to corresponding discrepancies in the decisions themselves. It is quite possible for a psychiatrist to diagnose 'mental disorder' when there is simply a clash of values between the patient and the psychiatrist, who may be conforming to patriarchal values. A collection of summaries of case histories from the practice of the family psychiatrist Susan Penfold illustrate this point. The relevant descriptions concern encounters between male psychiatrists and female patients. In particular, they reveal that lesbian relationships may be viewed by psychiatrists as a mark of mental disorder, and by the patient as a preferred life-style.[32]

The diagnosis of 'mental disorder' may considerably decrease the self-esteem of the diagnosed person, who may also be encouraged to embark on a treatment programme which may be at best irrelevant and at worst deadly. The side-effects of some of the psychiatric drugs such as lithium and the phenothiazines may be death. If it desirable for the 'patient' to change her values, there are more relevant and humane ways of promoting this other than by medical psychiatric treatment.

There may be some instances of agreement on the values which underpin decisions about impairment, but this does not necessarily mean that such values should remain unquestioned. The values bearing on the acceptability of certain sorts of behaviour for women and the acceptability of other behaviour for men, relating to sex-role stereotypes, seem to be enormously widespread; also, they are commonly incorporated into the self-concepts of both men and women.[33] This might reveal the difficulty of trying to get a change, but in no sense invalidates feminist initiatives towards change.

The problems in the conceptualization of 'distress' and 'disability' are compounded in the new clause: that the syndrome is associated 'with a significantly increased risk of suffering death, pain, disability, or an important loss of freedom'.[34] This introduces a new looseness into the definition. What is 'a significantly increased risk of suffering disability', for instance, when 'disability' is in the social or occupational realm? It could amount to a risk that the person will experience difficulties in the relationships with family and friends or employer, not that she actually does now. If there are biases in the determination of distress or disability as argued above, then these biases could certainly also affect the assessment of the risk of such suffering, and again this could relate to the interests of women.

An exclusion clause is added to the basic conceptual framework in DSM-III-R: 'Neither deviant behavior, e.g. political, religious, or sexual, nor conflicts that are primarily between the individual and society are mental disorders unless the deviance or conflict is a symptom of a dysfunction in the person.' This clause is an attempt to disassociate the concept of mental disorder from the realm of politics, but it doesn't work. A political difference could easily fall under the label of 'dysfunction' – for example, suppose one's political deviance amounts to rejection of authority figures and the desire to create egalitarian structures. It could be said that according to the DSM definition this deviance amounts to an occupational dysfunction – rejection of authority figures – and hence it satisfies the definition for mental disorder.

Conflict between an individual and society could always be seen as dysfunctional, given that normal functioning is defined in such a narrow way. The category of 'adjustment disorder with disturbance of conduct' mentioned above illustrates this point. This aspect of the definition of mental disorder is also of relevance to women. If it is the case that modern Western societies are dominated by patriarchal norms, then women rejecting such norms may find it very difficult for this position to be viewed simply as a conflict between an individual and society and not simultaneously dysfunctional.

The failure of the DSM to be clear about (and to examine) the values that are operative in the discussions about distress and disability is a serious weakness. In uncovering ways in which values do enter the apparently neutral diagnostic scheme, I hope to have shown how it may be used as a weapon to keep women 'in their place'. One positive move in the DSM-IV would be to drop the façade of value neutrality. At least if it is admitted that values enter into the conceptual foundations, then this could form the basis for a debate about their appropriateness – a debate that should extend beyond the domain of medicine because the values concern the right way to live, and medicine should not have any particular authority on that question.

Problems of subjectivity

Many of the descriptions of the categories in the DSM-III-R leave room for variable interpretations. There is also a strong element of subjectivity which will come into the application of various criteria contained in some of the descriptions.

This is of particular significance to women. It is women who are more likely to be persuaded, cajoled or forced to submit themselves for assessment by psychologists or psychiatrists. As already mentioned, the label of mental disorder can be devastating to one's self-image. It may also affect how one comes to be regarded by others. The label almost invariably sets one up as a candidate for drug therapy and the drugs currently in use often have significant irritating and/or damaging side-effects. Hence it does matter if someone is classified as mentally disordered or as sane, and if that classification depends to a large extent on certain subjective factors then it should be seen as problem.

Two diagnoses which are supposed to be much more commonly attributed to women than men are 'borderline personality disorder' and 'dependant personality disorder'. In the DSM-III field trials, this difference in attribution on these two disorders was confirmed and extremely significant for the diagnosis of 'dependant personality disorder'.[35]

The 'borderline personality disorder' is characterized by 'instability of mood, interpersonal relationships and self-image'. No single feature is invariably present.[36] One problem here is that what counts as instability is very much an open question. It will be up to the assessor to decide and there will be great variability in these decisions. Also the assumption that instability is a mark of mental disorder is not free of subjective elements. A further problem is the covert inclusion of homosexuality in the defining criteria. Increasingly homosexuality is regarded as a normal variant of human sexual experience and this is acknowledged in the DSM-III-R in the abandonment of the category of 'ego-dystonic homosexuality' (or being a homosexual and worried about it). It is inconsistent then to retain homosexuality within the definition of borderline personality disorder, and it leaves open the possibility that some psychiatrists will apply the criteria in a different way from others because they hold varying judgements about normal sexuality. This is of particular concern to women, as women more often receive the diagnosis of borderline personality disorder. The problem is that a disorder diagnosis could be given to someone who has simply chosen a life-style different from the norm.

The dependant personality disorder also contains subjective elements. The disorder is marked by 'a pervasive pattern of dependant and submissive behavior beginning by early childhood and present in a variety of contexts'.[37] This has a familiar ring. It is very close to what we are expected to be as women. If we succeed in our role as women then we may be diagnosed as having dependant personality disorder. If we do not succeed in our role as women, we will be punished in other ways.

Marcia Kaplan elaborates on the subjectivity of the description 'dependant personality disorder', pointing out three major assumptions: 1) that dependency is unhealthy; 2) that extreme dependency in women marks an individual dysfunction rather than merely reflecting women's subordinate social position; and 3) 'that whereas women's expression of dependency merits clinicians' labelling and concern, men's expression of dependency (for example, relying on others to maintain their houses and take care of their children) does not.'[38] She challenges the three assumptions. Williams and Spitzer have responded by pointing out that the description is open enough to cover dependency in males as well as in females.[39] This argument concerns the challenge to the third assumption, but it does not counter Kaplan's point that specific male behaviours are often not acknowledged to involve dependency when they are just as good candidates for this description as certain female behaviours. Kaplan's challenge to the first two assumptions is simply ignored.

Kass, Spitzer and Williams make another attempt to undermine Kaplan's position by citing empirical findings that show there is no overall tendency for women to receive a personality disorder diagnosis more often than men, and hence sex bias does not exist in the DSM-III criteria for personality disorder.[40] This misses the point: if a woman conforms to the female role, she runs the risk of being labelled under one of the categories 'dependent personality disorder', 'histrionic personality disorder', or 'borderline personality disorder'. Even if fewer women than men received personality disorder diagnosis, this would not show that this bias did not intrude.

Two of the proposed diagnostic categories in the DSM-III-R applying mainly to women are the late luteal phase dysphoric disorder and the self-defeating personality disorder.

The former has a tight definition in terms of onset, 'symptoms occur during the last week of the luteal phase and remit within a few days after onset of the follicular phase',[41] but a very loose definition in terms of symptoms. No change is necessary for the diagnosis but a range of changes covering many different mental and physical factors is sufficient. This is an improvement on the results in a 1985 survey of the literature and clinical experience relating to premenstrual syndrome, where the authors stated that at least 200 symptoms and complaints have been reported to occur premenstrually.[42] However, the DSM-III-R definition still has a 'catch-all' nature. Judith Bardwick comments on three of the listed symptoms – 'depression, irritability and hostility' – saying that they are 'predictable, normal, emotional states in women'.[43] This is another variant of the theme emerging from the Broverman studies, that it is normal for women to be disordered. Bardwick and others promoting this diagnostic category are implicitly adopting a male norm. Men are viewed as less changeable than women and men are used as the standard to evaluate acceptable levels of changeability. There may be positive aspects to fluctuations in mood, in energy levels and in levels of aggression. It may then be inappropriate to call such changes symptoms of a disorder.

Another aspect of the diagnostic description is that 'the disturbance seriously interferes with work or with usual social activities or relationships with others'.[44] This doesn't adequately keep in check the problems of subjectivity in the symptoms list. Suppose an irritable, angry, tense woman were to rebel against an oppressive work situation on two occasions just before the onset of menstruation. She may be labelled as suffering from the late luteal phase dysphoric disorder. Another way of looking at what is going on may be to regard her anger, etc., as giving her the strength to rebel against an oppressive occupational arrangement. The diagnostic category directs us to see what may be merely *changes* of emotional or bodily state as *symptoms* of a disorder. It also assumes that serious interference with past social or occupational arrangements is necessarily negative.

An alternative view is that the changes the woman experiences in the premenstrual phase may give her the motivation and energy to make positive alterations in her life.

While it cannot be denied that some women experience undesirable cyclical changes, the diagnosis of late luteal phase dysphoric disorder should not be introduced into the DSM-IV. The subjective nature of the proposed criteria could have very dangerous implications for women. The diagnosis could be used to defuse rebellious moves by women which may have a sound basis, and there are definite indications in the work of Katharina Dalton, a leading British researcher/practitioner in the field, that this diagnosis could be used to justify women's unequal position in the workforce.[45] (The whole question of this 'disorder' will be taken up again in Chapter 3.)

The diagnostic category of 'self-defeating personality disorder' also contains dangers for women. It is defined as follows:

> The essential feature of this disorder is a pervasive pattern of self-defeating behavior, beginning by early adulthood and present in a variety of contexts. The person may often avoid or undermine pleasurable experiences, be drawn to situations or relationships in which he or she will suffer, and prevent others from helping him or her. The diagnosis is not

made if the self-defeating behaviors occur only in situations in which the person is responding to or anticipating being physically, sexually, or psychologically abused.[46]

This definition is an improvement on the 1985 draft for 'masochistic personality disorder', but some of the problems raised by the American Psychiatric Association Committee on Women remain, namely, 1) it is implicitly sex-biased and will be misapplied primarily to women; 2) it ignores the fact that our culture fosters behaviours in women that could be misinterpreted as self-defeating (there is a striking parallel between this proposed disorder and Pope John Paul II's 1988 pronouncement on the role of women);[47] and 3) it describes normal responses to the experience of victimization.

The new definition attempts to handle (3) by the clause 'the behaviors do not occur exclusively in response to, or in anticipation of, being physically, sexually or psychologically abused.' This clause does not go far enough, however, as the determination of actual abuse may sometimes be difficult to make. There could well be variable judgements about whether abuse has occurred, especially psychological abuse. Many women complain, perhaps rightly so, that most men are blind to their perpetration of psychological abuse. Will a male psychiatrist within a patriarchal culture see the situation from a women's point of view? Also as noted by Franklin, 'it often takes a long time and an unusual amount of trust between a client and a therapist before the patient will admit to being a victim of abuse.'[48]

Whether or not a woman anticipates abuse will also be very difficult to determine. If the diagnosing psychiatrist has no evidence of actual abuse, he may find it difficult to accept that there is anticipation of abuse; yet it is rare for women not to anticipate abuse, whether it is through their desire to exercise the physical freedom that men experience – for example, by walking the city streets at night – or to enter traditional male domains in the social, religious, occupational and sporting arenas.

Another reason why this clause is an inadequate response to (3) is that victimization may fall short of actual abuse and still exercise a constraining effect on one's thinking and behaving.

The main danger in introducing this diagnosis is that it will act to obscure the extent of the oppression of women within modern culture. Many of the problems that women suffer seem to be attributable to their unequal social position.[49] So if the aim of psychiatry is to improve mental health it should not be introducing categories which could perpetrate that inequality.

Narrowness of focus

Not surprisingly the focus of the DSM-III-R is on problems within particular individuals rather than problematic features of a particular social context. The consistent lack of a broader perspective is likely to encourage diagnoses of 'mental disorder' when there is far more disturbance in the social environment than in the mind of the diagnosed person, and where the 'treatment programme' should be directed towards fixing up that environment rather than continually trying to make the disturbed individual fit in with the disturbing environment. Marcia Kaplan also mentions this problem when she states that, in some instances, 'it is difficult to say when society should be labelled unjust and when an individual should be labelled crazy.'[50] She obscures this issue, though, and leaves herself open for attack when she also claims that 'it is difficult, if not impossible, to say when a disturbance is only brought about by a conflict between an individual and society.'[51] As Williams and Spitzer correctly point out, this can be read simply as asserting that societal pressures may contribute to mental disturbance,[52] a claim which is not very controversial and much weaker than the assertion that the disturbance is wrongly attributed to the individual.

A study which could be used to throw light on this distinction was reported by Stone in 1987.[53] He looked into certain features of the diagnosis of borderline personality disorder, including homosexuality, displays of temper and suicidal threats. He found that parents' lack of acceptance of their offspring's homosexuality as manifested in mockery and abusiveness appeared to have led their children into suicidal gestures and inordinate anger.

One point that is relevant when reflecting on Stone's study is that, as mentioned above, many people now regard homosexuality as a normal variant of human sexuality. The problem here may be more with parents' intolerance. The suicidal gestures and anger could at least in some instances be seen as normal reactions to what is viewed as oppressive and unfair criticism.

The narrowness of focus in the DSM-III-R is a problematic feature of other diagnostic categories too. The descriptions of the categories 'cyclothymic disorder' and 'dysthymic disorder', for instance, pay too little attention to the social context of people fitting the descriptions. The cyclothymic disorder is characterized by fairly mild changes in mood from depression to elevated states, perhaps with intervening periods of normal moods. The dysthymic disorder is characterized by periods of mild depression separated by periods of normal mood (possibly of a few months' duration). Both are diagnosed more in women than in men. By directing our attention away from the social context, these descriptions prevent us from viewing the relevant mental states as normal responses to a disappointing or frustrating social context. Yet it might be more appropriate to view them in this way, to deny that there is disorder in the individual and to impute a problem to the social context, if indeed there is a problem at all. It could be that the normal variability in the context is reflected in the variability in people's moods, which will come out as a problem in the social or personal domain only if it is assumed that stability, or non-variability, has a higher value. This is quite debatable, especially if one seeks a rich and complex life.

Two studies have pointed out a sex bias in the diagnosis of histrionic personality disorder, with clinicians tending to diagnose female rather than male case histories as histrionic personality disorder, even though the diagnostic information is the same.[54] This bias seems to relate to the diagnostic label rather than the specifics of the criteria, leading Ford and Widiger to conclude 'removing sex-typed features from the criteria sets may neither eliminate nor substantially inhibit sex bias.'[55]

These are just a sample of the problems that affect a wide range of diagnoses in the DSM-III-R stemming from a narrowness of focus. The scheme brings in broader considerations under what is called Axis IV, but these are restricted to psychological stresses. The diagnostician will not be alerted to the fact that cultural biases might inappropriately affect diagnoses – for example, biases relating to sex or sexuality or the desirability of narrowly defined emotional stability.

This takes us back to the point mentioned above, that values are very important in the diagnostic process, a fact obscured by the use of medical terminology. It is possible that the problems of the narrowness of focus will be adequately addressed only when the façade of value-neutrality is dropped.

The DSM does not attempt to provide us with a list of the causes of mental disorders. It does attempt to lay down a definitive way of looking at problems of madness or mental distress. It is coming from the world 'experts'. It purports to be objective. I hope in the above discussion to have shown that it is not beyond scrutiny, that it is not objective in the sense of being free of values, and that the values it does contain often work against the interest of women. In future chapters I will try to develop alternative ways of looking at these problems. An important lead has come from recent research in the field of 'personality disorders'.

Personality disorders

There are several 'personality disorders' listed in the DSM which warrant special attention, as they may be useful in understanding mental distress in new ways. Women outnumber men to a significant extent in the diagnoses of multiple personality disorder, borderline personality disorder, self-defeating personality disorder, dependent personality disorder and histrionic personality disorder.

Following on the argument of the previous section, a case can be made for regarding the last two disorders as bogus categories. They amount to different ways of being human – in particular, different ways of being female. To call them disorders amounts to saying that only males can be normal, and then only males that fit the North American ideal of an individual autonomous subject.

There are also problems with the diagnosis of borderline personality disorder, which I have outlined above, and the category is so broadly defined that almost anyone could fall under it. However, there are some people who engage in self-mutilation, which is supposed to be one of the signs of this disorder, though not a necessary sign. It is hard to deny that self-mutilation is a problem. It is also hard to imagine that conceiving of oneself as 'borderline' is going to be helpful. I regard calling someone 'borderline' as an insult. It is perhaps instructive that there is no such diagnosis in the other major classification scheme of psychiatric disorders: the *International Classification of Diseases*, 9th edition (ICD-9). There is one extremely odd report by Dr Alan Ali in the *American Journal of Psychiatry* from 1990 noting 'a strong correlation between having this disorder and having multiple ear piercings per earlobe'.[56]

Certain difficulties with the classification of self-defeating personality disorder were mentioned above and, although I will argue that it may be inappropriate for psychiatry to corner this field, it is an area that needs attention. The multiple personality disorder has not been mentioned yet. This is described as follows:

The existence within the person of two or more distinct personalities or personality states. At least two of these personalities or personality states recurrently take full control of the person's behavior.[57]

Is this a problem? It would certainly make for a very confusing life or lives and a life or lives difficult to live. The curious twist with this disorder is that it is scorned within the profession, with many psychiatrists expressing extreme scepticism and distaste. There are very important reasons for this which I will return to below.

Some questions that arise from this brief run-through of the female personality disorders are: how should we understand self-mutilation; why do many women behave in a self-defeating way; and what is going on when women develop multiple personalities?

Personality disorders and biological psychiatry

Psychoanalytic accounts have dominated interpretations of these disorders up until now, but there has not been a consensus view even among analysts. Psychoanalysis is at present experiencing a decline, especially in the United States, where it has been a major force within psychiatry. Along with this decline is a strong surge of interest in biological psychiatry, roughly conceptualized as a position which posits a biological base for psychiatric disorders. Insiders believe that their strongest support lies in the evidence for a biological basis for depression and schizophrenia, a position I will contest later in this book. In the last few years psychiatric papers have started to emerge pointing to the relevance of a biological orientation in the understanding of the above personality disorders. This amounts to no more than wishful thinking.

With multiple personality disorder (MPD) the research has focused on the psychophysiological differences that occur between personality states, and such factors as cerebral electrical activity measured by EEG, galvanic skin response and skin temperature, cerebral blood flow, thyroid function, voice, posture, motor behaviour, response to medication, perception, and visual functioning. Some studies on small numbers of subjects have found differences, but as one researcher comments: 'this research . . . is complicated by an almost equal number of studies that find little or no difference in physiological functioning across personalities of individuals with MPD.'[58]

Computerized tomography imaging, a fashionable research technique used by biological psychiatrists, has been employed to try to detect differences between the different personalities as well. In a study done with one person and no controls, Saxe et al. claim that there were cerebral blood flow differences in the temperal lobes of the woman in her different personalities. From this they conclude that 'the temporal lobes may be mediating structures for the phenomena of MPD',[59] a rather brave hypothesis given the scanty evidence. With the research to date, there is nothing approaching a causal account.

One line of research with the borderline personality disorder (BPD) has been to look for biological markers (biological features common to these subjects), and some studies have suggested that subjects with this disorder have different sleep patterns.[60] This seems to be the area where there is most agreement, but even this finding is disputed by Jonathan Fleming, whose research detected the same sleep patterns in insomniacs, patients with altered sleep/ wake schedules and even some normal subjects.[61] In any case, a biological marker is a long way from a biological cause.

Some other supporters of biological psychiatry express a hope that BPD will be explained in its terms without offering any evidence. Thus Gardner and Cowdry state, 'we believe our understanding of borderline personality disorder can benefit greatly from adaptations of the same aggressive biological approach used over the past several decades in the study of affective disorders and schizophrenia.'[62] Paris and Zweig-Frank put forward the idea that there is a biological vulnerability behind the BPD, without saying how they came by this idea. No research is cited.[63]

There is a suggestion in the research from biological psychiatry that self-defeating behaviour is to be understood as a physiological addiction to the victimizer.[64] No direct evidence has been provided for this view, however. It is based again on the desire to get a biological explanation for all psychiatric disorders and a refusal to acknowledge that there might be irresistible social or economic reasons for a woman to stay with a victimizer. In the course of elaborating this desire, Kolk makes a further contentious claim that 'victims of rape who blame themselves have a better prognosis than those who do not assume this false responsibility: it allows the locus of control to remain internal and prevents helplessness.'[65] He doesn't cite a basis for this claim. I suspect that there isn't one, and there are certainly other ways of preventing helplessness for rape victims – for example, bringing a charge against the rapist.

In summary, biological psychiatry does not seem well equipped at the moment to answer the questions that I raised above concerning female personality disorders. Is there another line of enquiry which may be helpful?

Personality disorders and child abuse

In the discussion of self-defeating personality in the above section on diagnosis I pointed out that it is difficult to think about this supposed disorder separate from abuse, anticipated abuse, or other forms of victimization. Perhaps we need go no further in looking for a cause. This line of thinking is backed up by emerging information about multiple and borderline personality disorders. Recent papers in medical journals in North America and the United Kingdom report that alarming numbers of women sufferers have a history of child abuse.

In 1979 Richard Kluft stated that multiple personality was a syndrome which follows child abuse, including physical brutalization, psychological assault and sexual violation.[66] This position was endorsed by two speakers at a 1984 symposium on multiple personality. David Speigel claimed that MPD occurs in individuals who have a history of abuse or neglect,[67] and Cornelia Wilbur stated that it is etiologically related to child abuse.[68] It was not until 1986, however, that a major study was conducted by Putnam and others of 100 people suffering from MPD. They found:

> A history of significant childhood trauma was absent in only 3 patients. Sexual abuse was the most frequently mentioned form of trauma, occurring in 83%. Generally, sexual abuse occurred in the form of incest (68%). Repeated physical abuse was reported in 75% of the cases; in 68%, sexual abuse and physical abuse occurred in the same patient. The witnessing in childhood of a violent death, usually of a parent or sibling, was reported by 45% of the patients.[69]

This finding has been supported by a further four studies using a large number of subjects.[70]

There were three small studies published before 1989 which suggested a link between histories of childhood abuse and the borderline personality disorder.[71] Then there were three major studies all pointing in the same direction. Judith Herman et al. reported that 71 per cent of their subjects diagnosed with BPD has suffered physical abuse and 68 per cent had suffered sexual abuse.[72] Studies led by Zanarini[73] and Ogata[74] also found a significant link, especially to sexual abuse. More research reported in 1990 was along the same lines.[75] Summarizing the data in 1990, Steven Shearer et al. say that 'the prevalence of childhood sexual abuse in adult women with a diagnosis of borderline personality disorder ranges from 67 per cent to 86 per cent.'[76]

Self-defeating personality disorder is a new diagnostic category, and there is an attempt in the description to divorce the disorder from abuse: 'the behaviors . . . do not occur exclusively in response to, or in anticipation of, being physically, sexually, or psychologically abused.'[77] One would not expect, then, to find studies that link this disorder with abuse. However, given the evidence that does exist showing a very strong causal link between abuse and self-defeating behaviour,[78] it is a reasonable conjecture that not many women will be diagnosed with the self-defeating personality disorder.

Reflecting on the questions posed above concerning female personality disorders, together with the information about child abuse, it seems that there could be a common answer, that the abuse experienced either in childhood or as adults could give rise to self-mutilation, a splitting into multiple personalities or behaving in a self-defeating way. There are several studies which show that profoundly self-destructive behaviour emerges after victimization.[79] Also the extremely high incidence of sexual abuse in women diagnosed with MPD strongly suggests that this is to be understood as a way of coping with or denying the trauma. Finally, as the work by Paula Caplan[80] shows, it is quite clear that self-defeating behaviour is linked to abuse. If the self-defeating personality disorder excludes abuse by definition, then it's likely to be an empty category.

These findings on child abuse and personality disorders need to be set against other recent research, which reveals a very high incidence of child abuse – especially sexual abuse in women diagnosed with many different psychiatric disorders. Some suggest the whole range,[81] but depression and eating disorders feature prominently. Reports from New Zealand[82] and Austria[83] join ones from North America[84] and the United Kingdom.[85]

Furthermore, there is mounting evidence concerning a high rate of sexual abuse in some Western communities. In a study done in the mid-1980s with 930 women from San Francisco, Diana Russell found that 16 per cent had experienced incest abuse and 38 per cent reported childhood sexual abuse.[86] A New Zealand study found a

13 per cent incest rate in a cross-sectional study of women in Christchurch.[87]

The figures on child abuse, whether related to psychiatric disorders or not, are alarming, especially given the difficulty that abused women have in speaking out, the difficulty that helpers have in mentioning it and the fact that it is not a routine part of psychiatric enquiry. If abuse is so widespread, does that throw doubt on the appeal to abuse in answering the questions raised above concerning personality disorders? I don't believe so. Women can have very different ways of responding to abuse, and abuse also has many variations which the figures don't capture.

What is remarkable is the fact that we are only just finding out about the incidence of abuse. When Freud began the practice of listening to female psychiatric patients, this is what he heard too, but he theorized away his knowledge. It is likely that Freud's elaborate theory about what was really going on when women complained of this abuse is largely responsible for the refusal of later psychiatrists to accept the truth of the reports. In fact the influence has not been restricted to psychiatry. Jeffrey Masson's book *The Assault on Truth*,[88] which clearly documents Freud's acceptance and then rejection of the reality of sexual trauma in the etiology of hysteria, first appeared in 1985, and it is from that time that there has been a proliferation of papers published in the medical literature on the widespread influence of child abuse in the causation of many psychiatric problems in women. Another related factor is the declining influence of psychoanalysis, which might mean that fewer people in the helping professions and fewer women sufferers are seeing their abuse in psychoanalytic terms (as a childhood fantasy) but instead are acknowledging its reality. Also the accelerating strength of the women's movement has made it easier for women to be open about the truth of abuse. It is possible too that abuse has increased in line with the general level of violence in many Western cultures. It is impossible to make a comparison with earlier times as there are no reliable figures for those times.

The medical profession responds to child abuse statistics

These findings are being accepted for publication in medical journals, but they are also generating incredibly defensive responses on the part of the medical profession. Some are sceptical about the reports. Some believe that the subjects are lying.[89] Some refuse to inform themselves on the issue[90] and some express outright hostility. Eugene Bliss comments on the reception of his work on child abuse and MPD:

> During the first few years when I was studying and treating patients with MPD, the attitude of colleagues and war personnel ranged from scepticism to hostility. Because I was formerly a 'respectable' investigator as well as the past chairman of the Department of Psychiatry, I was spared open abuse. The general sentiment was that I had lost some of my wits in one of the presenile changes evident in aging academics. I could ignore local opposition but I became frustrated with the rejection of articles by journals and an inability to get grant support to finance investigation. My observations and ideas were evidently preposterous.[91]

Paul Dell conducted a survey of MPD therapists and found that more than 50 per cent reported 'that they and their patients had repeatedly been subjected to malicious harassment, contemptuous ridicule, and deliberate interference in the medical care of the patient.'[92]

Another defensive response has been to dismiss the findings on the incidence of MPD as mere fashion, charming us 'with its drama and the promise of interesting criminal defenses when one of the "distinct and separate" personalities turns villain'.[93]

Yet another tack is to accept the statistics but soften their impact, for example, by blaming the victims. Arshad Husain and James Chapel describe incest as 'liaisons' and claim that the daughters 'may not violently resist'.[94] David Speigel claims that women who develop MPD after child abuse are vulnerable to abuse.[95] Others deny that there are serious consequences from abuse.[96]

A further defensive move is to accept the reality of child abuse but to keep it as an item of disconnected information, not letting it have any impact on theories or therapies or the assessment of psychiatric patients. As Carmen et al. suggest, 'increasing awareness of the extent of violence in this society leads us to suspect that psychiatric patients are more likely to have experienced physical and/or sexual violence than to hear voices, yet clinicians are systematic in their inquiries about hallucinations while overlooking the reality and importance of violent assaults.'[97]

There have been efforts to respond to the credibility problem, with research attempting to get independent validation of child abuse. From the research conducted by Herman and others, there is a 5 per cent rate of unsubstantiated complaints.[98] In a study by

Coons and Milstein they were able to confirm the trauma through outside sources in 85 per cent of cases.[99] This would seem to be pretty good backing for the claims. It should also be noted that psychiatric theorizing in other areas makes extensive use of retrospective reports, and it is uncommon to demand independent corroboration.

Why is there such an extreme reaction to the child abuse studies? Of course it is true that no one wants to believe that the abuse is that bad, and there could still be a Freudian influence, but I think something more is at stake. The news is very threatening to the biological model which is dominant in research and teaching, and it is this model which attracts research funding, often from the pharmaceutical companies. One can imagine that this funding would be under threat (as indeed Bliss found out) if causal accounts of psychiatric disorders don't appear to relate to biology.

A different non-defensive reaction is also taking place with some psychiatrists and psychologists. They are suggesting that we should view the psychiatric symptoms arising from abuse basically as reactions to stress independent of the particular type of symptom. Some suggest that the diagnosis of post-traumatic stress disorder should be employed.[100] This is a diagnosis already in the DSM, which is characterized by

> symptoms following a psychologically distressing event that is outside the range of usual human experience. The stressor producing this syndrome would be markedly distressing to almost anyone, and is usually experienced with intense fear, terror, and helplessness. The characteristic symptoms involve re-experiencing the traumatic event, avoidance of stimuli associated with the event or numbing of general responsiveness, and increased arousal.[101]

Another suggestion has been to talk about a 'post-sexual abuse syndrome'.[102] Laura Brown, a feminist psychologist, presents a detailed proposal for a category of abuse/oppression artefact disorders.[103]

These moves would be resisted from anyone who thinks that the enterprise of psychiatric diagnosis is worthwhile, as they really amount to giving up on diagnosis. If the overwhelming majority of female psychiatric patients have experienced abuse, then the above suggestions would place them in the one category. In response, however, a classification scheme based on causation is surely preferable to one based on a grouping of symptoms, as it would give us a much better lead on prevention. The DSM is currently based on groupings of symptoms, and there are constant debates in the journals about whether certain categories are discreet or not, debates which would be quelled if there was more certainty about causation. Perhaps defenders of psychiatric diagnosis could accept the role of child abuse in the causation of many disorders and go on to maintain that there are other disorders which have to be explained in other ways. That position will be scrutinized in the next two chapters.

The idea of positing one abuse disorder is certainly more positive than the defensive reactions noted above, but it still seems to me to be unsatisfactory. I question the need to think about a disorder here at all. The manifestations of the disorder in the above proposals are so vague and diverse that the only clear part of the diagnosis relates to the cause. What these descriptions may capture is the range of *normal* reactions to abuse. This is not to deny that people may need comfort and help, just like those who suffer from other terrible events. The 'abuse disorder' approach directs attention away from the questions 'how can abuse be prevented?' or 'what should be done in the event of abuse or threatened abuse?' Instead the following question is seen as more relevant: 'what should be done when abuse is a memory?' Meanwhile it is reasonable to conjecture that high rates of abuse still continue. We could draw a parallel with house theft. Many people are distressed after a robbery in their home and react in diverse ways. The mechanisms to deal with this problem in modern Western culture are to fortify one's home with locks, alarms and dogs, to take out insurance against robbery and to catch and convict the thief. If, as a society, we treated robbery in the same way as abuse, then we would have articles in learned journals about the devastating psychological effects and a few articles in popular magazines about protecting houses. Meanwhile thieves would have pretty much an open go on our homes without much risk of conviction. Social chaos would ensue. There is every reason to think that we should protect our bodies even more vigorously than our houses. The realities of child abuse call out for a social/political account. Whereof more anon.

3 Shifting Trends in Diagnosis

Depression is the most common psychiatric diagnosis in the twentieth-century Western world, and up until recently it has been thought to be primarily a female problem. It has the sort of 'catch-all' nature that 'hysteria' had in the nineteenth century. I want to argue, perhaps surprisingly, that there is another diagnosis waiting in the wings to take over from depression, and that diagnosis is the premenstrual syndrome. In Chapter 1, I mentioned the usefulness of a catch-all female diagnosis of 'hysteria' for psychiatry. It was an important tool in the moral guardianship role that psychiatry usurped. It allowed 'protests' or manifestations of frustrations with the female role to be read as 'symptoms' and treated as such. Could the same be true of depression? Also, the keenness to defend a biological base for psychiatric disorders that held strong in the face of failure in the nineteenth century is still with us today. Is it meeting with more success? If there is a biological base for depression then it wouldn't make much sense to talk about it as a protest, or socially induced discontent.

Depression

What is the nature of depression? Is it just an inappropriate level of unhappiness? Medical psychiatrists believe that most people who are depressed are not only unhappy, they have a biological fault. The unhappiness is a manifestation of this fault. There is, however, no agreement on what this fault is, so diagnosis cannot come from detection of a biological problem.[1] It is based on supposed symptoms of the underlying disorder.

The *Diagnostic and Statistical Manual of Mental Disorders* lists two types of depressive disorder: major depression and dysthymia. Major depression is characterized by one or more major depressive episode. A major depressive episode is diagnosed when at least five of the following symptoms have been present for at least two weeks and one of the symptoms is either (1) or (2):

1   depressed mood
2   loss of interest or pleasure
3   appetite disturbance
4   sleeping too little or too much
5   psychomotor agitation or retardation
6   decreased energy
7   feelings of worthlessness or excessive and inappropriate guilt
8   difficulty thinking or concentrating
9   recurrent thoughts of death and suicide.[2]

Dysthymia is supposed to be a milder condition, characterized by depressed mood and at least two of the symptoms (3), (4), (6), (7) and (8) above or 'feelings of hopelessness'.[3]

There may be difficulties in working out whether a person has these symptoms or not. Some researchers applaud the development of rating scales where the person to be diagnosed writes answers to questions such as 'Do you feel guilty?'.[4] There are two problems here, however. Firstly, the questions can be interpreted in different ways and, secondly, no account is taken of a person's motivation or likelihood of fabrication. This could have a significant bearing on the reliability of the scales.

When assessment is made in conversation, the danger may be that the psychiatrist could prompt an answer of a particular sort that doesn't accurately represent the person's state of being. Marilyn Scarf, in the book *Body, Mind and Behaviour*, mentions the approach of the psychiatrist Myrna Weissman, whose advice is as follows: 'One of the things you do right away in working with a depressed person is to ask: "Do you feel a little like life is not worth living?" And if the person says that he or she does, then you may go on and say: "Have you ever thought that you would be better off dead?" And then you ask if he's made any actual plans and what those plans might be. And you continue probing very carefully, going through a whole scale of levels of questions to make very certain that you've covered the waterfront.'[5] I believe that such a line of questioning may prompt varied responses and not necessarily accurate or verbal ones.

One leading researcher in the field of biology of depression, M. Zimmerman, despairs at what he calls the 'idiosyncrasies in interpreting criteria'.[6] In his study conducted in 1988 he found that different research groups interpret the same criteria of depression differently.[7] He admits that this throws a cloud over the results of research into the causes of depression, but there are many who have not been so cautious.

Within medical psychiatry it is generally assumed that underlying the symptoms of depression there is usually a biological fault and this is why depression is thought of as an illness or disorder. The *Diagnostic Manual* states that depression is far more common in women than in men.[8] This could lead some into the belief that women are biologically weaker than men because they are more prone to depression, and some justification for the subordinate status of women could then be provided. I am not claiming that this is a view commonly espoused in medical psychiatry but merely that it may appear to some to be a natural development, a development that has a parallel in the story of hysteria in the nineteenth century.

It is possible, however, to be sceptical about the results of the biological studies of depression, to question whether depression should be regarded as an illness, and also to doubt the fixed nature of the sex ratio in depression statistics and hence the significance that can be attached to such a ratio.

Biological studies of depression and diagnosis problems

Kraepelin distinguished two types of depression: 1) disorders of the brain (endogenous depression) and 2) disorders caused by a stressful environment (reactive depression).[9] Many psychiatrists have retained this distinction and researchers into the biology of depression often say that they are making claims about endogenous depression and not reactive depression. Indeed it is assumed that a biological malfunction in (1) but not in (2) explains the distinction between the two. The reasoning here was always going to be on shaky ground while the biological malfunction remained unidentified. The current lack of consensus about the biology of depression does nothing to shore up the distinction, but more crucial in its growing unpopularity are the studies which fail to show that patients diagnosed as reactive have significantly different environmental stresses from those diagnosed as suffering from endogenous depression.[10] There are stressful events in the lives of most people diagnosed as depressed.[11] Levitt et al., in a very elegant report, reveal the methodological defects in the studies that argue for two types of depression. In particular, they show that what diagnosis is given to patients varies with the beliefs of the diagnosing psychiatrist. If the latter believes that two types of depression exist, this will be borne out in his or her clinical assessment.[12] But the argument for the existence of two types of depression rests on clinical assessment, as biological findings cannot yet form the basis. Given that clinical assessment is biased by beliefs, the results of these studies on two types of depression cannot be used to support a distinction between the two.

One way out of this circularity might be to try to establish diagnosis other than by clinical assessment of symptoms. Some have attempted a defence of a distinction between endogenous and reactive depression based on treatment outcomes. Thus if a depressed person responds well to electro-convulsive therapy (ECT), a diagnosis of 'endogenous' depression will be made. If she responds poorly to ECT but better to various drug therapies, then a diagnosis of 'reactive' depression will be made.[13] Unfortunately there is the possibility of bias in these studies too. As Levitt et al. point out, 'response to therapy may be used as a diagnostic indicator',[14] bringing in circularity again. Also the responses to treatment could be a function of the *intensity* rather than the 'type' of depression.

Will the distinction disappear? The DSM-III-R does not mention a distinction between endogenous and reactive depression. Some see 'major depression' as a substitute for the former.[15] Certainly many researchers assume that there is an underlying biological fault in major depression, but this assumption is sometimes made for dysthymia also, so that classification cannot be seen as a new label for reactive depression.

Many writers have tried to hang on to the idea of 'disturbance of mood' as the core problem in depression,[16] but according to the DSM-III-R this is not an essential feature. In the classification criteria noted above, it is necessary for the patient to have 1) a depressed mood or 2) loss of interest or pleasure in order to be diagnosed as depressed. Exactly what depression is seems to be slipping through our fingers. There are some theorists who would be unhappy about not including (1) as a necessary diagnostic feature. Levitt et al., writing in 1983 before the acceptance of the DSM-III-R, state that 'one symptom . . . must be included in the criteria for depression. It would be entirely unreasonable, even ridiculous, to exclude the symptom of expressed mood of unhappiness from the eventual pattern. Otherwise why use a word like depression at all?'[17] Of course it isn't true that the DSM-III-R has excluded 'depressed mood', but it is no longer necessary to include it in every diagnosis of depression.

I began this chapter by asking whether depression was an inappropriate level of unhappiness. It looks now as though it may be, but it need not be. Some writers claim that 'the depression concept has accumulated all the ingredients necessary for a first-rate muddle.'[18] I believe that the DSM-III-R is quite clear conceptually but, by specifying only sufficient conditions and not necessary conditions for depression, it introduces a complexity which makes the basis for research quite tricky. Subjects with different symptoms could be placed in the same diagnostic category. It would presumably be easier for biological researchers if they were attempting to find the base of the same symptoms.

In 1979 van Praag wrote that 'the Achilles heel of biological depression research still lies in psychiatric classification, making it difficult to compare the results obtained from the various investigators.'[19] In 1990 he wrote: 'today's depression classification is as confusing as it used to be 30 years ago. All things considered, the present situation is worse. Then, psychiatrists were at least aware that diagnostic chaos reigned and many of them had no high opinion of diagnosis anyhow. Now, the chaos is codified and thus much more hidden.'[20]

Research into the biological base of depression

This research has been mainly into genetics and biochemistry. Diagnostic problems have plagued the studies into the genetics of depression. Most studies were conducted before major depression was divided off from manic-depression. The latter is now thought of as a quite distinct disorder. Most of the 'genetics' studies look at incidence of psychiatric problems in families where one member is diagnosed as depressed. If other family members also suffer from depression, this is used as an argument for some genetic involvement. Recent estimates show that the risk of relatives being diagnosed as depressed if one person in the family has this diagnosis is 7 per cent.[21] This is low and certainly does not impel us to accept genetic involvement. The social contagion of unhappiness could easily explain the results.

If identical twins are reared apart it is often thought there is more chance of detecting genetic effects. In a recent summary of such research with twins diagnosed as suffering from major depression or dysthymia, genes could not be implicated in the causation.[22] Also Kendler et al.'s major study of twins who were not reared apart strongly supported 'the causative importance of environmental factors in depression'.[23]

Some writers in this field have suggested that X-linkage can explain the greater incidence of depression in women,[24] as X-linked dominant disorders are more common in women. The idea is that the gene for depression is located on the X chromosome. There seems little current support for this view. Perhaps because 'studies of X-linkage . . . have inconsistent and contradictory results'.[25]

There are two main lines of biochemical research into depression: 1) concerning serotonin and 2) concerning the dexamethasone suppression test (DST). The first centres around the action of certain drugs and levels of serotonin, a neuro-transmitter. (A neuro-transmitter is a specialized chemical which transmits information from one neuron in the brain to another.) In the 1960s it was found that resperine, a drug used in hypertension, led to depression in 20 per cent of patients.[26] Resperine depletes serotonin. Certain mood-elevating drugs increase serotonin. This led to the hypothesis that depletion of serotonin is the cause of depression.

Serotonin cannot be directly administered to check this hypothesis, but certain precursors of serotonin have been tried. These chemicals had only a limited anti-depressive effect.[27] Some claim indirect support for the hypothesis but the results are not consistent.[28] One finding which goes against the hypothesis is that some new drugs effective in relieving depression don't alter the functioning of serotonin.[29] Qualifiers are now introduced; for example, Trimble says that 'serotonin is depleted in some patients with affective disorder.'[30] Shopsin draws back even further: 'a *susceptibility* or *vulnerability* to serotonin as *perhaps* etiopathogenic in *at least some* depressions'[31] is suggested by drug research. This is not to suggest very much. More recent research is similarly inconclusive.[32] The cause of depression has not been found in this area. It cannot even be asserted that depleted serotonin is a correlate or biological marker of depression.

A great deal of interest has been focused on the dexamethasone suppression test (DST) as revealing something significant about depression. The object of the test is to suppress a certain hormone, cortisol, with a dose of dexamethasone. Normal subjects suppress cortisol for 24 to 48 hours after dexamethasone. An abnormal result is found in some depressed patients. Recent studies suggest that about 45 per cent of depressed subjects show this abnormality.[33] This result is not strong enough, however, to establish a causal basis for depression. It needs to be shown that there is some feature shared by all the people diagnosed as depressed. To claim that some depressed people have a certain feature and others do not tells us very little about the nature of depression. It has been common for research reports to describe insufficient suppression of cortisol following application of dexamethasone as a biological marker for depression.[34] But if such an abnormality is only turning up in 45 per cent of patients then inadequate support is given to even this conclusion.

One interesting result that has emerged from the DST research is that people suffering from anorexia nervosa have a high rate of abnormal test results: 36 to 40 per cent.[35] Current work in this area suggests that what was initially thought to be a function of faulty biology is really the result of weight loss and a starvation diet, a point I will return to in the next chapter. Could the same be true for depression? Many people in a depressed state are likely to give scant attention to diet and to sustain weight loss. Appetite disturbances are listed above as one of the defining characteristics of depression in the DSM-III-R. In an extremely relevant study conducted by Fichter et al. into depression, anorexia nervosa and nutrition, healthy volunteers were examined before, during and after a three-week period of complete food abstinence.[36] DSTs were administered and 'dexamethasone suppression was abnormal already after minimal acute weight loss and normalized quickly within days with resumption of food intake.'[37] The disturbances in cortisol secretion that occurred in these healthy subjects with their starvation diet had the same pattern as the disturbances observed in depressed people, in sufferers of anorexia nervosa, and in other conditions where malnutrition may exist, for example, alcoholism and bulimia.[38] The most likely conclusion, then, is that abnormal results on the DST tell us something about the diet and/or weight of the person rather than isolating a biochemical abnormality responsible for depression (and anorexia nervosa, etc.).

The serotonin hypothesis and the DST hypothesis are put forward as the best supported ideas about the biological basis of depression. Yet there are these grave weaknesses.

It is commonly thought that the biological account of depression is on firm ground at least in the area of 'post-natal depression'. However, while it is true that there are hormonal changes during this time there is no evidence that these changes give rise to depression. Not all women experience depression after childbirth, yet all mothers have the hormonal changes. Also there are major social changes beginning for the new mother which might be behind the depression that is experienced, perhaps by many women. This was borne out in the research conducted by Paula Nicolson,[39] who was also able to trace back the depression that some of the mothers experienced to medical complications and hospital care.

Is depression an illness?

There has been endless controversy over what constitutes an illness, but a widespread view is that an illness is a disturbance of bodily structure or function. If depression has an established biological base then this would give support to the view that depression is an illness. We have seen, however, that the research to date has not established a biological base. The research into social factors mentioned in the next section also threatens the illness model, as the basic fault is not located in individual biology but rather in social inequity. Trimble illustrates the confusion in the illness debate when he states that it is important to distinguish 1) major depressive illness from 2) understandable reactions to adverse circumstances.[40] Yet he welcomes the loss of the endogenous/reactive dichotomy in the DSM because 'it has falsely assumed a classification based on aetiology . . . the evidence that depressions are somehow either provoked by external circumstances or are the result of a mysterious internal process does not stand up.'[41] However, the distinction that Trimble puts forward in (1) and (2) above is based on aetiology and aetiology of precisely this sort. There seems to be a straightforward contradiction here.

There is also fundamental conflict between different writers on this issue. For example, Hamilton says: 'it is important that we should not confuse "depression", by which we mean an affective illness of depressive type, with depressed mood.'[42] Yet Levitt asserts that 'there is a broad consensus that depression is an affective disorder . . . and . . . the unmistakable meaning of "affective" is that an alteration in mood is the primary symptom.'[43]

Hamilton makes the point that 'normal functioning' for 'writers, artists, actors (and actresses), our inventors and scientists', may be different from normal functioning for the average citizen and that this should be borne in mind in making a diagnosis. He suggests that if there is a clear-cut deviation from the person's own normality then a diagnosis of depression may be made. For Hamilton, all depression is illness. It may constitute a 'trivial disturbance' or 'the grossest disablement'.[44] He does not offer any basis for the illness label and he makes another claim about depression which leaves me wondering what he would count as evidence. Hamilton says that depression 'tends to recur, though the interval between phases can sometimes be so long that it is greater than the span of life of the patient'![45]

If we go back to the DSM-III-R it is interesting to note a contrast with the DSM-III. In the earlier system major depression was referred to as an illness[46] even though the stated intention of the manual was to do away with talk of 'mental illness' in favour of the term 'mental disorder', for all psychiatric categories. In the later scheme, depression is referred to as a disorder, now in line with the basic conceptual framework of the manual. If, however, 'major depression' is simply a disorder, it is hard to imagine how it is distinguished from 'dysthymia', which has been regarded as a personality disorder distinct from an illness. Indeed if we compare the list of symptoms for the two 'disorders' (see above), they do seem to be very close. In summary, it looks as though the DSM is moving towards one model of depression which does not have illness status. We should be cautious of this interpretation, however, as even though the label 'illness' has been dropped, the way of conceptualizing the problems of both major depression and dysthymia is still closely tied to medical terminology. The following terms are liberally used in both cases: 'symptoms', 'impairment', 'chronic course', 'episode', 'complications', etc.[47]

There seems to be some reluctance on the part of medical psychiatry to give up the idea that depression is an illness, but there is increasing recognition that there are inadequate theoretical and/or empirical grounds to back this position. If depression is a disorder then the risk from the medical psychiatrists' point of view is that it will slip out of their domain, a real risk if the findings on the sociology of depression are correct. What are these findings?

The sociological challenge to biology

An indirect attack on the biological model has turned up in the field of sociology with the claim that depression is related to social factors. In a broadly based study undertaken by Brown and Harris in the late 1970s it was found that vulnerability to depression in women is related to the following factors: 'loss of mother before eleven, presence at home of three or more children under fourteen, absence of a confiding relationship, particularly with a husband, and lack of a full- or part-time job.'[48] This research finding is now widely accepted but of course completely inexplicable if biology is the prime cause of depression. Also, as Jordanova comments, 'if George Brown and his co-workers are right about the large numbers of depressed women with pre-school children, then agitation for nursery and other facilities for children would be better than Valium.'[49]

Psychiatrists with a biological orientation display some of the same defensive reactions to the Brown and Harris research that were mentioned above in connection with multiple personality disorder and child abuse. They may simply ignore the finding. Some proceed as though it is a piece of information, disconnected to the real biological cause of depression.

Unsatisfactory aspects in the lives of women diagnosed as depressed were also highlighted in a study by Agnes Miles, documented in the book *Women and Mental Illness*. She found that the stress inherent in the role of housewife could lead to depression.[50] The sources of stress in housework are 'long working hours, monotony and an absence of rules, isolation, confinement and a heavy measure of responsibility and . . . its unending nature'. She believes that the way out of problems of depression is to change the unsatisfactory aspects of life, for example, by taking up outside employment, but because depression is misconceived as some inner insufficiency, employment outside the home is often not seen as a solution.[51] Instead a medical solution will be sought. Yet in Miles's study the factors which led to improvement or recovery from depression were major events involving profound changes in the lives of women, such as 'divorce, separation, moving house, relief from difficult caring roles, obtainment of satisfactory employment'.[52] Lack of improvement occurred when there were no major changes in the lives of the depressed women.[53] This study also sits uneasily with a biological approach to depression.

Brown and his co-workers have recently looked at recovery from depression, and what they unearthed is quite similar to the material in the Miles study. Recovery was most often associated with a 'fresh start', for example, a new boyfriend, rehousing or employment outside the home.[54]

The success of these sociological studies and the lack of success of the biological research might lead easily into the view that depression in women can be understood as a protest, an unwillingness 'to go on' or as an expression of frustration with the female role, especially the restrictions of that role. This is surely part of the story. However, it's not possible to ignore the statistics on child abuse and depression. The link is quite strong. In a 1987 study of 66 female psychiatric patients, Bryer and others found that 58 per cent of the depressed women had experienced sexual and physical abuse in childhood.[55] A New Zealand study in 1991 found that 22 per cent of 138 women diagnosed as depressed had experienced childhood sexual abuse.[56] Sheldrick presented a summary of the research literature in 1991. She claimed that depression was the most common psychiatric disorder reported by adults sexually abused as children.[57] Also, in a large US study reported in 1990, Winfield and others found a significant relationship (12.93 per cent) between sexual assault and depression.[58] Perhaps the experience of abuse is another way into depression, or perhaps having had that experience predisposes one to become depressed from the frustrations of the female role. If depression is just what is deemed 'an inappropriate level of unhappiness', then it doesn't take a big imaginative leap to regard abuse or frustration as causal; and, as I have argued above, psychiatry has not presented a convincing picture or a consensual view of what depression is, if it isn't just inappropriate unhappiness. There is another question which should be raised here: who decides what is 'inappropriate'? Perhaps it is appropriate for a sensitive human being to be extremely unhappy after being raped or trapped in a boring environment for years. The appropriateness of the depression does not mean that change should be resisted, however, as most would prefer not to be depressed and, as a protest, depression is not usually very effective. The studies cited above give some directions. It may be harder to eradicate the unhappiness caused by abuse, but, looked at in societal terms, it is necessary to toughen the laws, to make more use of the laws, and to put efforts into prevention, a point I will return to in Chapter 8.

A further line of research which is problematic for the biological approach and offers some hope to women concerns the sex ratio in depression statistics. A common finding has been that women exceed men in the rate of depression, and this has seemed to hold even when confounding factors are taken into account such as women's greater willingness to admit to problems of this sort or to the greater frequency with which we seek medical help.[59]

In three large epidemiologic studies that have recently been reported the incidence of depression in men and women is evening out.[60] The studies span the United States, Sweden, Germany, Canada and New Zealand. A factor that is constantly mentioned in attempts to explain these changes is the increased participation of women in the workforce[61] or, as Murphy et al. say rather inelegantly, 'where women are concerned, work in the marketplace has consistently been associated with lower levels of symptomatology in the domains of depression and anxiety.'[62]

We do not have to be satisfied that this is a complete or even partial explanation of the changing statistics if we want to use these changes to undermine the notion that depression is primarily a female problem. There is enough information coming through now to back the claim that the sex ratio in depression is not fixed. Hence those who want to make claims about 'women's nature' on the basis of their greater prevalence of depression are misguided. Depression will probably continue to be a catch-all diagnosis for both men and women for many years, but if, as I suspect, the sociological account gains strength, then those who wish to support an idea of the inherent psychiatric weakness of women will need to look elsewhere. There are early indications that the diagnosis of premenstrual syndrome will be presented as fulfilling this role. It offers hope for biological psychiatry, as it seems to be transparently obvious that such a syndrome must be based in female biology.

Premenstrual syndrome (PMS) – defined?

In the 1987 revision of the DSM-111, PMS is listed as a proposed mental disorder under the label 'late luteal phase dysphoric disorder', and some doctors are currently writing about it as 'the world's commonest disease',[63] with claims that it is experienced by 80 to 100 per cent of women.

Hippocratic physicians wrote about the occurrence of physical and psychological changes just prior to menstruation,[64] and Icard in the nineteenth century said 'the menstrual function can, by sympathy, . . . create a mental condition varying from . . . a simple moral malaise, a simple troubling of the soul, to actual insanity, to a complete loss of reason, and modifying the acts of a women from simple weakness to absolute irresponsibility.'[65] However, it was not until 1931 that these changes became formally identified as a medical syndrome. The American doctor Robert Frank drew the attention of the New York Academy of Medicine to 'a large number of women who are handicapped by premenstrual disturbances of a manifold nature'. He explained this syndrome in terms of faulty ovarian function.[66]

More recently, Katharina Dalton, a major theorist on PMS, who has spent many years as the head of a large London clinic, claims that the term 'PMS' covers a wide variety of symptoms which regularly recur in the same phase of each menstrual cycle followed by a symptom-free phase in each cycle. This phase may be anywhere from ovulation to four days into menstruation. She explains that the term PMS was chosen at a time when it was not realized the symptoms can occur at menstruation and ovulation.[67]

Dalton asserts that the term 'premenstrual tension' covers only the psychological symptoms: depression, lethargy and irritability. PMS includes these and somatic symptoms, for example, asthma, epilepsy and migraine.[68] In the book *Once a Month*, Dalton elaborates on the psychological symptoms. She says that 'the image of women as fickle, changeable, moody and hard to please'[69] and our periodic irrationality[70] can be explained in terms of the 'ebb and flow of the menstrual hormones'. Dalton claims that the symptoms of PMS are worse during the four days prior to menstruation and the first four days of menstruation. She used the term 'paramenstruum' to cover these eight days.[71] These days are linked with low levels of progetserone, and she regards PMS as a progesterone deficiency disease.[72]

Judith Bardwick supports the view that depression, irritability and hostility form a part of the PMS but says they are 'predictable, normal, emotional states in women'[73] – another variant of the theme that it is normal for women to be disordered, which I mentioned in Chapter 2.

In a 1985 survey of the literature and clinical experience concerning PMS, Halbreich and others state that 'at least 200 symptoms and complaints have been reported to occur premenstrually'[74] and some of the 'symptoms' are positive – for example, increased affection and sex. They call this the Increased Well-Being Syndrome. To their credit, they use this finding to distance themselves from calling PMS a *disorder*. They prefer to talk about premenstrual *changes*.

Rubinow and others in another survey in the same year claim that over 150 symptoms representing every organ system have at one time or another been attributed to PMS and that there are no symptoms which are either necessary or sufficient for the diagnosis. They offer the following operational definition of PMS: 'a cyclic disorder with symptoms that are of sufficient severity so as to interfere with some aspect of living and that occur with a consistent and predictable relationship to menstruation', but they point to the wide variability of claims regarding which time is supposed to be relevant.[75] The catch-all nature of the definition then starts to emerge. Thus, it is not surprising that some put the incidence of PMS at 100 per cent of women. It is strange that it went undetected for so long, however, as it is not supposed to be a product of social circumstances but rather of our biology. Dalton claims that 'very few of the doctors in practice today had any training in diagnosing or treating what we now know is the world's commonest disease, the premenstral syndrome.'[76]

The breadth of the definition should, I think, lead to suspicion about what is going on. It seems much more likely that the newness of the diagnosis is not to be accounted for in terms of some empirical discovery but rather it is produced by decisions to group certain attributes together. Some researchers isolate particular moods, behaviours and bodily states, a small subset of the 150 to 200 symptoms mentioned above. Other researchers provide a different list. Some point to certain times in the cycle, others focus on different times. It is commonly assumed that the cyclical changes, whenever they are and whatever they are, are negative. Judith Bardwick states that many of the mental characteristics attributable to PMS are normal emotional states for women. The fact that she and nearly all other writers still persist in seeing them as signs of a disorder – PMS – means that once again women are judged by a male norm, a point discussed in Chapter 2. A refreshing alternative perspective to the PMS push is the suggestion by Stewart and co-workers that women tend to be abnormally pleasant and nice three weeks out of four. They fail to experience or express normal annoyances and anger a great deal of the time, and are dismayed when these emotions surface during premenstrual days.[77]

Despite the lack of agreement on definition, some causal theories have been suggested. These are in a rather weird position as there is no consensus on what the effect (PMS) is. Perhaps they can help us to understand the effect? Is there anything in the causal research which could provide a justification for any of these decisions on a new category?

PMS: the causal research generates puzzles

Many theories concerning the cause of PMS have been advanced. I will consider three main contenders in the *psychiatric*/medical area.

I have already mentioned Dalton's hypothesis that PMS is a progesterone deficiency disease. The reasoning is as follows: cyclical changes occur in women; they are worse when progesterone is low, hence it is progesterone deficiency that causes the cyclical changes. Dalton introduced this view before accurate measurements could be made of hormone levels, but she claimed support for her view in observing the effectiveness of progesterone as a cure for PMS.[78]

Recent developments in the testing of hormone levels have not supported Dalton's hypothesis. Women with high degrees of cyclical mood change have not shown any difference in progesterone level from women with low degrees of cyclical mood change.[79] Also a fairly consistent finding is that progesterone is no more effective than a placebo as a therapy for PMS.[80]

This is the most popular psychiatric/medical theory of PMS and it seems to amount to a mere conjecture based on a simple coincidence in time; that progesterone change occurs in the paramenstruum, along with the heightened PMS. It would not be appropriate to regard this as a theoretical breakthrough giving backing to the diagnostic category. In fact, in the early days of Dalton's theorizing, she wrote about PMS ranging from ovulation through into menstruation. It is only in her recent work that she brings in the notion of the paramenstruum as the main time when PMS occurs, which does coincide with the time when progesterone levels are low. This suggests to me that she has defined 'paramenstruum' to fit her theory about progesterone. Many other writers contend that PMS finishes with menstruation, but that does not fit in with the progesterone deficiency model. Dalton has noticed when progesterone levels are low and stipulated that this is the time when PMS occurs – namely, the paramenstruum. So it is not even the case that she has discovered a coincidence. It is rather the case that she has invented one.

Judith Bardwick claims that 'recent data suggest that women have a surge of testosterone production premenstrually',[81] and others attempt to link PMS with fluctuations in this androgen,[82] a perspective which fits in neatly with recent psychiatric theories about male criminality. These theories attempt to explain criminal behaviour biologically by relying on a postulated relationship between aggression and crime. Some theorists further claim that the male hormone, testosterone, affects the level of aggression. The basis given is that castration seems to have a calming affect and that males are more aggressive than females.

There are many problematic features in this approach. Not all crimes committed by men are related to aggression, and it is not the case that all males are more aggressive than all females, even though all males in the reproductive age group produce much greater quantities of testosterone than females. Also recent more accurate chemical tests have not backed the theory that testosterone production is linked to PMS.[83] The story of testosterone and PMS is illustrative of a common move in psychiatric methodology where a theory that is around but is not well supported in one area is taken over in another area. The lack of support in the old area is somehow glossed over and thus the fact that it has simply been around in the first area acts as support for it in the new area.

Many theorists associate PMS with neurotransmitter malfunctioning[84] and suggest that psychotropic drugs may alter the neurotransmitter functioning. This is a similar package of speculations and treatment recommendations that have been applied to depression. As I have suggested above, opposing ideas are gaining ground in that area, with depression increasingly being seen as a social rather than a biological problem. From the psychiatric literature it is clear that the diagnosis of PMS is taking over from the diagnosis of depression as the catch-all female category. Although this package of theory and treatment recommendations is also adopted by many, no direct evidence has been found linking PMS with neurotransmitter malfunction[85] nor cures for PMS with psychotropic drugs.[86] What would be the motive, then, in importing the package? It is puzzling but perhaps relates to the influence of the pharmaceutical industry on some directions within psychiatry and the potential loss of sales if depression is looked on as a social problem requiring social rather than biological cures.

None of these theories concerning the cause of PMS are well enough supported to provide a basis for grouping certain characteristics together and claiming that this group constitutes PMS. What, then, is going on in the promotion of this category? There are notes of caution in leading psychiatric journals. Halbreich and others, writing in the Canadian Journal of Psychiatry, state: 'an evaluation of the literature . . . leads us to the conclusion that at present there is no solid evidence for any of the hypothesized pathophysiological mechanisms of premenstrual condition.'[87] Rubinow and Roy-Byrne write in the American Journal of Psychiatry that 'despite 50 years of study there is still surprisingly little known about menstrually related mood disorders; questions of etiology and treatment are largely unanswered.'[88] One of the major British medical journals has published editorials emphasizing the doubt that exists about the scientific basis for claims made about PMS.[89] Even Robert Spitzer, who is behind the inclusion of PMS in the DSM, agrees that 'little is known about the etiology and treatment . . . as yet, research has not revealed any biological abnormality, such as endocrine disturbances, in women with severe premenstrual symptoms.'[90] He claims that it will aid research to have the diagnosis in the DSM. That is incredibly dubious given the lack of agreement on diagnosis.

In summary, the apparent variability and arbitrariness of decisions to group certain characteristics as constituting PMS is not dissipated by the causal research. It is so inconclusive that the puzzle of this diagnosis looms even larger. The research has not even come up with a biological marker for PMS despite at least 50 years of study. How are we to understand the PMS story?

Questions about the PMS diagnosis and its role in the discipline of women

The problem concerning the newness of the diagnosis of PMS was mentioned above. If it is a widespread biological fault, why is it only now being recognized, especially as some report the incidence to be 100 per cent of women? *Is* it now being recognized or is it now being invented? I want to reject both these answers and argue that the high incidence of PMS is produced by a combination of factors and that it is not known which are the most important.

1) Some women do experience cyclical changes in mental and or bodily states.

2) The subjects in PMS studies do not constitute a random sample of women. Rather, they are women seeking the help of the medical profession or being tried in criminal courts. If the former, then they may have a problem in living which mistakenly gets diagnosed as PMS. It is possible that the patient will comply with this diagnosis for a variety of reasons: acceptance of expert opinion, desire to medicalize problems to avoid other means of handling them, wanting an excuse for anti-social acts and so on. Women criminals may have an additional motive to medicalize their crime in the hope of getting greater leniency of sentence. (PMS and crime will be discussed further in Chapter 5.)

3) Beliefs and expectations may produce experiences of our bodily states which may differ with changing beliefs and expecta-

tions. Diane Ruble conducted studies in which she purportedly convinced one group of women that they were in their 'premenstrual' phase and found that they reported higher levels of menstrually related pain than did those who had been told that they were in the middle of their cycle. This coupled with the background assumption that we believe or expect the premenstrual time to be painful is taken to show that beliefs about the menstrual cycle can influence women's descriptions and experiences.[91] I find the gullibility of these subjects hard to accept, but the general idea that beliefs and expectations influence experience is well supported in other areas (for example, with the placebo effect), and the background assumption just mentioned is gaining support from current theories such as Dalton's. It is quite possible, then, that some women's experiences of PMS are produced by evolving cultural beliefs about the premenstrual time. This is further supported by the research by Koeske and Koeske, who found that both men and women were willing to attribute negative but not positive moods to PMS. Positive mood changes were more likely to be viewed as related to the situational context, while negative ones were viewed as biological. The belief that negative moods are biological may even cause further negative moods which might get labelled PMS.[92] The research by Chandra and others, especially comparing Indian and Canadian women, reveals cultural variations in the experience of positive as well as negative premenstrual experiences;[93] and so does the research by Janiger et al. with American, Japanese, Nigerian, Apache, Turkish and Greek women.[94]

4) Nearly all of the studies on PMS have used retrospective data. Yet recent studies employing prospective and retrospective data indicate that retrospective ratings in this area overestimate symptoms experienced[95] or that the symptoms do not turn out to have any relation to the menstrual cycle.[96] This suggests that data on PMS are produced by a particular method of collection, and if the method was changed the reported incidence of PMS would drop significantly. This indeed did occur in the research conducted by Rivera-Tovar and Frank in 1990. Using a 30 per cent or greater premenstrual change as an index of PMS and prospective ratings, they found a prevalence rate of only 4.6 per cent in a sample of university women.[97] Even prospective reporting can be problematic, however. Englander-Golden et al. found that women who knew they were in a study of PMS reported more cyclic symptoms both retrospectively and prospectively than did women who were not aware that the study was of PMS.[98] AuBuchon and Calhoun found

that the reports of negative psychological and bodily symptoms increase when the subjects are informed that the menstrual cycle is the focus of study.[99]

5) A spokesperson for the National Women's Health Network in the USA 'stresses that a lot of PMS is iatrogenic. It often appears for the first time after a women has stopped taking birth control pills, after tubal ligation or even after a hysterectomy.'[100]

6) Some researchers claim that women experiencing PMS may not actually be aware that they are doing so. According to Judith Bardwick, 'one seems to see the cyclicity of the affect response more clearly in measures which are less self-aware or conscious probably because people perceived themselves as being more consistent than they actually feel.'[101] This perspective means that a great deal of scope is given to the doctor to read the syndrome into women's experience and thus inflate the incidence rates.

7) Many women still suffer from role restrictions, and psychiatry has traditionally provided opportunities to conceptualize discontent – without of course this being an overt aim. There are also 'fashions' in this conceptualization. It is no longer fashionable to be diagnosed with hysteria. PMS is in vogue in the popular health magazines, which also promote a range of 'cures' – none of which have been shown to be any more successful than placebos.[102] However, it is increasingly difficult for many women, especially those unexposed to feminist political analysis, not to think about their negative emotions in terms of PMS.

Because of all these compounding factors in the diagnosis of PMS, we have no way yet of knowing how many women do suffer from a biological malfunction that is labelled PMS. It may in fact be quite rare. The popularity of the diagnosis cannot then be explained by appeal to biology, but there are ideological factors that make sense of it. As I have pointed out above, there is starting to be a move away from the diagnosis of depression as a diagnosis applied primarily to women. If psychiatry is to perpetuate its position as a moral guardian of women and defend the scientific respectability of that position, then another catch-all diagnosis is needed, and preferably one which can be shown to have a biological base. Then it can be asserted with some authority that most women are mentally disordered, and this is because of our inherent nature. The need for a new generalized diagnosis, from the point of view of biological psychiatry as moral guardian, is becoming particularly urgent with the failure of the biological research on depression. Another factor is that the 'female role' is now under severe challenge in the Western world and conservative forces need to mount strong resistance if that challenge is to be met. The PMS diagnosis must look promising. It has the appearance of being quite specific. It is said to apply to a very large percentage of women and it seems perverse to deny that the cause is biological. The reality is that it is totally non-specific and has not been shown to be biological.

The diagnosis of PMS is already being used to discipline women in invalidating our anger, in defusing the political impact of women's crime (a claim I return to in Chapter 5) and in providing a rationale for restriction of employment opportunities. Dalton asserts that 'the cost to industry of menstruation is high',[103] and then details the harmful effects in various industries in Sweden, the UK and the USA, for example: 'in the retail and distributive trades there may be a variety of effects ranging from errors in stocktaking and billing to bad-tempered service to customers and breakages from clumsiness. In the office the irritability may result in a sudden argument with the boss, the cleaner spilling the bucket of water across the room, the secretary hurling spoilt letters into the basket.'[104]

Dalton recommends that employers handle these problems by giving women time off or assigning us to less skilled jobs, such as 'packing and stacking . . . rather than remaining on tasks which are harder to remedy later, such as soldering or filing.'[105] This could easily be taken as encouragement to employers not to employ women at all. Dalton's approach very easily leads into the view that women's unequal position in the workforce is in fact fair. Personnel management is beginning to follow this lead. In a recent article in a human resource management journal it is claimed that 'approximately 70 per cent of women experience some adverse symptoms prior to menstruation, with anywhere from 20 to 40 per cent experiencing incapacitation.'[106] The authors then list work-related consequences such as errors of judgement, memory loss and poor concentration. The source cited for these assertions is Katharina Dalton.

It seems that the PMS diagnosis can serve the same sort of ideological function that the diagnoses of 'hysteria' and 'depression' served. In general it can explain why it is appropriate to regard women as inferior to men, and then in specific areas it can be used to justify unequal treatment. Although the depression diagnosis is still widely used, it is a reasonable bet that PMS will take over in the near future. There are currently journal articles claiming that depression statistics are inflated because they have assessed women in the premenstrual part of their cycle. The PMS sufferers are incorrectly diagnosed as depressed.[107] This foreshadows a smooth 'scientific' transition from depression to PMS.

In conclusion, some aspects of modern psychiatry are pointing in a very dangerous direction for women, not that it has ever been otherwise. There is no problem is accepting the idea that there may be cyclical changes in our moods, our levels of aggression, our sexual desire. Such changes may even have a positive value. (According to Jacquelyn Zita they may constitute 'windows of sensitivity', 'which grant the human female fine tuning with her environment'.[108]) The next step is the problem, where these and other changes are incorporated into a syndrome, a disorder or disease that is so widespread that it may affect all women. This step gains some credibility because there are women who experience painful episodes before menstruation, but the extent of this group is presently unknown and could in fact be quite small. It would also seem more appropriate for such episodes to be treated within gynaecology rather than psychiatry. The promotion of the psychiatric diagnosis of PMS must be seen as a tool in the discipline of women.

Some of the problems which have surfaced when looking at the diagnostic categories of depression and PMS are epistemological. They relate to the definition of the object (the disease entity or disorder) under scrutiny and the methods for gaining knowledge about these objects. These epistemological problems within psychiatry are not unique to the diagnoses discussed. In the next chapter I will show how they pervade the theorizing about some other disorders applied primarily to women. In addition I will look at the category of 'schizophrenia', which is supposed to provide the strongest backing for biological psychiatry. If it is indeed on strong ground here, then perhaps an argument could be put that it is only a matter of time before the epistemological problems that pervade other categories will be overcome.

4 Epistemological Problems with the Dominant Medical Psychiatric Perspective

Two key epistemological concerns for a developing discipline are 1) clarification of the objects of study; 2) some endorsement of the theoretical position adopted, in particular establishing that the theory will uncover *causes* of the objects studied. In the previous two chapters I have illustrated the problems that medical psychiatry encounters with (1). The objects of study, the mental illnesses or mental disorders, are by no means conceptually clear. Nor is this improving as new categories such as the premenstrual syndrome are introduced.

Turning to the second epistemological concern: some maintain that the theoretical position of medical psychiatry has been endorsed by decades of research, which has discovered causes of at least some mental illnesses or disorders. Others are more cautious and maintain that, while causes have not yet been identified, at least some biological markers have been found. These markers would allow us to determine when a person has a disorder and when they do not. Then there are the critics who claim that it is not even the case that biological markers have been found and that this should lead to a questioning of the whole theoretical orientation. My discussion on depression and premenstrual syndrome in the last chapter is an attempt to support this critical perspective. I will continue the argument by looking at the 'schizophrenia' studies.

'Schizophrenia'[1]

Firstly, there is a problem in definition and diagnosis. These have been very loose and with changing features since Bleuler introduced the term early in this century. In fact Mary Boyle presents a convincing case that what Bleuler described was encephalitis lethargica, the odd collection of behaviours and experiences recently brought to light again with the film *Awakenings*[2] by the brilliant combination of Oliver Sachs, Robyn Williams and Robert de Niro. During this century and in different countries 'schizophrenia' has been variously defined – usually much more broadly in the USA than in Europe and differently again in Russia. It has been common, however, for one or another of the following to be emphasized: thought disorders, incongruent emotions, and hallucinations and delusions, but no one common defining characteristic has been used. The DSM definitions of 'schizophrenia' have changed right up to the latest scheme, where the key characteristics are poor performance in the areas of work, social relations and self-care, together with delusions or hallucinations or thought or feeling disorders with delusions or hallucinations.[3] The alternatives in the symptom list mean that people with very different experiences will fall under the label of 'schizophrenia'. Also people whom psychiatrists and others regard as normal can have these experiences. Another factor is that a great deal of the schizophrenia research was conducted before the 1987 DSM was published, and samples of schizophrenic subjects are likely to be quite different to present-day samples. Finally, changes have already been suggested for the DSM-IV diagnosis of 'schizophrenia', which will again affect the people demarcated as 'schizophrenic' for research purposes.[4] Problems arise in comparing research findings as the object of the study, 'schizophrenia', takes on different meanings. It is common for these problems to be overlooked. Is that justifiable in the light of the research findings? Do they allow us to see the object of study with greater clarity or do they merely add to the problems?

There are three major lines of research into 'schizophrenia': studies in genetics, drug studies and brain imaging work. The results claimed for the last are fairly conservative, indicating at most that brain abnormalities have been found in some schizophrenic patient samples. The 'dopamine hypothesis' developed from the drug studies has been described as the 'most influential biologic hypothesis of schizophrenia for more than two decades',[5] yet the certainty of the findings has been disputed and there are few papers on it in recent journals. Others claim that 'the genetic contribution to schizophrenia is the most clearly established etiologic factor.'[6] This has also been challenged, and many working in the area currently assert that the cause for schizophrenia is unknown,[7] questioning Solomon

Snyder's confident claim in 1974 that, 'through careful clinical observations over the years and more recently because of rigorous genetic studies, we can affirm that there does exist a disease called schizophrenia.'[8]

Genetic studies of schizophrenia

The genetics studies fall into two categories, those using twins and those using adopted children. One of the most famous twin studies was undertaken by Franz Kallman. This study purportedly showed that schizophrenia is more likely to be shared between identical twins than fraternal twins.[9] Snyder claims that such findings 'provide fairly convincing evidence that a strong genetic element determines whether someone will become schizophrenic'.[10] Leon Kamin has, however, published a strong critique of this research. He points out that the diagnosis of one of each pair of twins was from hospital records, and, for the other twin, Kallman relied on a variety of sources which does not instil confidence about the reliability of the diagnoses. Kallman acknowledged that the task often involved

> formidable difficulties . . . we were dealing with inferior people . . . They sometimes escaped our search for years . . . Quite a few were bad-humored . . . we had to overcome the suspicion with which certain classes regarded any kind of official activity . . . Whenever we encountered serious opposition we found ourselves to be dealing with either officials and members of the academic world, or people with exaggerated suspicions, . . . our private sources of information were amplified from the records of police bureaus . . . In making inquiries about people already dead or living too far away, we employed . . . local bureaus and trusted agents.[11]

More recent studies do not overcome the problems of diagnosis – still diagnosing one of the twin pair after death, depending on the word of relatives or others – but Kallman's results have not been replicated. The general trend is for there to be less and less of a difference between identical and fraternal twins on the liklihood of both getting 'schizophrenia'. In a 1984 study, aware of the problems of diagnosis, the authors used more than one measure of schizophrenia and came up with different results. Some of these results show no inherited component in schizophrenia.[12] When 'schizophrenia' is quite strictly defined no inherited component is found. When it is broadly defined, to include 'probable schizophrenia', then the results show an inherited component. This may, however, simply be an artefact of the measure used to define 'schizophrenia'. Apart from these enormous diagnostic problems, alternative explanations can be given of the findings such as Kallman's. Identical twins look alike and for that reason are more likely to be treated alike than fraternal twins. Supposing schizophrenia does exist, one hypothesis could be that it is brought about by relationships between people, the sort of psychological environment in which one is placed. These two considerations would be enough to explain Kallman's findings, and taken together they do away with the need to postulate a genetic element in 'schizophrenia'.

Even if it is agreed that there is a genetic element in schizophrenia, that by itself does not give credence to the medical model. The controversial point is whether schizophrenia is a disease entity or not. Merely revealing that schizophrenia is genetically linked is insufficient to decide this controversy. Some critics of the medical model regard schizophrenia as a special strategy that a person adopts in order to live in an unlivable situation.[13] It is quite consistent with this to maintain that some people have a genetic predisposition to adopt such strategies. Consider the analogy with aggression. Some claim that this is genetically linked, but there is no suggestion that it constitutes a disease.

Before the twin studies can be used to provide convincing support for the medical model, several problems have to be overcome. These include the diagnostic variability, and hence the difficulty of knowing whether a relevant sample has been used, the plausibility of alternative hypotheses and the fact that a genetic link is not necessarily anything to do with illness.

Other studies, using adopted children, purport to support the medical model[14] in backing up the claim that 'genetic factors are important in the transmission of schizophrenia'.[15] The idea of these studies is to identify some adopted children who are schizophrenic and then to look at the incidence of schizophrenia in their biological families and in their adopted families. If there is a higher incidence of schizophrenia in their biological families than in their adopted families, this could be used to lend support to the view that the children's schizophrenia is genetically transmitted. This is the idea but it has never quite made it into practice.

The major problem with these studies centres around the diagnostic categories used. What the authors claim to have shown is that chronic schizophrenics (i.e., people who are supposed to have been suffering from 'the schizophrenic disease' over a long period) have a very high incidence of *schizophrenic-related disorders* in their biological families but not in their adopted families.

A relationship between schizophrenia in the adopted children and schizophrenia in their biological parents has not been found, but it is claimed that a relationship has been detected between chronic schizophrenia in the adopted children and a broad collection of disorders which are supposed to include schizophrenia and other disorders related to schizophrenia in their biological parents.

These studies are highly questionable because of the problems in defining and diagnosing 'schizophrenic-related disorders'. As indicated above, there are problems with the diagnosis of schizophrenia and, if that category is expanded, the problems become even bigger. 'Schizophrenic-related disorders' include 'borderline schizophrenics'. Such people are characterized as follows: their thinking is a bit vague; they experience episodes of feeling strange and confused under stress and are never very happy.[16] Many, perhaps most, people in Western culture answer to this description. How do we separate such people from normal people not suffering from a disorder? There is also a further question about whether a person so described is really disordered. In one of the main studies a further category was used entitled 'uncertain borderline schizophrenic'.[17] This was included as a 'schizophrenic-related disorder'. The uncertainty of that diagnosis speaks for itself.

If we take out of the study those parents diagnosed as having borderline schizophrenia or uncertain borderline schizophrenia, then no relationship remains between chronic schizophrenia in the adopted children and schizophrenic-related disorders in the biological parents. Thus the findings appear significant only when extremely dubious categorizations of disorders are used. If the subjects who fall into the dubious categories are eliminated or regarded as normal, then the evidence for the biological transmission of schizophrenia, from these studies, falls away.

In a more recent article, Kety, Rosenthal and Wender, who have played a key role in these adoption studies, acknowledge the problematic nature of the concept of schizophrenic-related disorders, but they decide to retain reference to such 'disorders' 'in the hope that our studies might shed some light on their relationship to chronic schizophrenia'.[18] This simply repeats the weakness of the earlier report. The supposed disorders that fall under the category 'schizophrenic-related disorders' may not really be disorders at all. The adoption studies have, as yet, too many flaws to support a claim about schizophrenia and genetic links.

Some research based in molecular genetics has been put forward as providing support. Sherrington et al.[19] claim to have demonstrated a genetic linkage on the chromosome 5 to schizophrenia in seven British and Icelandic families. There are several methodological problems with these studies, however. The findings do not in fact reach the level of statistical significance that the authors themselves agree should apply; also, as in the adoption studies, the category of 'schizophrenia' has been extended into impossible vagueness, with 'schizophrenic spectrum disorders'. A research team headed by James Kennedy did not duplicate Sherrington's results[20] and nor has more recent work.[21] Sherrington's confidence that we are close to the point of genetic counselling for families where chromosome 5 linkage can be reliably established has turned out to be premature. The suggestion was possibly quite damaging given that it was published in *Nature*, a widely read magazine. Attempts to establish other genetic linkages to schizophrenia have also failed.[22]

As mentioned above, even if a genetic component to schizophrenia is established, this is not necessarily support for the medical model. Mere genetic transmission tells us nothing about whether the factor transmitted relates to illness or disorder. Also, far from shedding light on the diagnosis of schizophrenia, these studies compound the problems by introducing an even broader category.

Schizophrenia and body chemistry

Another line of research purportedly supporting the medical model relates to the action of certain drugs. There is a great deal of conjecture about the effects on the brain of drugs which are used to treat schizophrenia, for example, chlorpromazine. Although this drug does not bring about a cure, it is thought to alleviate the symptoms. The fact that chlorpromazine does bring about a change in the behaviour and experiences of some people diagnosed as schizophrenic is insufficient to support the medical model, however. Instead of saying the drug works by changing the chemistry in the brain which was previously malfunctioning, an alternative hypothesis could go as follows: when a person is diagnosed as schizophrenic she is acting in an unusual way because of the environmental pressures upon her. There is no physical malfunctioning of the brain present. This hypothesis is credible given the reported psychological effects of taking chlorpromazine:

It provokes not any loss of consciousness, nor any change in the patient's mentality, but a slight tendency to sleep and above all 'disinterest' for all that goes on around him.[23]

Under the influence of chlorpromazine people seemed to pay little heed to their environment and to be perceptually indifferent, even though their sensory abilities were fully intact and they were awake.[24]

If so-called schizophrenia is a way of reacting to environmental pressures, and if a diagnosed schizophrenic loses interest in her environment because of the action of chlorpromazine, then it is understandable that the symptoms of schizophrenia would disappear. There is no need to postulate the existence of a brain disease. Also the alternative explanation suggested need not bring in the assumption that schizophrenia is a disease, whether physical or mental. Changes in behaviour and experience are possible without it necessarily being the case that one state is disordered or ill and another is ordered and healthy. This point is taken up again in the final chapter.

Other drugs that have been studied in connection with schizophrenia are the amphetamines. Amphetamine psychosis is the name given to the condition experienced by some people addicted to amphetamines who have consumed large amounts of the drug gradually over a period of several days. According to Snyder, this condition 'closely mimics paranoid schizophrenia'.[25] In 'amphetamine psychosis', the drug affects the brain in some way to make it malfunction. As 'amphetamine psychosis' is thought to be similar to schizophrenia, the conclusion is drawn that schizophrenia must have a chemical basis too.

Given the difficulties in defining and diagnosing schizophrenia, this argument is very dubious. Even within the proponent's own terms there are difficulties. Snyder believes that schizophrenics are supposed to suffer disturbances of thought and feeling. There is no evidence that 'amphetamine psychotics' have such disturbances. Snyder simply states that they must suffer from them, as they have often been diagnosed as 'schizophrenic'.[26] But he agrees that it is very difficult to diagnose on the basis of these disturbances and he claims that diagnosis of schizophrenia usually rests on whether hallucinations are present or not. He also admits, however, that hallucinations are neither a necessary nor a sufficient condition for schizophrenia.[27] Given all these problems, there is no solid ground on which to make the judgement that 'amphetamine psychosis' is similar to 'schizophrenia'.

A related and similarly problematic argument used by Snyder for the medical model runs as follows: amphetamines activate latent schizophrenic symptoms; it is then implied that brain chemistry must be at the basis of schizophrenia.[28] If accurate diagnosis of 'schizophrenia' is difficult, then surely accurate diagnosis of 'latent schizophrenia' will be even more so. In fact, it will not be possible to make such a diagnosis until after the person has shown some symptoms, if at all. Once the symptoms appear, it will be impossible to say whether they amount to schizophrenia revealing itself or are simply the effects of the drug.

The strongest line of defence for the view that schizophrenia involves a malfunctioning of the brain is thought to come from the studies done on the neurotransmitter dopamine.[29] It has been observed that most anti-psychotic drugs reduce the activity of dopamine-dependent systems in the body. This led to the view that the dopamine system in schizophrenic patients is hyperactive. Many studies have tried to estimate the concentrations of dopamine and its metabolites in the cerebrospinal fluid of patients or in brain tissues post-mortem. However, 'most investigators have been unable to find significant, still less specific, changes in the concentrations of dopamine and its metabolites in schizophrenia.'[30] Even if 'positive' results were to be found, there is a known effect on neurotransmitters from the anti-psychotic drugs. Most of the research subjects are on these drugs, which is likely to confuse the results. Also the value of the dopamine/schizophrenia hypothesis rests largely on the acceptance of the assumption that the anti-psychotic drugs are antagonistic to schizophrenia exclusively. If the drugs produce a generalized effect then it could be argued that, in the process of bringing large segments of the human nervous system into a resting phase, the intensity of the schizophrenic's unwanted experiences are also diminished.[31] As pointed out above, the drugs do have a generalized effect. This further undermines the position that the drug studies support the view that there is a malfunctioning of dopamine in schizophrenia.

There is now speculation about the possibility of a more fundamental abnormality lying somewhere else in the body chemistry and giving rise to problems with dopamine. No agreement has been reached, however, about where or what this abnormality is.[32]

All these drug studies are plagued by the problems of diagnosis, perhaps even more so than the genetics studies considered above. Some of the experiments with drugs have been done on animals. One researcher reports a study he conducted on schizophrenia in spiders![33] This condition is supposed to be revealed by the erratic webs that the orb weaving spider weaves after it has been injected with the blood from human schizophrenic patients. Some of the spiders in the study didn't in fact produce abnormal webs but, more importantly, what a leap of imagination has taken place here to call abnormal web-building a sign of schizophrenia! Most proponents of the medical model would agree that non-human animals cannot have schizophrenia. So the conclusions drawn about schizophrenia from animal experiments must be inconclusive.

Cowdry and Goodwin, in a recent survey of the theories which attempt to explain dopamine irregularities, conclude that 'the paucity of reproducible biological findings suggests that gross clinical groups [such as "schizophrenia"] may not correspond well to identifiable single pathophysiologic derangements, at least as reflected in neurotransmitter studies.'[34]

Another branch of research concerns certain neurotransmitter-related enzymes found in plasma or blood cells. Dopamine b-Hydroxylase (DBH) interacts with dopamine. If dopamine is implicated in schizophrenia, then perhaps one would expect to find some irregularity in DBH. However, the studies reveal no difference in plasma or serum DBH between schizophrenic patients and controls.[35] The enzyme Erythrocyte Catechol-O-Methyl Transferase (COMT) is important in the degradation of dopamine. Again, if dopamine is important for schizophrenia, perhaps one might expect that this could be detected in the level of activity of this enzyme. Studies have not borne this out.[36]

The enzyme platelet Monoamine Oxidase (MAO) is thought to function in a regulatory fashion for several components of neurotransmitter metabolism. Some studies do show that platelet MAO activity is reduced in chronic schizophrenic patients in comparison with controls.[37] One large study does not, however, confirm this result.[38] Also, whether this relation exists or not, reduced MAO activity cannot be taken to be the central malfunction in chronic schizophrenia as 'first-degree, well relatives of patients with . . . schizophrenia and well twins in a study of monozygotic twins discordant for schizophrenia all manifested equivalent reductions in MAO activity when compared to their ill relatives.'[39] Murphy and Buchsbaum, in a survey of the research on enzymes, conclude that the 'data now available . . . do not strongly support [the speculation that] one or another of the enzyme differences might prove to be a biological "cause" for psychiatric diagnostic entities like schizophrenia.'[40]

A final point needs to be made about these studies into the chemistry of schizophrenics and others: if an organic difference is found between schizophrenics and normal people, this does not in itself establish the medical model. According to this model, schizophrenia has as its basis a physiochemical malfunction. The organic condition of schizophrenics need not, however, be the *basis* of their schizophrenia. The basis may be elsewhere. Whatever mental states we are in presumably have a correlate in terms of brain functioning, and that brain functioning may take on a particular pattern if our mental states form a pattern. Thus all people who play chess may, to some degree, share a certain sort of mental state during play, and there may be something similar in the functioning of their brains. It is obviously absurd to say in this case that it is the organic condition of the brain which causes the chess-playing behaviour. Similarly people who, over a period of time, behave in a way that gets labelled 'schizophrenic' may have certain similarities, in terms of brain functioning, with others who receive this label. This brain condition could be a mere correlate of their mental state, or it may be causally produced by the mental state. If 'schizophrenics' are shown to be different from others in some physical or chemical condition, whether in the brain or elsewhere, this is insufficient to establish a physiochemical basis for so-called schizophrenia.

Furthermore, supposing there is a particular organic condition which separates schizophrenics from non-schizophrenics, the medical model needs to show that this amounts to a *malfunction* in the former case, rather than a mere difference. If there is no malfunction present, there would be no basis for regarding schizophrenia as an illness. However, if a difference is established, it cannot simply be assumed that such a difference amounts to a malfunction.

In conclusion, although there are some interesting findings about dopamine and the action of chlorpromazine, and although these findings have led to speculations about the basis of schizophrenia, the status of the research is such that alternative explanations of the phenomena are possible. This research does not overcome or even confront the problems of definition and diagnosis. It has not produced a consistent, well-supported theory concerning the basis of schizophrenia. If it is successful in the future in revealing an organic condition peculiar to 'schizophrenics', that will still be a long way from supporting the medical model.

Brain imaging studies of schizophrenia

In the last 15 years computer technology has been used to try to detect specific abnormalities in the structure or function of the brains of schizophrenic patients. Computerized tomographic imaging (the CT scan) is employed in combination with EEG data to produce a map of the brain. A further mapping technique involves 'positron emission tomography' (PET). The subject is injected with radioactive substances which localize in the brain. The radioactive atom decays and releases a positron, and through detecting the action of the positron, biochemical function can be worked out. A further imaging technique that has been used is magnetic resonance. This involves no radiation but is less sensitive than PET.

While some researchers would like to see these techniques as probing the causal basis of schizophrenia, others claim that at best they would provide biological markers.[41] The research has not even fulfilled this limited, second aim. While some people diagnosed as schizophrenic have been shown by these methods to have certain brain abnormalities of either structure or function, others with the same diagnosis do not always have those abnormalities. They may have different ones or no abnormalities at all. One leading research group in the field asserts that 'the brain structure of the majority of schizophrenic patients looks normal.'[42] Furthermore, control subjects from the 'normal' population have been shown to have some of the abnormalities detected in some 'schizophrenic' subjects.[43] One confounding factor is the fact that most of the patients in the research are on medication for schizophrenia which is believed to affect the results of brain imaging, but in unknown ways. The results then are very inconclusive[44] and, as Seeman et al. claim, 'no dependable or diagnostic markers have yet been found despite the extensive array of plausible hypotheses.'[45]

Some researchers argue that schizophrenia is too broad a category, and they suggest subgroups defined by particular brain abnormalities. There is, however, no consensus on such subgroups. This move is a type of *ad hoc* modification of a theory in the face of disconfirming evidence that Karl Popper argued so strongly against in *The Logic of Scientific Discovery*.[46] The theory that there is an isolable brain abnormality in schizophrenia is falsified by research. Instead of rejecting the theory, it is modified to try to take account of the falsifications. The modifications do not have any independent support. They are introduced solely to bolster the original hypothesis. Popper claims that such a move is illegitimate. My own view is that this claim is too tough but is worth taking into account if no independent evidence is forthcoming in the long term.

There are also ethical problems raised by the PET studies. The intervention is not thought to be therapeutic, and perhaps it will have damaging long-term effects from the radiation, currently unknown. One research group states:

> Although at this stage of development it may seem as if we are asking our patients to undergo radioactive procedures which will not benefit them directly in any way, we must recognize that we are on the brink of a new era of discovery. If the brain can yield its mystery, at least in part, to the advances of new technology, then our patients in time to come will be diagnosed more accurately, treated more specifically and will suffer less.[47]

Even if one were to believe this rhetoric – and there is no compelling reason to do so – an ethical problem remains: why should today's 'schizophrenics' be put at risk to help future patients?

Looking at the schizophrenia research overall, an interesting picture emerges. None of the detailed theoretical lines have established biological markers for schizophrenia or the biological cause. Yet this is supposed to be the area of greatest strength for biological psychiatry. The studies do not even lead to clarification of the object of study: schizophrenia. They produce greater confusion with the introduction of the category of schizophrenia-related disorders. Yet there is a pervasive aura of confidence in the field. Those who work in one area, for example, brain imaging, recognize the inconclusive nature of their research but suggest that the direction is bolstered by the more secure findings in the genetics area. Those working in genetics refer to the established results from the dopamine hypothesis, but not genetics. Those working on the dopamine hypothesis hold out more hope for the genetics studies than their own work.

Perhaps the persistence of the biological model in the face of failure can be understood by the lack of alternatives? In fact a very promising alternative was suggested by Laing and Esterson in 1964 in the book *Sanity, Madness and the Family*.[48] They did not provide a social cause of schizophrenia. They showed how it was possible to explain the behaviour and experiences which had been taken to be 'the signs and symptoms of schizophrenia' without assuming that schizophrenia was an isolable condition. They argued that such an assumption was not only without foundation but that it was dangerous. The timing of the presentation of this position was unfortunate. In the mid-1960s the genetics and chlorpromazine studies were just beginning, and many believed that they would put psychiatry firmly on a biological footing. Research money poured into that direction – especially, of course, the money provided by the pharmaceutical industry.

Even in the present, when we are immersed in this particular historical epoch when the medical model is so dominant, it is difficult to question the idea that schizophrenia is an illness or disorder which afflicts specific individuals. Yet undercurrents of criticism are very much alive. Franco Basaglia has achieved great success in Italy in shifting the theoretical and practical basis of psychiatry.[49] Sarbin and Bentall are presenting exciting alternative hypotheses to the English-speaking world.[50] These authors are not attempting to give an alternative causal theory of schizophrenia but rather to question the validity of the category. It may be granted that some people experience hallucinations, some are deluded and so on, but we are likely to come closer to understanding the meaning of these experiences if we refuse to reify them into a 'condition' and instead look at their meaning in the person's context. Sarbin, preferring to talk about 'imaginings' rather than hallucinations, says: 'each person has his or her own story, and the expressed beliefs, the atypical imaginings, the instrumental acts of withdrawing from strain-producing situations are intentional acts designed to solve identity and existential problems. The actions designed to keep one's self-narrative consistent are not invariant or machine-like outcomes of postulated disease processes.'[51]

Perhaps, patient reader, you think that the technical overload of this discussion is diverting from the main topic of this book. 'Schizophrenia' is usually diagnosed more in men than in women. However, if I have been successful in showing that there are epistemological problems in this area, then weaknesses in other areas that do relate more to women can be seen in a clearer perspective. We may be less convinced that those weaknesses can be overcome. Also it has recently been suggested that the fact that more men are diagnosed with 'schizophrenia' is simply because the definition included 'early onset', and women are likely to have a later onset. In any case there are issues of vital concern to women in the genetic linkage studies. If positive results had emerged there, it is a short step to genetic screening, to recommended abortions for those who carry the 'schizophrenia gene'.

Furthermore, as Elaine Showalter has argued, the schizophrenic woman has become as central a cultural figure for the twentieth century as the hysteric was for the nineteenth. She documents this by reference to literary texts and films, claiming that 'modernist literary movements have appropriated the schizophrenic woman as the symbol of linguistic, religious, and sexual breakdown and rebellion.'[52]

As we move further into the 1990s another association between women and madness is gaining ground, a link to eating disorders. This area is useful to investigate on the second epistemological concern mentioned at the beginning of the chapter to see whether the perspective of medical psychiatry is endorsed. It also reveals how epistemological issues merge with ethical ones.

Eating disorders

In looking at what psychiatric medicine says about how to conceptualize and understand eating disorders, the epistemological questions of this chapter, I also want to examine the role of values. I will argue that, given the framework of understanding that flows from biological psychiatry, certain treatment directions will be indicated and other ways of understanding a phenomenon will be excluded. Yet if the psychiatric medical approach is unsubstantiated, then there is a moral problem in recommending those treatments which do not have a good record of success, and there is a moral problem in excluding from consideration directions that could lead to a richer understanding.

According to the DSM, there are two rare eating disorders that occur in babies, and anorexia nervosa and bulimia nervosa. Anorexia nervosa is defined as follows:

A. Refusal to maintain body weight over a minimal normal weight for age and height, for example, weight loss leading to maintenance of body weight 15% below that expected; or failure to make expected weight gain during period of growth, leading to body weight 15% below that expected.

B. Intense fear of gaining weight or becoming fat, even though underweight.

C. Disturbance in the way in which one's body weight, size, or shape is experienced, for example, the person claims to 'feel fat' even when emaciated, believes that one area of the body is 'too fat' even when obviously underweight.

D. In females, absence of at least three consecutive menstrual cycles when otherwise expected to occur (primary or secondary amenorrhea).

(A woman is considered to have amenorrhea if her periods occur only following hormone, e.g. estrogen, administration.)[53]

The diagnostic criteria for bulimia nervosa are as follows:

A. Recurrent episodes of binge eating (rapid consumption of a large amount of food in a discrete period of time).
B. A feeling of lack of control over eating behaviour during the eating binges.
C. The person regularly engages in either self-induced vomiting, use of laxatives or diuretics, strict dieting or fasting, or vigorous exercise in order to prevent weight gain.
D. A minimum average of two binge eating episodes a week for at least three months.
E. Persistent overconcern with body shape and weight.[54]

Some investigators disagree with these criteria, not wanting, for instance, to include amenorrhea,[55] and questioning whether body perception disturbance is a consistent feature of anorexia nervosa.[56] All seem to agree that the disorders are much more common in women than men.

The attempt to isolate the biological fault in eating disorders follows a similar pattern to other areas of psychiatry:

1   there is an appeal to genetics to argue that some people have a genetic disposition to develop anorexia nervosa. I believe that while this may be true, the research to date has not established that conclusion, and, even if it did, the conclusion on its own is not enough to support a medical orientation.
2   there is an assumption that the disorders are caused by faulty chemistry, and research is done into various possible chemical faults. The argument I wish to put here is that, while there may be certain chemical *differences* between a person diagnosed with one of these disorders and others, we don't need to conclude that these chemical differences are the cause of the disorder.
3   new computer scanning techniques are used to attempt to isolate abnormal brain patterns in those suffering from the disorders. Here I want to claim that interesting correlations might emerge, but these correlations may not tell us anything about causation.

If this critique of the medical psychiatric perspective is successful it could still be argued that the treatments which emerge from it have a pragmatic value. The most commonly used medications for anorexia nervosa are the anti-depressants. They are not, however, superior to placebos when tested under double-blind conditions. The anti-schizophrenic drugs have also been used, but a recent survey of the effect of these drugs for anorexia nervosa failed to show any marked benefit.[57] Bulimia nervosa is sometimes treated with anti-depressants, but trials have not substantiated any claim as to their effectiveness. Also, the cause of death in a significant number of people with eating disorders who die is an overdose of anti-depressants.[58] Extremely dangerous drugs called MAO inhibitors have also been used for bulimia nervosa. They are dangerous for several reasons. One is that if you take them with certain common foods you can die. It is hard to evaluate their effect in treating bulimia nervosa, as most subjects drop out of the tests because of intolerable side-effects.[59] In summary, it cannot be argued that the treatment proposals that emerge from the biological model of eating disorders have a pragmatic justification.

The biological research into eating disorders

I shall now move on to more details of the argument – firstly, the genetic evidence. Is there a genetic component to the eating disorders? Some of the research here has simply looked at the incidence of anorexia or bulimia in family members. Some studies claim to have found that if one member has an eating disorder then there is a slight possibility that another family member will be so affected. Other studies do not replicate this result.[60] None of these studies provide a strong basis for the claim that there is a genetic component to anorexia or bulimia, as even when more than one member has a disorder this could be caused by the family social context. There are strong suggestions coming out of the literature to support the view that families which include members with eating disorders give health and fitness an exceptional priority[61] and that they also place greater than average importance upon food and eating.[62]

One study using twins indicated that about 50 per cent of 24 pairs of 'identical' twins both had anorexia nervosa. Methodological problems lead to scepticism about this result. There is, for instance, a question about whether all the pairs were identical.[63] As non-identical twins share about the same number of genes as ordinary siblings, a finding of concordance for a disorder in non-identical twins may not be telling us anything about genetics. In a recent study that is constantly referred to as establishing a genetic base for anorexia nervosa, Holland et al.[64] found that 9 out of 16 pairs of identical twins shared anorexia nervosa but for 14 pairs of non-identical twins only one pair shared the disorder. They claim to have sorted out the methodological problems of previous studies by using a more precise measure of zygosity (a measure which determines whether the twins are identical or not). However, they do not escape another methodological problem. The authors knew whether the twins were identical or not at the time they made the assessment of whether the person had anorexia or not. There is the possibility of the well established problem of experimenter bias here, and it is puzzling why the researchers did not proceed in a way that would avoid it. The certainty of their results is undercut by this weakness. Also there is a further criticism that people who look alike tend to be treated alike, which might explain why a disorder is shared by identical twins – if it is – quite independently from any genetic theories.

Finally, it may be true that anorexia has a genetic component without it being the case that anorexia should be regarded primarily as a biological disorder. Along the lines argued above, it may be true that musical ability has a genetic component, but we are not tempted to say that this is a biological disorder. Thus to agree that there is a genetic component to anorexia nervosa is not to accept the view that anorexia nervosa is primarily a biological disorder.

The second strand of the argument for the biological model of eating disorders delves into body chemistry. The dominant theory along these lines asserts that the disorders are a disease of the neuroendocrine system.[65] The endocrine system controls hormones which have an effect on bodily function and metabolism and this system is closely linked to the brain. The brain both influences and is influenced by the endocrine system. Hence we can talk of a neuroendocrine system. The menstrual cycle is part of this system, and the cycle stops in women affected by anorexia nervosa. Indeed, those suffering from anorexia nervosa have low levels of the sex hormones.[66] These hormones are under the control of another hormone released by part of the brain called the hypothalamus. It is not possible to measure the hypothalamic hormone directly, but indirect measures show that there are abnormal levels of the hypothalamic hormone in women suffering from anorexia nervosa.[67] The hypothalamus is involved in the control of appetite, satiation, sexuality and emotion, all of which are changed in anorexia nervosa. Drawing all these strands together, it is argued that anorexia nervosa is a primary disease of the neuroendocrine system, notably of the hypothalamus and the related areas of the brain.[68] A more specific hypothesis makes the claim that there is an increase in the chemical triggers which decrease feeding in anorexia nervosa. There is some evidence for this.[69]

The mere fact of cessation of periods in women with anorexia nervosa forces us to grant that there is a biological change, but we do not need to accept that the basic problem is biological. Weight and level of nutrition in the diet seem to be the keys to understanding the neuroendocrine changes, as when the weight and nutritional content of the diet are restored to normal the hormone levels return to normal too.[70] Weight on its own is not a sufficient explanation, as not all anorexic subjects regain normal endocrine and menstrual function as soon as their weight is back to normal.[71] However, these functions return to normal as the woman moves off a starvation diet and gains weight. Thus it seems most likely that the dietary restraint causes the neuroendocrine changes rather than the other way around.

In bulimia nervosa a rather similar story is emerging. Periods do not cease and weight may remain normal, but in some other respects the neuroendocrinology of bulimia overlaps with that of anorexia nervosa.[72] It is also thought that the triggers that signal satiety may be set differently from normal, which may prompt binge eating. There is some indirect chemical evidence along these lines.[73] Further indirect evidence comes from a study which showed that bulimic subjects were less responsive to chemical signals that lead to the termination of meals because they were hungrier at the end of meals than control subjects.[74]

Can we say that the basic fault in bulimia nervosa is a neuroendocrine one? Although some researchers draw this conclusion,[75] alternative explanations seem more plausible. Some writers claim that weight changes bring about the neuroendocrine changes,[76] but this won't account for those suffering from bulimia nervosa who retain normal weight. Schweiger and others have demonstrated that, in spite of their weight status, bulimic sufferers are often effectively in a state of starvation, and they claim that it is this nutritional deprivation that causes the neuroendocrine changes. A further piece of relevant research is that neuroendocrine disturbances may result from reduced caloric intake, not just in those with eating disorders, but also in normal subjects.[77] Levy, in 'Neuroendocrine profile of bulimia nervosa', states that the person with bulimia nervosa may be in a 'normal weight malnourished state', but suggests that malnourishment needs to be defined in ways other than by weight parameters.[78] If the primary problems are isolated as weight and lack of adequate diet, then we are not forced to posit a biological cause.

A further line of reasoning that tries to pin bulimia nervosa down to a biological fault runs as follows: there is an association between bulimia nervosa and depression. Depression is caused by a biological fault, therefore bulimia is caused by a biological fault.[79] As I have shown in the previous chapter, this claim about the cause of depression doesn't stand up under scrutiny and this style of argument is an example of the 'sleight of hand' manoeuvre – a weak piece of reasoning in one area is used to back weak reasoning in another.

A variant of this theme is put forward by Pope and Hudson, with the idea that bulimia is the result of an underlying depression.[80] Nothing beyond correlation is offered in support of this claim, and the mere fact of correlation is too weak to support a causal conclusion. Indeed it would be surprising if bulimia sufferers did not experience some depression related to their eating practices, so a causal link may be in the opposite direction from that proposed by Pope and Hudson. Other research reports bear on this issue. Laessle et al. draw attention to the fact that depression in bulimia is no more common than in any other psychiatric condition, and they suggest that it may be secondary to low carbohydrate intake.[81]

I shall now turn briefly to the third line of evidence for the biological model – that involved in computer scanning. Using cranial computerized tomography (CT), certain structural changes have been observed in the brains of subjects with anorexia nervosa (enlargement of the external cerebrospinal fluid spaces and/or a dilation of the ventricles). Also recent CT studies of bulimic subjects with normal weight have revealed morphological brain alterations similar to those found with anorexic subjects.[82] There is dispute about whether these changes can simply be regarded as the effects of starvation or not.[83] The research is quite new and further work with control subjects is needed to clarify this issue. At most what this research reveals to date is that structural brain changes are a biological marker of the eating disorders. The research does not help us sort out what is causally primary. Also, before anything definitive can be said about the biology of either of the eating disorders, the biology of starvation needs to be further researched. Recent work is indicating that any physical abnormality surfacing in anorexia or bulimia might simply be the result of starvation.[84]

Another line of investigation which challenges the biological model is into the historical and cultural variability of eating disorders. Anorexia nervosa has been recognized at least since the seventeenth century.[85] Yet even in the 1970s one of the key workers in the field declared that anorexia was 'rare indeed'.[86] In 1984 'it was estimated that one in every 200–250 women between the ages of thirteen and twenty-two suffers from anorexia and that anywhere between 12 and 33 percent of college women control their weight through vomiting, diuretics and laxatives.'[87] Ben Tovim et al. assert that 'in just a few years bulimia has gone from being virtually unknown to being described as a "major public health problem" and a disorder of "epidemic proportions".'[88] Other writers agree.[89]

Perhaps to some extent the incidence of these disorders was hidden before lists of criteria were specifically developed, but that is unlikely to be a sufficient explanation of the apparent historical variability. This feature poses obvious problems for a biological medical approach, as presumably women's biology has not varied that much or that suddenly.

This historical variability of eating disorders should also be considered in connection with the cultural variability. The above statistics refer to Western culture, specifically North America and Western Europe. Anorexia is virtually unknown in China or in the Chinese community in Hong Kong, less frequent in Russia and Eastern Europe, uncommon in Latin American countries, rare in Malaysia and increasing in Japan[90] and Australia. One generalization that seems to be supported is that where there is a genuine shortage of food these disorders are rare.[91] These cultural variations are ignored in writings defending the biological approach, but they do pose difficulties for it.

Non-biological accounts of eating disorders

There have been many attempts from psychoanalysts, often with a feminist orientation, to provide explanations of eating disorders. Several inconsistent positions have been suggested with unfortunately no clear reason to prefer any of the directions. For instance, the view that eating disorders are caused by an unconscious conflict resulting in a rejection of femininity is at variance with the view that anorexia is an exaggerated striving to achieve femininity.

Waller, Kaufman and Deutsch claim that 'anorexia stems from disapproval by parents of their adolescent daughter's sexuality resulting in her defending it by regression to the orality of infantile sexuality.'[92] Chernin also believes that

At the heart of an eating obsession is a regression to the infantile conditions [to fulfil] a need to regain a relationship to the . . . mystery of
female being – a mystery conferred inalienably upon women's lives by
our ability to create life and food from the female body . . . It is as if we
are trying to remind ourselves, through our obsessive overvaluation of
food, that we have been starved of this positive sense of an inherent
female creative power on the basis of which we could elaborate a new
and meaningful female social identity.[93]

While this focuses on fantasies underlying anorexia nervosa, Hilde
Bruch stresses the actual deprivations experienced by those suffering from eating disorders. These deprivations are a result of 'abnormal patterns of family interaction' in infancy.[94] The infant's needs
are not appropriately met and ego boundary problems arise. This
surfaces most clearly in adolescence. She writes of the patient as
someone who is not 'seen or acknowledged as an individual in her
own right, but . . . valued as someone who would make the life and
experiences of the parents more satisfying and complete.'[95]

Caskey puts forward a Jungian account that 'anorexics are caught
in a relationship to the animus as it is projected onto the father
. . . Anorexia is the result of a peculiar kind of incest which involves
a psychic relationship rather than a physical one.'[96]

How can these competing accounts be evaluated? The general
problems in the evaluation of psychoanalytic theories could be applicable here. Karl Popper argues that psychoanalysis is unscientific
because every conceivable observation can be explained in its terms.
Nothing serves as a possible falsification. This, according to Popper,
makes the view empty.[97] While I believe that Popper's conclusion is
too strong, there is certainly a difficulty in getting a basis to judge
the different theories. Also an evaluation in terms of the success of
treatments that emerge from the perspective is difficult to make
because of the lack of long-term follow-up studies.[98] Another source
of suspicion of the psychoanalytic approach to eating disorders is
that one of the main proponents, Hilde Bruch, actually opposes the
use of psychoanalytic interpretation in the treatment of anorexia,[99]
and Selvini-Palazzoli, who for years treated anorexic patients with
psychoanalysis, has abandoned it for a more directive, strategic
intervention.[100]

There has been some research linking eating disorders and child
abuse, and it might be suggested that psychoanalysis is still covering up this reality in the way suggested in Chapter 1. However, a
fairly consistent finding is that about 30 per cent of subjects diagnosed with eating disorders have experienced such abuse, and this

figure is in line with rates for the general female population in the USA and also the psychiatric population.[101] So there does not seem to be any *special* relationship between child abuse and eating disorders. One response to the abuse may be to develop an eating disorder, but, for many women with such a disorder, another explanation is needed.

Alternative accounts of eating disorders coming from non-psychoanalytic perspectives have been proposed and they constitute a greater threat to the medical view than psychoanalysis. Susan Bordo views anorexia as a cultural phenomenon linked to the particular situation of women in modern Western culture.[102] It is 'a symptom of some of the . . . distresses of our age'.[103] The key cultural phenomena that she claims are important in understanding anorexia are:

1 the belief in dualism: the mind/body split. 'This is manifested in the anorexic by a battle between the mind or will and appetite or body . . . in this battle, thinness represents a triumph of the will over the body.'[104]
2 the importance put on control of the body. 'The anorexic, typically, experiences her life and her hungers as being out of control.'[105] She feels powerless.
3 the cultural emphasis on the slenderness of women and the denigration of women. This phenomenon is manifested in anorexia by a disdain for traditional female roles and social limitations, and a 'deep fear of "The Female" with all its more nightmarish archetypal associations: voracious hungers and sexual insatiability'.[106]

Many aspects of eating disorders fall into place if this account is accepted. In particular, a plausible explanation can be given of the historical and cultural variability in incidence of the eating disorders. The rising incidence of the eating disorders in recent times parallels the decreasing estimates of the ideal body weight in Western culture.[107] This ties in with Bordo's third point. The cultural variability mentioned above is also easily accounted for in Bordo's explanation. The greater incidence of eating disorders in Western culture could be related to the above three factors, which are not so significant in other cultures.

Bordo does accept that anorexia is pathological. Eva Székely goes one step further in her socio-cultural account of what she calls the relentless pursuit of thinness. She believes that the practices which have been labelled 'eating disorders' do not represent a radical departure from the lives of other women in similar socio-historical contexts.[108] Hence she rejects the pathological status of anorexia and in fact avoids talking about 'anorexia' and 'bulimia'. The key question then becomes: what in the socio-cultural contexts of women's lives has created the possibility and the necessity for women to engage in the relentless pursuit of thinness? The answer suggested is that the context is one where 'appearance is considered to be woman's major asset, where what women are able to do matters far less than what they look like, where people are raised to be never satisfied in the midst of plenty.'[109] She points to the pressures on women to be thin in order to obtain and keep a job, and in order to find and keep the 'right calibre' of man.[110] Correlatively, 'women have been given the message that their efforts in improving and perfecting their bodies would be rewarded by success in both their personal and professional lives.'[111] One strand of support for Székely's argument comes from the ideals of female beauty. Studies carried out on Miss America contestants from 1979 to 1988 show that their body weight is 13 to 19 per cent below expected weight for women in that age group.[112] Yet some fashion magazines speak of the 1980s as a time of 'sexy excess' and rejoice in the 'bony backlash' of the new waif models, the 'imp-ingenues of string-bean proportions'. A leader of a top New York modelling agency comments on the new models: 'they're not tall, they're not buxom and sexy and '80's and rich and decadent-looking. They're kind of like nothing, frail, real people.'[113] Real people or real women? It is not men who are asked to be 'like nothing'. Although it is difficult to escape from this web of cultural expectation, one way forward is to see that it does operate and to ask whose interests it serves. It appears to conflict with the interests of the majority of women.

A final problem with the biological psychiatric approach is that it directs our attention away from accounts such as Székely's, and yet when one bears in mind the historico-cultural variability of so-called eating disorders it seems clearly the direction to take. Deflection from this direction by biological psychiatry could well be dangerous given the lives and suffering that are at stake and given the dubious effectiveness of biological cures.

In conclusion, medical psychiatry does not exist in a value neutral realm. The area of 'eating disorders' is one of the new fields of interest, but it is illustrative of what has happened in the research and treatment of 'schizophrenia' and 'depression'. A particular model of understanding is presented which defines a research direction and a treatment programme. When one theory falling under the model is successfully criticized, another is presented. A string of unsubstantiated theories emerge. The treatments are tied into the biological model but not to the specific theories. Hence the treatments can remain the same through the succession of theories. If the treatments could be claimed to work then perhaps there is no great ethical problem, except that certain other possibly more fruitful research directions aren't taken up. If, however, the treatments are not shown to be very beneficial and carry significant dangers, then an ethical problem emerges quite clearly. I have mentioned the dangers in the biological treatments of eating disorders. Breggin, in the book *Toxic Psychiatry*, presents a strong case for the hazardous and sometimes deadly nature of biological psychiatric treatments in general.[114] Also the fact that other research directions don't get a look-in is not just of academic interest. If Brown and Harris, Sarbin, Bordo and Székely are on the right track, then they not only provide a way of conceptualizing depression, schizophrenia and eating disorders which reveals why the medical psychiatric perspective must fail, but they also open up considerations for all women in modern Western culture to help us to understand the covert forms of oppression. Thus, in diverting our gaze from these directions, medical psychiatry colludes in the maintenance of the subordination of women, belying its value neutrality.

Psychiatry began in the late eighteenth century with a promise, a promise that the future would endorse the biological theoretical orientation. As we move towards the end of the twentieth century, this endorsement is thought to lie in the fields of genetics, neurophysiology and computer technology. These fields have a respectable scientific status in their own right. What I have argued above is that there are no solid findings from genetics, neurophysiology or computer studies which show that biological psychiatry is on the right track.

Some alternatives to medical psychiatry have been mentioned, and from Chapter 6 on I will draw these together with some other reflections which provide a basis for a non-biological approach to the problems of women and mental distress. Firstly, however, I would like to allude briefly to the extension of biological psychiatry into the area of women and crime.

5 Women, Psychiatry and Criminality

From the perspective of biological psychiatry, nearly all women are disordered. Even if we take into account only depression and premenstrual syndrome, it is difficult to imagine many women falling outside this net. It is no surprise, then, that criminal women are viewed as psychiatrically disordered. One of the themes that has been developed in earlier chapters concerns women's rebellion against the constrictions of the female role, and the power of psychiatry to pathologize this rebellion and to recommend treatment. This theme is relevant to the topic of women's crime too.

Female crimes and appropriate female behaviour

Young girls who break sex-specific norms by being promiscuous or 'ungovernable' may be convicted of an offence, and the fact that such offences are predominantly female is a reflection of attitudes about these activities in boys and girls. Sex bias determines whether promiscuity is an offence and a promiscuous girl is much more likely to be punished by institutionalization. A promiscuous boy may not be regarded as deviant at all. Similarly, 'ungovernability' may be understood in terms of hostility and violence, features which, in boys, may not be regarded as deviant at all or the importance of which is played down. In this way, sex-role stereotypes influence whether the same behaviour is regarded as an offence or not.[1]

In a study undertaken of children's courts in New York, it was revealed that if girls committed acts against sexual taboos, or against parents, this was enough to lead the probation officer to assume that psychiatric help was needed – but not so for boys. Carol Smart, in *Women, Crime and Criminology*, comments that 'This attitude towards female delinquency reflects the commonly held belief that deviancy by a female is a sign of a much deeper pathology than deviancy by a male.'[2]

Prostitution in adult women is often criminalized in Western countries. It also amounts to a break with the demand that women be sexually monogamous, and psychiatry enters to tell us that prostitution cannot be the result of a rational mind. Rather it is a form of sexual aberration – an activity that a woman is compelled to perform because of a mental disturbance. This is asserted without evidence and in the face of attractive alternative hypotheses, for example, that female prostitution can be understood in terms of certain broad social factors such as the relatively limited opportunites for women to earn a living wage, to win promotion, to achieve a secure career and to become economically independent of men.[3] It is also clear that a sex-biased logic is at work in not thinking about the men who go to prostitutes as criminal.

The crime of shoplifting shows quite clearly how sexist assumptions come into play in thinking about female crime. Women shoplifters generally steal food, usually of little value, and clothes, different things from what men usually steal, and their actions are quite in accord with the female role – women as providers of food and snappy dressers. If shoplifting takes this character it may not be regarded as irrational, but it will be seen as a crime nonetheless. If the theft cannot be so easily thought about within the confines of the female role, it may then be described as 'kleptomania', a psychiatric disorder which involves an irresistible impulse to steal. In a startling example of the strain that psychiatry needs to put on language in order to usurp the field of criminology, the *Diagnostic and Statistical Manual of Mental Disorders* talks about the 'impairment and complications' of kleptomania as follows: 'impairment is usually due to the legal consequences of being apprehended, the major complication of this disorder.'[4] The label of kleptomania may enable the woman to avoid criminal prosecution only by accepting that she is psychiatrically disabled.

Increasingly abortion has been decriminalized, but when it is regarded as a crime, a common thought is that one would have to be crazy to agree to such a procedure, as it cuts across the 'maternal instinct'. Moves in the United States to reverse the decriminalizing trend have been met with justified alarm by feminists. Michell

Oberman, writing in the *Berkeley Women's Law Journal*, reaches the conclusion that if legalized abortion comes to an end then 'women simply cannot exist'. This is because the US culture is a 'rape culture – one in which women's lives are restricted by the fear of ubiquitous sexual violence . . . all women live with the risk of male sexual intrusion', and an unwanted pregnancy. If the state will not allow abortions then 'the only true means of avoiding state intrusion into a woman's life will lie in sterilization.'[5] I suggest that even sterilization doesn't avoid state intrusion, as presumably one would not go down that path if abortion was a legal option.

Women who kill their infants overturn the female duty to nurture the young, and there is a further psychiatric assumption that such women are deranged by the birth experience. This is built into the law in some Western countries, where the infanticide plea is available. In English law the plea applies when a woman, by any wilful act or omission, causes the death of her child when it is under one year old, because the balance of her mind was disturbed by reason of her not having fully recovered from the effect of giving birth or by reason of the effect of lactation consequent upon the birth of the child. The reason why this plea is available only to women is because of some implied biological cause, but this is in fact still merely a conjecture. I believe the deeper reason for the designation of this crime as sex-specific is that it cuts across the supposed maternal instinct.

In the most extensive study carried out on women charged with the killing or attempted murder of their children, d'Orban claimed to have found that 41 per cent had a psychiatric disorder at the time of the offence. The most common classification was a personality disorder characterized by dependency and submissiveness or antisocial behaviour.[6] This seems to do little to fill out what it means to be deranged by the birth experience, which might give a fuller understanding of the infanticide plea. A feature of d'Orban's results which seems to be more instructive is the finding that 71 per cent of the subjects suffered from severe marital discord with their husband or cohabitee, often involving violence.[7]

In an analysis of 22 successful infanticide pleas in England in the 1980s, Wilczynski found that 'virtually any type of perceived psychiatric, emotional, personality or mental problem whatsoever *can* be interpreted (if the psychiatrists, lawyers and/or judges so choose) as the severe mental illness *theoretically* required for the *Infanticide Act*.'[8] Wilczynski argues that, although this may lead to sympathetic treatment for the woman, it obscures the social, economic and psychological stresses that play a dominant role in maternal infant-killings. Such stresses include 'caring for an infant who may be unwanted or difficult, lack of social and or spousal support, economic difficulties, unrealistic expectations of motherhood, and the stigma of an illegitimate child.'[9]

In Australia's most well-known criminal trial, Lindy Chamberlin was convicted of murdering her baby and sentenced to life imprisonment on the basis of having a public persona which did not meet the societal demands for how a mother should act if her baby disappears. She did not stay very long in the camping area where her baby was last seen while others conducted an extensive search; she did not always appear sad; she was assertive and hostile to lawyers. Outside the coroners court, the press took photos of Lindy Chamberlin arguing with her lawyer:

> Lindy had her hands planted on her hips. Her handbag swung from a shrugged shoulder. She looked attractive and bossy, three quarter face with upturned nose and pert mouth, a young woman who was well used to calling the shots even to her lawyer, and editors ran it front page all over the country.[10]

It was this sort of image built up from the press that determined the verdict. The baby certainly disappeared but there were no eyewitnesses to the disappearance; there was no body to prove that death had occurred, no weapon to illustrate the manner of it and no motive to betray deliberation or intent. There were, however, dingoes in the park where the family was camping. After years in prison and a number of appeals, Lindy Chamberlin's conviction was quashed. It was decided that a dingo took the baby. What the case illustrates is that violations of expected female behaviour consequent upon the loss of a child are adequate to bring a murder conviction. In the eyes of the public and the jury these violations were so horrible that they did not want to allow her the 'excuse' of insanity (not that she wanted to use it, as she never wavered in maintaining her innocence). She represented some 'unfathomable evil.'

Looking at the crime statistics in 42 countries, a 1992 United Nations survey found that, while female convictions have increased slightly, they are still a tiny percentage of male convictions. The types of offences have remained the same.[11] The differences between countries are of course flattened out in this sort of survey, and some writers mention changes in law enforcement practices which may be sufficient to explain the increase in female crime rates. The survey, in common with most crime statistics, fails to take account of the hidden enormity of corporate crime,[12] which, ironically, is particularly rife in the pharmaceutical industry.

Biological psychiatry and female crime

In 1895 Lombroso and Ferrero dogmatically asserted that women in general were deficient in 'moral sense', but their lesser involvement in crime was a result of their lower intelligence. In *The Female Offender*, Lombroso and Ferrero stated that women who do commit crimes have inborn traits reflecting primitiveness of development which lead them to behave in a 'savage' fashion. In fact they claimed that 'the criminal woman is . . . a monster',[13] clearly displaying their belief in the intermix of biology and morality. Although these assertions were based on pure speculation, they have had an enormous influence – in particular as a basis for the entry of biological psychiatry into the field of female crime, which had previously been theorized within sociology.

Since Lombroso's time biological psychiatry has sought to explain female criminality in terms of hereditary factors, neurology/ physiology or hormones, but there has been very little research conducted. This is curious given the widespread conviction that the perspective is correct. Also most of the research has deep methodological flaws. I will briefly mention some of the key studies and problems.

Cloninger and Guze studied 66 convicted women felons and claimed that they were all psychiatrically ill, suffering from sociopathy, alcoholism, drug dependence, hysteria or homosexuality;[14] further studies with 28 female felons revealed a higher incidence of family members with pathology relative to other females.[15] The first problem here is the classification of sociopathy, etc., as illnesses. In the 1970s, when this research was done, 'sociopathy' was a term used to describe 'the behavior pattern of marginal criminal types'.[16] This was the 'psychiatric illness' found in 65 per cent of the sample. Yet it is completely circular to argue that criminal behaviour is caused by sociopathy – in other words, the behaviour pattern of marginal criminal types.

The second problem with the research if it is used to back a biological understanding of crime, is that shared criminality between biological relatives does not establish biological causation, as there may be common environmental factors. A similar cloud hangs over the twin studies, which show a slightly higher likelihood of shared criminality in twins from the same ovum than in twins from different ova.[17] As mentioned in the last chapter, twins who look alike are often treated similarly and may share more environmental influences than twins who do not look the same, and it may be the environmental influences which cause the crime.

In the largest adoption study of criminality, a relationship between criminal convictions in biological parents and convictions in their adoptive children was found,[18] but the crime rate in the children (2.8 per cent) was very close to the population average (2.2 per cent), so the significance of this result can be questioned. Leon Kamin has also pointed out the problem of selective placement in this study – the lack of random assignment of adoptees to adoptive homes – which undercuts conclusions that might be drawn about a biological base to crime.[19]

There have been sporadic reports of chromosomal abnormalities in some delinquent females and adult criminals,[20] but the frequencies are very low and do not justify a claim about biological causation of crime.

Some point to neurological studies as indicating a biological cause. Shanok and Lewis found that delinquent girls in general had more adverse medical histories than non-delinquent girls, particularly central nervous system trauma, usually from child abuse.[21] I have already indicated above problems with the conception of delinquency in girls, but there is the further point that the delinquency might have been caused directly by the abuse or inadequate parenting, rather than faulty biology.

Some research suggests a physiological difference between women prisoners and 'normal women' in responses to certain questions concerning lying and stealing,[22] but the sample size is small and the results open to variable interpretation. There is little basis even for saying that this whole body of research since Lombroso's time is suggestive of a biological base to female crime. Some biological psychiatrists, however, put greater store on the hormonal studies, especially the work that has been done on the premenstrual syndrome. It is worthwhile, then, to consider this work in a little more detail.

Premenstrual syndrome and female crime

In Chapter 3 I mentioned how the premenstrual syndrome (PMS) is gaining ground as the new catch-all psychiatric diagnosis despite the conceptual unclarity and lack of reputable research. There have also been attempts to use the diagnosis to explain female crimes, especially crimes of violence. Even in the nineteenth century Icard was arguing that disorders of menstruation gave rise to klepto-mania, pyromania, homicidal mania, suicidal mania, lying etc.[23] Otto Pollak, writing in *The Criminality of Women* in 1961, also suggested a strong link between women's crime and menstruation, especially for shoplifting, arson, homicide and resistance against public officials.[24] Katharina Dalton, the current key theorist on PMS, refers to these criminal categories and relates them to the premenstrual phase or to menstruation. She adds to the list suicide attempts, citing a lecture given by Pollitt to the Royal Society of Medicine in 1976, where he said that the timing of suicide attempts helps to explain their failure: 'killing oneself is not easy, success requires careful planning. Women in the premenstrual phase show a marked tendency to be careless, thoughtless, unpunctual, forgetful and absentminded. This inefficiency at a time when they are more likely to try to end their lives may result in a disproportionate failure.'[25] Dalton also relates assault to PMS. 'There are those cases of assault where in a sudden fit of temper the woman throws a rolling-pin at her neighbour, a typewriter at her boss, or tries to bite off a policeman's ear. There are the cases of baby-battering, husband hitting . . . and so on.'[26] Theft, being drunk and disorderly and all crimes of violence are related, by Dalton, to PMS, and she claims that information from the courts and police in the UK, the USA and France support her position. The phenomenon of 'battered husbands' seems to interest her particularly. She sympathetically reports the views of two American researchers that there are 12 million battered husbands in the USA, and that it is the 'most unreported crime', affecting 20 per cent of husbands.[27]

Judy Lever, in the book *The Unrecognised Illness*, adds wife-battering to the crimes of violence attributed to PMS. This occurs when the wife provokes the husband by her own violent behaviour when suffering from PMS.[28]

In two English court cases in 1981 Dalton gave the 'expert evidence' that PMS diminished responsibility of the women killers. The judge accepted PMS as a strongly mitigating factor and they walked out of the court with no punishment. In other cases of arson and assault where Dalton appeared as an expert witness, PMS was admitted in pleas for mitigation of sentence.[29] PMS has been accepted as a mitigating factor in the sentencing of two women in Canada on shoplifting charges[30] and in plea bargaining in the

United States. It is recognized in the French legal system as temporary insanity.[31]

In the courts, PMS is usually brought in as an explanation of crimes of violence, and when the violence is out of character or untypical of stereotypical female behaviour. A normal woman could not behave like this – she must be sick. There is a trend to see violent criminal women as doubly disordered – by not complying with the female role and as suffering from PMS.

The causal account of PMS that comes closest to explaining a link between PMS and crime is the testosterone theory, but, as I have argued in Chapter 3, a little analysis shows that to be very weak.

Despite all the problems with the PMS diagnosis it must be granted that it is *defence* lawyers who are introducing it on behalf of their female clients. It is these lawyers who are medicalizing the criminality, presumably with the agreement of the women suspects. It also must be granted that it has worked to the advantage of some women, resulting in acquittal or lighter sentences than otherwise. I believe that there are two important difficulties in allowing PMS as a defence or mitigating factor: 1) there are difficulties at the theoretical level (these surface if one tries to answer the question: what is it about PMS that takes away responsibility for a crime?); and 2) there are enormous dangers for the perception of women in general.

An obvious stumbling block to answering the question in (1) is the lack of consensus about the defining characteristics of PMS explored in Chapter 3. The only point that is agreed on by those who believe there is a category here at all is that it involves some change, not necessarily a disorder, which occurs in a cyclical fashion. Even if the changes are severe there needs to be some rationale for thinking that they impact on responsibility before they have relevance to criminal proceedings. Dalton and others have not done the theoretical work necessary to develop this rationale. A study reported in 1980 by d'Orban and others[32] makes this rationale appear very illusive. The study was conducted with 50 women charged with violent offences. Seventeen women (34 per cent) reported the presence of premenstrual symptoms, which the researchers, here take to include 34 different bodily, mental or behavioural changes. The results were spread out over these changes, but more women did report depression and irritability than any other symptom. Recalling that Katharina Dalton defines the paramenstruum as the first and last four days of the menstrual cycle, the results of this study appear to overturn her ideas. No link was found between committing the offence in the paramenstruum and complaining of premenstrual symptoms. Only five of the 17 women with symptoms committed their offence at this time. There were 22 women who offended during the paramenstruum but only five had premenstrual symptoms. However, the fact that 22 out of the 50 women did commit their offence in the paramenstruum has led the authors to believe that the offenders' behaviour was caused by their biology even though they were not consciously aware of a premenstrual symptom. They asserts that the women's 'only "symptom" may be an offence of violence or increased aggression during this period', and then add:

> Perhaps too much emphasis has been placed on premenstrual tension symptoms as an aetiological factor in female crime; it is cyclically recurrent, observed behavioural changes (of which the woman herself may be unaware) rather than subjective symptoms which should be looked for.[33]

If this is the case then we are no nearer to understanding how PMS can operate as an excuse for criminal behaviour, as PMS has now been reduced to the criminal behaviour itself.

Ellis and Austin summarize the findings of a number of studies which show a marked increase in aggressive behaviour during the ovulatory phase of the cycle,[34] so the generalizability of d'Orban's findings has to be questioned anyway.

The second problem with PMS as a criminal plea concerns the effects that it could have on perceptions of women in general. The ramifications could be very damaging. In the first place it would reinforce the idea that PMS is a psychiatric disorder, even though it is psychiatry that is supposed to be giving the backing to the plea, and then all the criticisms of this direction outlined in Chapter 3 come into play. In particular, given the scope of the definition, the sanity of nearly all women could be called into question. It would fuel notions of female irresponsibility and strengthen arguments for the subordinate status of women. It would defuse the political impact of female aggression or crime and it would divert attention from other more promising lines of thought about female crime relating to the social context and level of violence surrounding the offender.

The dangerous nature of the plea is highlighted for me in a letter by Robert Wilson to the *Canadian Medical Association Journal* in 1988. He is reflecting on a criminal case where women committed arson. They did not bring in PMS in their defence. Wilson argues that this defence should have been looked into, as the women were reported as experiencing symptoms and behaviour often found in patients suffering from severe premenstrual syndrome, namely: alcohol abuse is highly prevalent; the offence is committed alone; the offence is not pre-meditated; suicidal gestures and self-mutilation are common; recurrence of offences such as fraud and theft and previous instances of arson are common; sexual promiscuity is common; the mean age of female offenders approaches 30 years.[35]

He claims that, if the women committed the arson during the paramenstruum, then the possibility of automatism should be considered. In Canadian law this is 'used to describe unconscious, involuntary behaviour, the state of a person who, though capable of action, is not conscious of what he is doing.'[36] What Wilson fails to recognize is that there is no consensus about these symptoms of PMS and behaviours supposedly common to sufferers of PMS. For instance, there is no overlap at all between his list and the list used in the 1980 study just mentioned. In any case, there is a huge leap from agreeing that a person has those characteristics and accepting that they are not conscious of what they are doing.

The apparent rise in the female crime rate has been one factor leading to the need to develop a theory of women's criminality. Yet if the changed incidence of female crime is accepted then it would be reasonable to assume that such crime must depend on some factor which has *changed* rather than some constant factor such as biology. It might be relevant, for example, that more opportunities have been opened up for women to organize robberies because of women's changing social role.

I have canvassed some of the difficulties with two psychiatric defences that are available only to women if they are available at all: the infanticide plea and the appeal to PMS. There are other psychiatric legal defences. Are they also of questionable theoretical standing? Do they also carry dangers for the interests of women in general? It is not possible to explore these questions thoroughly here but I would like to indicate some key considerations.

Psychiatric legal defences and the interests of women

Although the laws differ within and between Western countries, there are two psychiatric defences that have fairly widespread currency – the defence on the basis of mental illness and the defence of automatism – and the plea of diminished responsibility is increasingly available. The first defence captures the idea that, if an accused person was mentally ill at the time an offence was committed, then the jury should return a verdict of not guilty by reason of mental illness. It is often further stipulated that, for the defence to work, the mental illness must have rendered the accused into a state where they are incapable of appreciating the nature and quality of the act or knowing that it was wrong.

Focusing on the use of the notion of 'mental illness', we can ask how does it act to impair responsibility? As far as I can ascertain, the legal codes in various Western countries do not define 'mental illness' but leave it up to expert (psychiatric) witnesses to advise the courts. Even they are in a difficult position because the most widely used system of psychiatric diagnosis, the DSM, does not define the term. In fact it shies away from referring to 'mental illness' at all. As mentioned in Chapter 2, 'mental disorder' forms the core concept in the DSM. 'Mental disorder' is such a broad notion that it includes, for example, problems with reading and arithmetic, with giving up smoking and with mild mood swings, hardly excusing conditions for killing. Perhaps it is certain sorts of mental disorder that are relevant to the legal defence, but which they are and why they are relevant are not questions that have been faced. Referring to the psychiatric diagnosis most commonly given to criminal women is no help at all. In the first secion above on female crimes I mentioned the research which indicated that the most common psychiatric diagnosis of female criminals is a personality disorder involving dependency and submissiveness or antisocial behaviour. In the second section I mentioned the work by Cloninger and Guze which listed sociopathy (the behaviour pattern of marginal criminal types) as the most common 'psychiatric illness' in their sample of female felons. Finally, when discussing d'Orban's research, I pointed out that the PMS which their female criminals suffered from was simply violence. These findings all form a pattern in that the 'psychiatric illness' of the women criminals is conceptualized as immoral or illegal *behaviour* or, as in the first case, simply female behaviour. It is because she behaves in a deviant manner, violating social norms, that she is said to be suffering from an antisocial personality disorder or sociopathy. Referring back to the 'mental illness' defence, it is not behaviour that is thought to excuse the act but some mental incapacity or aberration. Killing someone could indicate an antisocial personality disorder, but it would then be circular to claim that the disorder to some extent excused the killing.

If we approach this point from another angle and look at the psychiatric categories in the DSM which incorporate criminality, then it becomes clear that they are all behaviourally defined. These categories are antisocial personality disorder, conduct disorders and adjustment disorder with disturbance of conduct.[37] As behaviour cannot excuse behaviour, it is not going to be helpful for the defence to employ these categories. Also why would it be relevant to point out that an accused person is suffering from any other psychiatric disorder? An easy answer might be to say that their judgement is impaired, but, even granting that is so, does that distinguish such people from other killers? It is fairly safe to assume that most people do not condone killing, so there is a sense in which anyone who kills has impaired judgement. If it was not mental disorder that impaired their judgement then perhaps it was abuse in childhood, a life of discrimination, poverty, etc.[38] Is it something else about mental disorders which gives them an excusing quality? Perhaps it could be argued that with certain disorders the sufferer loses control, it is as if some other agency is working through her, and hence she should be excused. This isn't satisfactory. It is the woman who performed the act even though she may not have thought so. She were mistaken – she suffered from impaired judgement. Hence this 'lack of control' approach collapses into a variant of impaired judgement. Nor does there seem to be anything else that could account for the excusing quality of a mental disorder.

Perhaps it is partly this conceptual mess which is behind recent moves in the United States to abolish or restrict the use of the mental illness defence and also its extremely rare use in the United Kingdom. Some US states have brought in the possibility of a 'guilty but mentally ill' verdict,[39] but this is not clearly preferable to a straight 'guilty' verdict.

The automatism defence was referred to above in discussing PMS. By definition the behaviour is involuntary and so the actor cannot be held criminally responsible. Canadian courts, for instance, recognize that automatism may result from a physical blow, carbon monoxide poisoning or a stroke. There are important differences between laws on automatism. The Canadian law is very extreme. It requires a 'total lack of consciousness' for a successful defence, whereas the Australian law requires only that the person be in a 'state of clouded or residual consciousness'. If one takes the Canadian view then it's clear why the automatic action is involuntary, but it is not obvious that any psychiatric disorder would qualify as automatic. It is not part of the defining criteria of any of the mental disorders that the person act from a 'total lack of consciousness'. Nevertheless two Canadian writers suggest that automatism is a promising potential defence for an accused who has PMS. Meehan and MacRae claim that women with PMS are not in control of their actions and cannot later explain their behaviour: 'this could fall under the definition of an unconscious state accompanied by involuntary actions. If the accused could establish that PMS produced these two states, a legal defence of automatism would be essentially established.'[40] As indicated in the discussion in Chapter 3, there hasn't been any research linking PMS to states of unconsciousness and there is of course the more central problem that there is no agreement that PMS is an isolable condition. In addition, in relation to this automatism defence, it is not even clear that it makes sense to claim that an act could be performed with a total lack of consciousness. Perhaps the Australian law has recognized this point. However, insisting on the weaker requirement of 'clouded or residual consciousness' could lead to questioning whether the behaviour is really automatic. It seems too weak a requirement to establish involuntariness. The High Court in Australia has stated that automatism may be caused by depression, tension, anxiety and fear, capable of giving rise to a complete defence.[41] To take an example, if an anxious person who kills has clouded consciousness, should that count as an automatic action? It is hard to envisage that a positive answer would ever be warranted. Part of the problem here is that the concept of automatism does not allow for degress. Perhaps, then, a plea of diminished responsibility is to be preferred when a psychiatric defence is sought, as at least this plea has the virtue of allowing degrees.

Diminished capacity or responsibility as defined in English and Australian law can be used as a defence to reduce a charge of murder to manslaughter when the state of mind of the accused was impaired at the time of the crime. The guilt of the accused is not denied but the impairment is thought to limit his or her accountability for the crime. The problem with this defence is not one of wondering whether it would ever apply. If there is a problem it is the reverse. Given the widespread socially valued taboo on killing, then of course a killer's state of mind is impaired at the time of the crime. The break with societal standards is a mark of this impairment, but that does not seem relevant to arguing that one's responsibility is diminished. If some other psychiatric notion of impairment is intended, then the problems that I raised with the defence of mental illness surface again. These problems work against a special defence on the basis of mental illness. However, it is undeniable that a variety of life circumstances and conditions of the individual can produce impairment of judgement and illegal actions. It would seem fair to open up the possibility of arguing diminished responsibility for all accused whether they have a mental disorder or not and for all offences. A person's judgement could be just as impaired by a brutal childhood or racism as by anxiety or depression. Also it is quite artibrary just to restrict the defence to murder trials. Of course such a direction would impact disastrously on the notion of free will, but that is a dusty old philosophical notion that I don't believe deserves a place in modern law.

There has been a great deal of recent interest in the 'battered woman syndrome' as part of a defence to killing in a situation of domestic violence. This is often portrayed as a psychiatric defence, but it is questionable whether it needs to relate to any psychiatric considerations. It is worth mentioning, however, as the discussion around this syndrome could lead to a revision of laws in a way that removes some of the biases against women.

Battered woman syndrome and the law of self-defence

The battered woman syndrome is a label introduced by Lenore Walker to describe 'the psychological impact of the common social and economic problems that battered women face. These problems include failure of the police and courts to protect women from abuse; the inability of battered women to leave their mates because they may have no job, child care, adequate housing or community social services; that battered women suffer severe isolation and shame, which strengthens their belief that they have no safe alternative; and that the lack of alternatives and the cycle of battering in which the men promise to reform leads women to cling to the illusion that the men will change.[42] While the focus of this description is on social and economic realities rather than psychiatric disturbance, when it has been used in the courts the result has often been a portrayal of women as helpless victims or as temporarily insane. The use of the word 'syndrome' could easily promote such a shift in thinking. Perhaps the word 'situation' should be substituted.

Portraying women who kill their abusive partner, whether male or female, as helpless victims undercuts an argument that they acted rationally, yet killing might in some circumstances be a reasonable action against a batterer. The constellation of circumstances mentioned in the above description of the syndrome might be sufficient. Also there is something paradoxical about acknowledging that someone has killed and describing them as helpless. It would seem that women who die from abuse are more accurately described as helpless.

To regard the 'battered woman syndrome' as a type of temporary insanity is also odd. If the killing is retaliation against serious violence, why should that be thought of as insane? Such retaliation is allowable in other contexts and the law of self-defence is introduced to excuse the action. The refusal to countenance the rationality of retaliation by a woman against an abusive partner is no doubt founded on beliefs about appropriate female behaviour and the underplaying of the significance of violence against women. Not only is it appropriate for an abused man to retaliate, it would be thought cowardly if he didn't. For an abused woman to retaliate is madness.

Apart from the problem that if the battered woman syndrome comes into a legal defence it is too easily thought of as implying helplessness or psychiatric disorder, there is the further point that those women who do not strictly conform to the syndrome might be left without a defence. If a woman wished to argue that the killing of her batterer was a rational act, could she simply appeal to the laws of self-defence? A common formulation of these laws involves the need to prove that 'she had a reasonable fear that she was in imminent danger of suffering unlawful bodily harm. She must have responded with only the amount of force necessary to counter the threatened harm; deadly force is sanctioned only in response to the use or imminent use of deadly force. In addition, she must not have been the aggressor, and . . . she must not have had an opportunity to retreat.'[43] As Gillespie has pointed out, these laws developed out of a response to men's needs, which arose in two situations: either a sudden assault by a murderous stranger or a fist fight between consenting participants which suddenly turns deadly. In these situations there was an assumption that both parties were male, that they were fairly equal in size, strength and fighting ability, and that the incident was an isolated one, in a public place, from which one or both could withdraw or escape, unless the attack was too sudden.[44] Women's needs were not addressed in the development of these laws and nor was the situation of women who wished to protect their children from violent assault.

It is the imminence requirement that has been the main barrier to many women's legal defences, with some judges ruling that the only evidence that can be used must relate to the confrontational encounter. The discussions around the battered woman syndrome have at least had the value of impressing the courts that more of the woman's history should be taken into account. Some feminist legal theorists recommend dropping the imminence requirement completely.[45] Perhaps a more realistic approach is to expand its meaning, as illustrated by a recent change in the Australian law, which states:

> the imminence of the threat will be established should the accused have honestly and reasonably believed that the perceived assailant remained in a position of dominance and in a position to carry out the threatened violence at some time not too remote, thus keeping the apprehension . . . ever present in the victim's mind[46]

Discussion of the battered woman syndrome has also led into valuable criticism of the requirement that the accused did not have the opportunity to retreat. Even if battered women are financially able to leave their homes, living separately is often not an escape as their batterers locate them to assault or even kill them. The police offer little effective protection to such women whether they stay in their homes or leave. Also, is it fair to require of a woman that she leave her home?

Thus while there is little to be gained by embracing the battered woman syndrome as a new psychiatric defence, the way that discussion of the syndrome has opened up questions about the laws of self-defence could have favourable results for women.

In the first four chapters I argued that, for psychiatry, the normal human being is male and, as the above discussion of self-defence indicates, for the law, the legal subject is male. The female legal subject is an anomaly and it is easier for the law to regard her as irresponsible or mad than to view her actions as stemming from rational intent. It is then thought possible to justify the very high level of use of psychotropic drugs in women's prisons[47] and to sympathize with the call for involuntary psychiatric treatment for all female criminals.[48] What the battered woman syndrome debate has highlighted is that the law does not allow a role for the female subject, so that before we accept the psychiatric domination of criminology there should be careful re-examination and rewriting of the law. This take I must leave to others as I move on to consider whether there are viable alternatives to psychiatry.

6 Contrasting Feminist Philosophies of Women and Madness: Oppression and Repression

Very few feminist theorists have looked into the area of women and madness from a philosophical perspective even though there are quite a few accounts from within feminist psychology. The distinction is not always easy to make, but it is useful nevertheless. A psychological account would locate the basic problem of a woman's madness in her mind and the treatment directions would centre around changing her mind using various psychological techniques. A philosophical account would focus on the concept of madness, perhaps developing arguments for exploding the category, but not fixing the concept in the domain of another discipline – psychology, biology, etc. Many feminist novelists do explode the category of madness and some of their writings will be discussed in the next chapter.

Two theorists whom it is useful to consider in developing an account of women and madness are Phyllis Chesler and Luce Irigaray. Chesler's book *Women and Madness*, published in 1972,[1] is still the most comprehensive account of the relevant issues. None of Irigaray's works have madness as their central theme but nearly all of her prolific writings since 1965 to the present day provide fertile ground for speculation on this topic.[2] I want to present a highly selective exposition of key aspects of the works of both these writers which relate to a philosophy of women and madness.

Phyllis Chesler

Chesler is interested primarily in problems of madness in women but she puts forward a general theory concerning women and men.[3]

Madness is to be understood in terms of sex roles – attitudes towards being female or being male – that exist in modern Western cultures. The female role is one of dependency, passivity and submission. The male role is one of activity, independence and assertiveness. The female role is regarded as inferior to the male role. According to Chesler, madness in women and in men is to be understood in terms of the devalued female role. A person may push this role to the extreme and become excessively dependent, passive and submissive. Chesler sees the female role, without going to extremes, as intrinsically unsatisfying, so if a person embarks on this course, she or he is likely to become very unhappy. This unhappiness may take the form of depression, anxiety, paranoia (fearfulness), suicide attempts or frigidity. These are then, incorrectly, regarded as forms of madness.

The basis for Chesler's claim about correct or incorrect ascriptions of madness seems to be that mere unhappiness in one's role does not constitute madness, but alienation from or rejection of one's role does. If a man acts out the devalued female role, he is likely, according to Chesler, to be labelled 'schizophrenic', and this is genuine madness. If a woman totally or partially rejects her female role she runs the risk of being labelled 'schizophrenic', and this would also constitute genuine madness. Men who push the male role to the extreme are more likely to be viewed as criminal than as mad. The following may be helpful in clarifying these claims:

Women	*Men*
Female role pushed to extreme: depression, anxiety, paranoia, suicide attempts, fridigity (not madness)	Alienated from male role: female role pushed to extreme: schizophrenia (madness)
Alienated from female role: schizophrenia (madness)	Male role pushed to extreme: criminality (not madness)

For Chesler, schizophrenia, which is genuine madness in women, as well as depression and other conditions that are wrongly thought of as madness, are to be understood in terms of oppression and conditioning. Females from an early age are channelled into the female role and punished when they step out of its bounds. The oppressive features of this role are covered over by romantic illusions: 'contemporary women are "free slaves", they choose their servitude for "love".'[4] Females more than males are starved of 'nuturance': 'the consistent and readily available gift of physical, domestic and emotional support in childhood together with the added gift of compassion and respect in adulthood'.[5] She cites studies from the 1960s and 1970s,[6] but there is every indication that this claim is still true today. Also it is most often males rather than females who benefit from valued female characteristics, such as tenderness, compassion and altruism. If this picture is correct, why do women continue to live out unsatisfying lives?

Chesler's answer is that women do so for male-imposed reasons, 'in order to survive economically and psychologically and because contraception and abortion are still either inadequate, illegal, expensive, dangerous or morally censured.'[7] Perhaps the latter is less true today. However, the 1993 killing in the USA by anti-abortionists of a doctor who performed abortions is a clear indication that the battle is not yet over.

Experiencing unhappiness with her lot, yet seeing no escape, a woman may become very depressed, frigid, anxious and fearful or attempt suicide, even though these paths may magnify the despair. In discussing frigidity, Chesler makes the point that women are sexually repressed by patriarchal institutions which enforce fear, dislike and confusion about female sexual and reproductive anatomy,[8] and 'women have had to barter their sexuality (or their capacity for sexual pleasure) for economic survival and maternity. Female frigidity *as we know it* will cease only when such bartering ceases. Most women cannot be 'sexual' as long as prostitution, rape and patriarchal marriage exist.'[9]

Genuinely mad women step outside the female role, becoming dominating, perhaps even hostile and violent, but usually retaining feelings of inferiority, helplessness and self-mistrust. (Chesler draws on three different studies conducted in the 1960s to support the latter claim.[10]) Such women may experience certain 'transformations of self ' where they incorporate the meaning of certain heroines, such as Joan of Arc or the Catholic Madonna. The delusional system of the female schizophrenic is then understood by appeal the cultural myths.

In the stories of Joan of Arc and of the Madonna, the woman is sacrificed for the purposes of male renewal (military victories or birth). Joan is physically and spiritually bold and a leader of men, although doomed. She began to step outside the realm of patriarchal culture, and for this she was killed. She is re-experienced by those women who are mad enough to wish to 'step outside' culture but who do not wish to be crucified for doing so.[11] Chesler believes that after such women grasp the meaning and limitations of Joan, 'they seek protection and redemption – from the Catholic Mary, the compassionate and powerful mother.' They wish to give birth to the world, and to themselves, anew. 'They wish to avoid Joan's crucifixion and can do so only by becoming Virgin-Mothers . . . Mary avoids crucifixion, but she is condemned to asexuality and sorrow.'[12] This path to overcoming female oppression leads nowhere.

Chesler wants us to understand genuine and non-genuine madness in terms of oppression. Occasionally she uses the language of the medical model but I don't think that this is of any consequence. She slips into talking about phenomena in both categories as 'diseases': 'Just as schizophrenia is no entreé into power for women, neither are "female" diseases such as depression, paranoia, frigidity and suicide attempts.'[13] Also when discussing 'schizophrenia', she says that what a particular researcher says about it is what the *disease* is about.[14] There are enough other statements and arguments in the book, however, to disclaim the view that madness should be regarded as a mental disease.

If the key to understanding women's madness lies in oppression, what should be done about it? Traditional psychiatric treatment in public mental hospitals is heavily attacked by Chesler. Also she is wary of individual help from a private psychiatrist as she believes most psychiatrists will adhere to a double standard of mental health for men and women and/or to patriarchal myths about femininity. All such psychiatrists are involved in the *institution* of private practice – an institution which she believes is like a mental hospital, which in turn is similar in structure to marriage and the family, with a power hierarchy that oppresses women. Her basic prescription is to work towards an end to female oppression. She acknowledges the problems. she is aware that women alone and in groups, even feminist groups, find it hard to abandon the double standard of male–female behaviour. However, she does think that this situation may change by growing awareness of women's oppression, by successfully organized accomplishments around such issues as child care, abortion and birth control, and by women working cooperatively in groups:

the only acceptable groups are those that, unlike the family, can function as places of authentic responsibility and joy; as ways of supporting our deepest cravings for individual liberty, security, achievement and love. Groups (ideologies, religions, 'solutions') which in any way kill the individual spirit; which despise and crucify that which it longs for; which enforce conformity, mediocrity, and conservatism – for any reason; which seek to diminish each person to 'manageable' and familiar levels rather than to enhance each person to 'unmanageable' and unique levels which the group supports – such 'groupings' are depressingly well known, such groupings are 'male' and 'female' rather than human groupings. They are doomed to spin out old patterns of martyrdom and oppression. Such groupings cannot provide women with the strength to gain power and redefine power, sexuality, and work.[15]

There is for Chesler, then, no short-term solutions to the problems of our so-called madness. What is needed is a breakdown of the rigidly defined male/female roles and an end to the oppression of women, but men, who hold the power, are opposed to absorbing female traits into the public sphere and to encouraging women to develop male traits for participation or domination in the public sphere. How are women, the powerless, to achieve these ends? Although Chesler claims that one step forward *could* be developments in child care, birth control, etc., she is also sceptical about what can be achieved here: 'Birth control "technology" by itself, like free twenty-four hour child care centres, will not necessarily lead to the abolition of sexism. It may lead to male-dominated totalitarian decisions regarding sexual activity and maternity, decisions over which the individual woman has as little to say as she did about her enforced maternity.'[16] The other step forward is her prescription for ideal groups, but this may be really ideal given that it is not the way most or any groups seem to function.

Chesler is an important writer even though her practical suggestions do not seem to go very far. Her importance lies in making very clear the need to look at features of the woman's role in trying to understand problems of madness in women. The distinction that she tries to forge between genuine and non-genuine madness does not, however, have an adequate rationale. From a traditional sexist point of view it does make sense to say that women who push their role to an extreme are not really crazy and those who are alienated from their role are, but from a feminist point of view this seems to have things the wrong way around. If the role is really as degrading and unsatisfying as Chesler says it is then alienation would seem to be saner than acceptance. Furthermore, Chesler acknowledges that both genuine and non-genuine madness can be debilitating, so there is no ground for distinction on this basis.

Another criticism is that Chesler suggests that a way out of the problems of women's madness would be to merge the roles of men and women with the aim of ending oppression. With the hindsight of 20 years since the publication of Chesler's book, it is clear that attempts at such merging usually end up with the disappearance of femininity. Women may gain power, but very often this is by 'becoming men'. Again this wouldn't matter if there was nothing of value in femininity, but that position is now being hotly contested, as Irigaray's work exemplifies. It seems that many women would like to have the oppression lifted but not in the process become like men. If the latter occurs then their sexuality is repressed. This is not to say that repression doesn't exist in patriarchal cultures. Rather it is saying that if women gain power this does not necessarily end repression. Perhaps it even masks the fact that it is still in place.

An account of madness that centres on sex roles and oppression while pointing to an important strand in the story is limited. The problems that women encounter are not just because they lack power. What other factors need to be taken into account? Chesler mentions repression in understanding frigidity but otherwise it does not feature centrally in her account. Irigaray's writings suggest that the repression of female sexuality is crucial to understanding women's madness. I will now investigate this idea.

Luce Irigaray[17]

To say, along with Chesler, that women are oppressed by their sex roles and that this oppression may give rise to 'madness' seems to make sense. With Irigaray matters are a little more complicated. One could say glibly that she believes that women's sexuality, identity and language are repressed in patriarchal cultures (i.e., all present-day cultures), and it is this repression that promotes madness in one form or another in most women – but is that readily understandable? We first need to look at the notion of repression in order to evaluate the reflections on women's madness. Irigaray believes that identity is tied up with sexuality and that under patriarchy women's sexuality has been conceptualized in male terms, that women have not been allowed to speak for themselves about their desire and their pleasure. This silence is kept in place by the linguistic and logical processes which structure thought.

Irigaray's claims stem from a version of psychoanalytic theory that she has developed from Freud, Lacan and Françoise Dolto.[18]

From Freud she takes over the idea of the stages in the development of female sexuality, not as a biological necessity, but as a historical phenomenon of patriarchal cultures. From Lacan she takes over the idea that sexuality is tied in to meaning – the importance of symbols and what they signify: the phallus as the primary signifier of desire. From Françoise Dolto she takes over the notion of the plurality of female sexuality.

In the course of normal female sexual development, according to Freud, the clitoris is the first genital zone which is important; then, later in life, the focus is shifted to the vagina. The activity associated with the clitoris in sexual play gives way to the passivity associated with the vagina. To be truly feminine is to confine oneself to vaginal eroticization. Also the erotic function in women is crucially tied in with the maternal function, rather than sexual enjoyment unrelated to maternity. The value of woman is meant to come from her maternal role and in other respects from her 'femininity'. There are, however, elements of this notion of femininity which mark women off as inferior to men: the clitoris may be regarded as a smaller penis and the vagina simply as a lack and as something 'out of sight' – in contrast to the male genitals which are visible – with visibility given a value over invisibility. Also activity is valued over passivity; so the passivity of mature femininity is devalued when compared with the activity of mature masculinity. According to Irigaray, this is an accurate picture of what happens in patriarchies, but it contains a view of female sexuality which is determined by male parameters. She wants to open up the question of what is to count as normal development of female sexuality. In particular, she rejects the idea that women's sexuality has a single focus in one of our bodily organs – the clitoris or the vagina. She claims that female erogenous zones include both of these, along with the labia, the vulva, the cervix, the womb and the breasts.[19] From a male perspective, it is understandable that women's sexuality is thought to be located in one area – the vagina. If we could move to a female perspective, we might see that plurality is more in accord with female desire. Furthermore, it is only from one standpoint that the vagina is regarded as a lack (or absence), and hence inferior to the penis, which is regarded as a presence and hence superior. Irigaray speaks of the vagina as a presence of a different sort and so fails to find any basis here for devaluation of the female.[20] One could also question the valorization of presence over absence. Similarly, there is nothing absolute about the positive value placed on visibility as contrasted to the negative value placed on invisibility. Irigaray notes that this is a dominant way of thinking in patriarchal cultures, however, and that it serves to enhance the status of men over women, as the male form is visible and the female form is not.[21]

Irigaray argues that the maternal role is narrowly conceived within classical psychoanalytic theory, in that it is inflexibly tied to the bearing of children. If women's pleasures are to be expanded, more recognition should be given to the fact that a motherly dimension may be satisfied in diverse ways: not only mothering children but, for instance, mothering friends; not only giving birth to children but also giving birth to mental creations, etc. Also, why should female sexuality be so closely tied to the maternal role, however broadly conceived? She claims that, although this is understandable in an economy and ideology of reproduction, it is nevertheless a mark of subservience to man's desire. Similarly, the passivity which goes along with mature female sexuality may simply be a state that women are coerced into in patriarchal culture. The stress on the multiplicity of sexual zones and the separation of female sexuality from the maternal role could liberate women from sexual passivity.[22] She puts in a plea for a 'truly free sexuality':

> Developing your sexuality doesn't involve reproducing (one more) child but rather transforming your sexual energy with a view to a pleasurable and fertile cohabitation with others. Society shouldn't demand the repression of our sexual desires, their denial or nullification, or that we keep them in their infancy or a state of animality. Rather, they should be incorporated into an individual and collective subjectivity capable of respect for oneself, persons of one's own and the other sex, an entire people, and peoples in general.[23]

For Irigaray a major problem with traditional psychoanalytic theory is that it leaves women's pleasure and desire out of account or that these are defined simply in male terms. The multiplicity and autoerotic character of women's pleasures are not recognized. In general, in patriarchies, 'femininity' is a role, image and value imposed on women by men's systems of representation.[24] As these systems of representation dominate our language, women are prevented from recognizing their desires independent from these representations and their pleasures are limited within the constraints of these representations. Irigaray believes that there has been a continuous effective repression of our desire, as old as Western civilization and embodied in our language: women's desire does not speak the same language as men's desire, and it has been covered over by the logic that has dominated the West since the Greeks.[25] Female sexuality cannot articulate itself, even minimally, in 'an Aristotelian type of logic . . . within this logic, which dominates our most everyday statements – while speaking, at this moment, we are still observing its rules, female sexuality cannot articulate itself unless precisely as an "undertone", a "lack" in discourse.'[26]

This 'logic' is a very broad conception of thought. It includes, for instance, syntax: the organization of sentences according to subject, predicate or subject, verb,object. 'Female sexuality is not unifiable, it cannot be subsumed under the concept of subject; which brings into question all syntactical norms.'[27] This 'logic' also places value on the visible, on discrimination of form and individualization of form (all of which are foreign to female eroticism but match very well the masculine sex). The phallus is a definable form and value is accorded to this form. Either the female is not thought to have a sexual form at all or the value of the female form is not seen. Tied in with the valorization of the male form and the invisibility or nonrecognition of the female form are the proper name (the name of the father) and proper meaning. Women have no 'proper name' and the language of women, if it were allowed to surface, could not be pinned down to single, literal meanings:

> One would have to listen with another ear, as if hearing an *'other meaning' always in the process of weaving itself, of embracing itself with words, but also of getting rid of words in order not to become fixed, congealed in them.* For if 'she' says something, it is not, it is already no longer, identical with what she means. . . . It is useless, then, to trap women in the exact definition of what they mean, to make them repeat (themselves) so that it will be clear; they are already elsewhere in that discursive machinery.[28]

Feminine language is characterized by multiplicity of meanings, by lack of unity. But rarely, if ever, do we hear this language of the feminine. It is repressed along with women's sexuality. If women try to let their desire come through in language, they must speak in a new way; to speak in the current language is to be trapped within 'male' systems of representation which cut woman off from herself and her closeness to other women. This language, which presents itself as universal, and which is in fact produced by men only, maintains the alienation and exploitation of women in and by society. Women's silence is connected to the repression of sexuality and this is behind women's madness.

How did this repression come into being? There is one suggestion for an answer in Irigaray's essay 'The bodily encounter with the mother', where she explores the Clytemnestra myth as an account of how patriarchy began and of how our imagination still functions. The mother and daughters are sacrificed or go mad, and Orestes, the matricidal son, founds the new order. Orestes' madness is overcome by male means (Apollo). He is not punished for the murder of his mother. Female madness is not overcome.[29] This is a strong cultural myth and what we see in reality in modern times is that the role of the maternal-feminine power is nullified. Furthermore, 'Desire for her, her desire, that is what is forbidden by the law of the father, of all fathers: fathers of families, fathers of nations, religious fathers, professor fathers, doctor fathers, lover fathers.'[30] There is something frightening in the relationship with the mother: 'threats of contagion, contamination, engulfment in illness, madness and death'.[31] These are man's archaic projections onto women, but they continue to dominate, generating a fear of the female. It is this fear which hinders the development of an autonomous and positive representation of female sexuality. It is this fear which lies behind the repression of women.

In cultural representations women embody madness, but this is a 'madness which is not ours'. Instead it is the weight of these representations and the repression that they entail which gives rise to madness. For instance, the lack of women's voice in 'normal' language is highlighted in hysteria, where through paralysis the woman communicates in a different language, a somatic language. In an early work, *Speculum*, Irigaray emphasizes the repression of speech experienced in hysteria.[32] In a later essay she points to 'a revolutionary potential in hysteria', as 'even in her paralysis, the hysteric exhibits a potential for gestures and desires. . . . A movement of revolt and refusal, a desire for/of the living mother who would be more than a reproductive body in the pay of the polis, a living,loving woman. It is because they want neither to see nor hear that movement that they so despise the hysteric.'[33]

Noting that women do not suffer as much from delusions as men, Irigaray says that this is because delusions need language and women do not have their language, except in bodily suffering. In some early research that Irigaray conducted with ten men and ten women diagnosed as schizophrenic, she found empirical support for this claim. The women did not have the verbal means to elaborate their madness but they suffered it directly in their body. The men could express their delirium verbally.[34] Women's suffering may also find expression in depressive collapses,[35] which along with anxiety can be understood as stemming from a lack of power and lack of a positive sexuality.[36] Irigaray is very scornful of psychia-trists' dismissal of women's anxieties about rape. She views these anxieties as memories of 'various traumatic experiences, as images of events undergone, seen or overheard, or as the effect of a whole series of restrictions, prohibitions, impossibilities, oppressions, omnipresent throughout the most day-to-day life of women'.[37]

Another path to madness is as follows: the daughter hooking in to the cultural devaluation of the mother, and the mother's lack of an autonomous identity, turns to the father leaving behind the mother; the father who doesn't prepare food for the daughter, the father who is governed by will:

> I do gymnastics. I practice the body exercises suited to my disorder. I'll become a schooled robot. I move my body, completely unmoved. I ad-vance and move about to the rhythm prescribed for my cure. Will, not love, regulates my gestures, my leaps, my dancing about. Each hour of the day finds me applying myself: trying to obey the doctors' orders.[38]

Irigaray turns around the conventional psychoanalytic under-standings of masochism as a natural female trait. She believes that the conventional understanding arose because what it is to be a woman is so much tied up with suffering: suffering of childbirth, suffering in sexual relationships and so on. If we could develop a different female identity in which sufferings were no longer the criteria for identification then 'masochism' would cease to be a problem.[39] A similar approach is presented for dependency in women. Women are in a 'familiar state of dependency upon man' because we cannot be ourselves; our desire has been submerged. Masochism, dependency and passivity are female traits in a male sexual economy:[40] 'What makes them 'passive' traps them in the roles described by 'femininity', in which their desire loses itself – which does not mean that they have none.'[41]

Frigidity is explained by appeal to the repression of female sexu-ality and the mismatch between female and male sexual techniques, with the latter's focus on orgasm.[42] Irigaray strongly attacks sex education classes in schools which analyse the reproductive genital mechanism but leave emotions out of account. She has some charm-ing suggestions for literature classes to set assignments such as 'A letter to my girlfriend or boyfriend'; for art lessons to involve creat-ing a face of a dream lover; and for photographic exhibitions at school of girls and boys who are close friends or loved ones.[43] Then we might have words and images taught in school that enable love to be. Looking at the various psychiatric categories applied to women, Irigaray always brings the explanation back to issues of desire, identity and language and, centrally, repression. To overcome women's madness, repression needs to be lifted. How is this to be done? Some suggestions have already been mentioned above, for example, freeing up sexuality, allowing a female language to develop, re-evaluating the mother–daughter relationship and promoting respect for sexual difference. Another is to encode more rights in law.[44] In 1977 Irigaray announced that the aim was not theoretical progression:

> the issue is not one of elaborating a new theory of which woman would be the *subject* or the *object*, but of jamming the theoretical machinery itself, of suspending its pretension to the production of a truth and of a meaning that are excessively univocal. Which presupposes that women do not aspire simply to be men's equals in knowledge. That they do not claim to be rivaling men in constructing a logic of the feminine.[45]

Not only theorizing but reason in general has come under attack, as indicated above, but this leads to paradox.

It is *argued* by Irigaray that women should pursue a new way of writing which gives expression to their sexuality. This writing would be an attempt to break with the dictates of reason. Syntax would be destroyed. Plurality would be a key feature, no determinate unique meaning would emerge, for 'at each moment there is always for women "at least two" meanings, without one being able to decide which meaning prevails.' The style of women's writing is to burn fetishistic words, proper terms and well-constructed forms. The tactile gains in importance over the visual. Fluidity is another key feature. Woman's 'style' resists and explodes every solidly established form, figure, idea, concept. This is not to say her style is nothing, as a language which cannot conceive of it would lead us to believe. But her 'style' cannot be supported as a thesis, it cannot be the object of a position.[46] But isn't Irigaray herself here making woman's style the object of a position? She acknowledges this paradox but regards it as temporary. She says that a language which is used to speak about women's language will have to be male.

Yet she does speak about women's language and the advantages of women's language over male language, namely that it will operate against the repression of women. In effect, she is using rational argumentation to say that we should move beyond the constraints of rational argumentation into a new mode. The paradox arises if it is simultaneously claimed that 1) the rational (male) language is a weapon of repression, and 2) the rational (male) language is a tool for opening up emancipatory possibilities. It is *conceivable* that the male language can have this dual use (just as a knife can be used to kill or conduct an orchestra) but, given Irigaray's characterization of the male language and the way in which it represses, it is difficult to see how (1) and (2) are reconcilable. Consider her claim: 'To speak *of* or *about* woman may always boil down to, or be understood as, a recuperation of the feminine within a logic that maintains it in repression, censorship, nonrecognition.'[47] It is possible to respond by saying that we are going to be caught up in irresolvable paradoxes while we stay within the confines of the rational (male) language. What we have to do is move into women's language and these paradoxes will disappear, but that amounts to saying that the task lies ahead. We cannot really gain an understanding of the new language until we are already in it, but if that is so, how do we know it is better than the one we have got, even granting the criticisms of the current language?

The problem that has surfaced here does not establish that Irigaray's position is false. It shows that when viewed from the standpoint of reason there are certain difficulties, but if one wants to break out of the constraints of reason maybe one should not be too concerned. It is like being given a low grade from an assessor one does not respect.

Nevertheless the prescription to abandon reason can be examined as a political strategy, and here too problematic features emerge. How can we be sure that trying to persuade women out of the use of reason and into another mode of thinking/feeling will be in their best interests (in whatever way we understand 'best interests')? Even if the enjoyment gained in using reason is not true to one's sexuality, it might still be desirable to experience that enjoyment. Also, given that rationality is currently valued over irrationality, to encourage a move towards irrationalism has very obvious dangers.

Linguistic recommendations of a rather different sort follow on from recent research conducted by Irigaray. This involved simple linguistic tests which revealed contrasting responses by men and women, highlighting the sexed nature of language. The subjects were asked, for example, to make a sentence using the words 'single, marriage, sexuality, child, etc.' Writing mainly about her results in the studies on the French language but foreshadowing further research in other languages, Irigaray says that 'anything believed to have value belongs to men and is marked by their gender'.[48] Linguistic gender is not arbitrary as is commonly believed, but 'the gender of words is, in one way or another, related to the gender of speaking subjects.'[49] From this finding she speculates that 'the same experience might be expressed by different grammatical genders depending on whether the culture . . . valorizes a sex or not.'[50] A further identification revealed in the research is the masculine association with 'living beings, animate, human, cultured' and the feminine association with 'lifeless objects, inanimate, non-human, uncultured'.[51] She claims that this reinforces the idea that only men can become social subjects, whereas women are objects of exchange between men (elsewhere she says that female psychiatric patients are objects of exchange between psychiatrists). Irigaray believes that the linguistic findings are a reflection of a social valuation but she also has faith in the possibility of linguistic transformations altering social realities. In the course of elaborating this position, Irigaray presents a slightly different recommendation for sexual liberation than the idea of developing a completely new, syntax-violating lauguage. For instance, she says that women should be 'more able to situate themselves as I, I-she . . . to represent themselves as subjects, and to talk to other women.'[52] It is still a reclaiming of language for themselves. It is still making an issue out of the sexed nature of language, but it falls short of the radical change advocated in her earlier writings (and perhaps still advocated as an ideal strategy).

Making space for women in language is in some respects parallel to Irigaray's next recommendation to end female repression, namely, to attribute more importance to the mother–daughter relationship, to establish a genealogy of women. This is to be understood as making a space for women in history, both personal and social. She claims that, in patriarchal cultures, mother–daughter relationships are subordinated to relations between men and, 'through incredible neglect and disregard, patriarchal traditions have wiped out traces of mother–daughter genealogies.'[53]

To make space for women in history in the personal realm means that the daughter need not give up her love for her mother. If she doesn't, she has a better chance of developing an identity which is not male-defined. Some practical suggestions presented by Irigaray for developing this bond are: 'learn once again to respect life and nourishment. Which means regaining respect for the mother and nature'; 'in all homes and all public places attractive images (not involving advertising) of the mother–daughter couple should be displayed' ; 'it's also important for mothers and daughters to find or make objects they can exchange between themselves so they can be defined as female'; and 'it would be helpful if, from an early age, mothers taught daughters respect for non-hierarchical difference of the sexes.'[54]

To make space for women socially is to give value to women workers, citizens, artists and politicians. This is not to denigrate motherhood but rather to refuse to define and value women exclusively by the maternal function. The aim is to develop positive, new values, which would pose a threat to the patriarchal order. For women to gain equivalent social status to men, Irigaray believes that it will be necessary to bring in new laws, for example, to protect the right to human dignity and the right to human identity for both women and men. This latter right would include the legal encodification of virginity (or physical and moral integrity) as a component of female identity, and the right to *motherhood* as a component (not a priority) of female identity.[55] Such laws would certainly change things around in an interesting way.

Irigaray points out that women's relation to religion is male dominated: 'if God is always imagined to be a father, how can women find in him a model of identity, a completed image or figure of themselves?'[56] What women need in order to develop a female identity is a relationship to the female divine: to women goddesses or figures such as Mary, and celebrations of female festivals centring around conception, birth, childhood and adolescence.[57]

This call for a female divine is problematic. While it may be true that gods and goddesses serve psychological needs they can't be erected as such. If they are, the religious realm would cease to be religious and would become therapeutic. The point of a religion is that it offers people something outside themselves as the object of their faith.

The other reclamation work which Irigaray advocates in lauguage, in personal and social life and in law, if it could be followed through, would obviously be a powerful means to lift repression, but it is terribly idealistic and one wonders about the practicality of the 'practical suggestions'. I will continue some of these themes in the next two chapters. The idea that we should work on language, position ourselves in language as a means to overcome oppression or repression, seems to be borne out in the work of many women writers who have experienced madness. In the next chapter I will explore some of their stories.

7 Women, Creativity, Reason and Madness

Creativity and madness are often linked in popular imagination and in reality many creative women have experienced mental distress. Madness is also a common theme in women's writing. Two sets of questions surface here:

A) Can we understand the literary link between women and madness along Chesler's lines as oppression possibly leading to alienation from the female role? Is it easier to provide an explanation in terms of repression or could both be working?

B) Can we understand creativity as a violation of reason and hence close to madness? Is reason so phallocentric that the only way women can be true to their nature is by irrationality?

These questions could take us in two different directions, as answers to the first cluster might lead to the view that many women writers are in fact mad. Answers to (B) might have us accepting that women's creativity will be called 'mad', a judgement based on male standards that does not need to be accepted. The distinction between the two sets of answers does not seem so clear-cut, however, when we think about the imposition of male standards as oppressive or repressive. This merging of the answers is portrayed most completely in the writings of Virginia Woolf and Janet Frame. Before discussing their works, I will briefly mention some other writers who offer insights on (A) and (B).

Charlotte Perkins Gilman, in the 1880s, experienced 'nervous depressions with a slight hysterical tendency'. She approached Weir Mitchell, a very prestigious psychiatrist specializing in female disorders. She had written down her history, bringing out the detail that her problems disappeared when she was away from her home, husband and child but returned as soon as she went back. He dismissed this history as 'self-conceit', ordered her to become more involved with her family and to give up writing. This made her much more distressed, but fortunately, in a 'moment of clear vision', she realized that she did not want to be a wife, she wanted to be a writer and activist.[1] In the fictionalized account of her experiences in *The Yellow Wallpaper*, Gilman writes of a woman ordered to rest, forbidden to write, seeing herself and others trapped behind wallpaper and desperately trying to escape – a true horror story.[2] A common theme in her writing is the attempt to break out of the limitations of the female role. In her utopia *The Man-Made World*, she concludes that 'to develop human life in its true powers we need full equal citizenship for women . . . an economic democracy must rest on a free womanhood.'[3] In the story *If I Were a Man* she places a woman's mind in a man's body and 'the world opened before her. Not the world she had been reared in – where Home had covered all the map, and the rest had been 'foreign' or 'unexplored country', but the world as it was – a man's world, as made, lived in, and seen, by men. It was dizzying.'

In Gilman's utopian novel *Herland* she describes a matriarchy, where women had no need for men except for breeding: 'to these women, in the unbroken sweep of this 2,000-year-old feminine civilisation, the word *woman* called up that big background, so far as they had gone in social development: and the word *man* meant to them only *male* – the sex . . .'[4] Gilman did not want to meet the normal expectations of womanhood; not realizing this made her extremely unhappy and the subject of a psychiatric diagnosis, acknowledging it jetisoned her into a life of writing. Some others with the same wants did not have such a clear trajectory.

Zelda Fitzgerald, who married Scott 1920, experienced extreme conflict over the female role. As she became more involved in creative pursuits, she spent less time as a wife and mother. This angered Scott, who attempted to disrupt her writing. Nancy Milford's biography of Zelda notes that Scott admitted in a letter to one of her psychiatrists that Zelda could have developed into a genius if they had never met, but given that they did meet and marry her insistence on her career as an author was hurting him and their daughter.[5] Zelda made many attempts to gain some independence from Scott, not by desertion or infidelity, but through creative expression in writing and in dance. He is portrayed as a dominating bully who gives her no support in these activities. One of the most outrageous inequities concerns the source data for both of their literary works. This consisted of Zelda's diaries and notes about her experiences as a glamorous and rebellious teenager in Alabama and about her later hectic social life with Scott. Scott tried very hard to deter her from using this material. He claimed that he should have the sole rights to it as he was a superior author to her. Zelda did manage to publish some stories, which is incredible given the impediments that Scott mounted, but she felt very frustrated that she could not do more.

The story of Zelda Fitzgerald is very disturbing. A bright, attractive and exuberant young girl with great promise is over the years beaten down into a submissive wreck of a person, leading a bare existence in and out of mental hospitals. Zelda's writing led her into conflict with Scott, which made her very anxious and brought about her hospitalization. While in hospital she was not allowed to write, which took away her very purpose in living, and of course made her more anxious.

It is interesting to read Scott's story *The Crack-Up*[6] in connection with Milford's biography. The former is a short survey of a large part of Scott's life when Zelda was with him, yet he does not mention her once by name and, as an aside, says he found it difficult to love those closest to him. He discusses his attitude to writing. If we recall along with these comments that Zelda saw writing as the key to her independence and identity, and that Scott made determined efforts to stop her writing, we can get some idea of the dreadful situation in which she found herself. He says, 'it seemed a romantic business to be a successful literary man – you were not ever going to be as famous as a movie star but what note you had was probably longer-lived – you were never going to have the power of a man of strong political or religious convictions but you were certainly more independent. Of course within the practice of your trade, you were forever unsatisfied – but I, for one, would not have chosen any other.'[7] Yet he did all he could to prevent his wife from choosing such a path. She died in a fire in a mental hospital.

Sylvia Plath committed suicide in 1963 at the age of 30. She achieved success as a poet and novelist (publishing some books under an assumed name). She also wrote *The Bell Jar*, an autobiographical novel. In one of her latest poems, 'Daddy', she rages against male power and the need to 'kill' the male influences in her life, namely her father:

> You do not do, you do not do
> Any more, black shoe
> In which I have lived like a foot
> For thirty years, poor and white,
> Barely daring to breathe or achoo.
>
> Daddy, I have had to kill you.

and her husband, Ted Hughes:

> I made a model of you,
> A man in black with a Meinkampf look
>
> And a love of the rack and the screw.
> And I said, I do, I do.
>
> . . . . .
>
> If I've killed one man, I've killed two.[8]

Even her own death is turned into an act of revenge in the poem 'Lady Lazarus':

> Out of the ash
> I rise with my red hair
> And I eat men like air.[9]

Her attitudes to the men in her life were not without ambivalence, however. In *The Bell Jar* she says: 'I thought how strange it had never occurred to me before that I was only purely happy until I was nine years old.' This was when her father died, and in her letters to her mother she expressed regret at her separation from Hughes.[10] While they were together she became depressed and was given electric shock treatment, a treatment which she regarded as merely punitive. After a description of this treatment in *The Bell Jar*, she says, 'I wondered what terrible thing it was that I had done.' In her short story *Johnny Panic and the Bible of Dreams*, electric shock treatment is depicted as one of the weapons used by psychiatrists to obliterate our dreams and bring us back to 'the crass fate these doctors call health and happiness'.

In the poem 'The Applicant' Plath presents an applicant for marriage, a 'living doll', who can sew, cook and talk, and in the poem 'Lesbos' she shows how the needs and dependencies of the husband can exhaust and limit the wife. Every day she must 'fill him with soul-stuff, like a pitcher'. In her own life she was highly motivated to write yet weighed down by domesticity. She expresses a tremendous release after her divorce and writes to her mother: 'living apart from Ted is wonderful – I am no longer in his shadow, and it is heaven to be liked for myself alone, knowing what I want.'[11] She completes the *Ariel* collection and announces: 'I have never been so happy in my life.'[12] The English winter then sets in, she has recurrent flu, difficulty getting help to look after her two babies and financial problems, yet still gets up early to write. Three months later she is dead.

Ted Hughes, in the introduction to Plath's diaries which he published after her death, even though she had decided against publishing them, says that her madness was due to excessive self-centredness.[13] Ed Cohen, claiming to be a friend of Plath's, wrote in the *New York Times* in 1989 that she suffered from a borderline personality at her very best and, 'while there is no consensus among the professionals as to exactly where that border is, most of them would agree that such people make those closest to them angry and uncomfortable a great deal of the time. . . . I find it remarkable that [Ted] stood it at all as long as he did.'[14] Wise words or further attempts at male domination? Perhaps Phyllis Chesler is closer to the truth when she says that Plath was 'lonely and isolated. Her genius did not earn her certain reprieves and comforts tended to the male artist.'[15]

Antonia White began writing in 1929. She married and divorced some years later. Her five books, all close to her own life, concentrated on the theme of a woman who is being crushed by the oppressive forces around her and her struggle for independence. The books also detail the unfruitful experiences with psychiatry. White suffered from depression and spent ten months in a London asylum. It was not psychiatry but her writing that helped her in the end.[16] A similar story with the same outcome is presented by Margaret Coombs in her autobiographical novel *The Best Man for This Sort of Thing*.[17]

If we look at these novelists, bearing the initial questions of this chapter in mind, it seems that we do not need to go beyond the idea that oppression, especially oppression related to the demands of the female role, is important in understanding problems of madness in women. It is perhaps the case that these women experience this oppression particularly acutely as they have something else that they urgently want to do, apart from looking after their husband and the house. Also, when they turn to psychiatry for help, none of them find relief. Rather, the oppression continues in a different form.

In answer to the (B) questions, these novelists did violate reason in the sense that they wrote personal stories or novels based on life. Such 'writing of a life' where madness is a key experience is obviously going to be very different from a traditional novel with a plot. It is likely to be viewed as irrational in a reason set by male norms. Also all these works challenge these norms, and, given that male norms set the general standard, such a challenge may always be viewed as irrational.

In addition to autobiographical novels and poems, there are straight autobiographies written by women depicting their experiences of madness and psychiatry. Frances Farmer, a film star and actor, rebelled against the demands of her family. Her parents had her committed to a mental hospital where she spent eleven years. In the hospital she was raped by orderlies and gnawed by rats. She writes that 'she cannot rationalize why it happened'.[18] Kate Millett was also hospitalized against her will because of the interventions of her female lover, who Millett claims is given by psychiatry 'nearly absolute authority over me, all power to decide whether I am sick or well, wrong or right (since that is the issue behind the first pair of opposites).[19] Millett views her madness as 'the crime of the imaginary', which is not apparent when people treat her as sane. The problem as she sees it is when 'I am approached with that hesitant, vaguely patronizing, coaxing firmness reserved for children and for maniacs, I become terse, short-tempered, cynical, sarcastic, impatient, annoyed – all sane responses perhaps, but in the context they are seen as positive and irrefutable evidence [of madness]. Stuck with this label, picked to be 'it', anyone could be manipulated into position, squirming for credibility, . . . it is like a game, a malicious game.'[20] She speaks of the hospital as a place where 'you will be examined and condemned by tests of reason themselves irrational, weighed and assessed by rules of logic which are illogical. And the drugs will make sure you fail. It is not mind or reason that is the issue but control.'[21] Both these authors deconstruct the concept of 'madness'.

The autobiographies of Shelagh Supeene, *As for the Sky, Falling*, and Marie Cardinal, *The Words to Say It*, take a different direction. Supeene began post-graduate work in philosophy in Canada. She had an affair with her professor and became pregnant. He wanted her to have an abortion and left her. She became very depressed, saw spirits, overdosed and then had numerous stays in mental hospitals. She turned to psychiatry because she did not know where else to turn for help. In retrospect, she views that 'help' as oppressive and as delaying her return to normality. This came when she was able to express her anger at psychiatry and male power. This anger allowed her to give voice to her life in writing. She concludes, 'merely reforming psychiatry wouldn't eliminate its abuse and oppression: they are an intrinsic part of the profession's self-definition. They are, often, what psychiatry means by "help," "care," and "therapy." Whatever genuine help a given person may receive, she will be harmed too. For many people the harm outweighs the help. The proportion varies from person to person, that is all.'[22]

Supeene did not doubt her madness and saw it as the outcome of isolation and the immoral treatment by those close to her. Marie Cardinal also did not doubt her madness. She experienced a 'Thing' inside her which made her bleed profusely. The 'Thing' controlled her life, causing anxiety and fear. Through eight years of psychoanalysis and through writing she gets in touch with a range of shocks and traumas in her early life and is able to dismiss the 'Thing'. She had been an unwanted child, and when she was ten her mother told her of all the ways she had unsuccessfully tried to abort her. Also when she was ten a man followed her home from school and, in the stairwell of her apartment, sexually abused her. She was reared by her mother under a strict regime: 'my needs were repressed, my desires, my impetus, they had been dammed up, painted over, disguised and imprisoned. After having removed my brain, having gutted my skull, they had stuffed it full of acceptable thought which suited me like an apron on a cow.'[23] She writes of herself in childhood as a 'submissive performer . . . a nice little girl who was being manipulated and who obeyed.'[24] She also views her married life as implicated in her madness: 'the Thing was fed by pregnancies, months of nursing, and the constant fatigue of a young woman with three children, a job, a house and a husband.'[25] Finally she comes to understand her life as dominated by a fear of male power, a fear passed on to her by her mother even in the abortion story, as this was told to her daughter to warn her not to trust men. Once she understands 'what it means to have a vagina', what it means to feel oppressed, she is able to regain her sanity. Both oppression and repression are clearly relevant here. Bruno Bettlelheim in an afterword to this autobiography focuses on the mother's desire not to have the daughter. He does not mention the sexual abuse or any other discontents with the female role.

There are other creative works which cannot be described as autobiographical novels or autobiographies but are still relevant to answering the questions posed at the beginning of this chapter, for example, the novels of Joyce Carol Oates. The women in her writings are nearly all attracted by the ideals of romantic love into a life of domesticity which brings pain and disaster. Her novels can be read as extremely comprehensive documents on the fine detail of the oppression of women trying to carry out the female role.[26] In one novel, entitled *Solstice*, Oates departs from this theme. She depicts a female painter who is fond of mixing with men in a non-sexual way, enjoying masculine freedom in pub crawls, dressing in a rough masculine style: she 'took up so much more space than her fairly thin frame required'. She experienced mood swings: 'in her speedy state she gave off an unnerving radiant heat, sheer energy, in the other state (for which there was no appropriate term) her voice was slurred and her body movement uncoordinated.'[27] Oates seems to be making a point here that there is no need to medicalize such experiences. When the artist is accused of being changeable, she says, 'I never change, I simply become more myself'. She views the different states of being as intertwined with her creativity, believing that she needed the depth and range of these feelings in order to paint adequately.

Finally there are the creative works by women which present strident images of female oppression and a complete rejection of the world of psychiatry. The 'Still Sane' exhibition in a Canadian psychiatric institution of sculptured images of the brutality towards women, and the book recording this exhibition, is one example.[28] It is about a woman who was hospitalized for her sexual preference – other women – and given shock treatment and drugs to try to cure her of this preference. Andrea Dworkin's novel *Mercy* expresses the anguish of a woman sexually abused in childhood and raped many times in adulthood, who has the desire to trust and love men beaten into a hatred and a karate-powered mission of revenge. She roams the streets of New York, attacking men with big swinging kicks. She says: 'I like one big one between the legs, for the sake of form and symbolism, to pay my respects to content as such, action informed by the imperatives of literature.'[29] Is she mad? She certainly doesn't think so. She believes that she is clear-headed and rational. Is she bad? Well, in her words: 'it is obscene for a girl to think about fair.'

In reflecting on the questions posed above, Virginia Woolf and Janet Frame are particularly instructive. Both were said to have experienced madness. Both wrote novels and autobiographies which help us to get a full picture of their lives and views. There is little doubt that they both experienced oppression and repression and thought that this was important in understanding how they lived their lives. It is unclear whether either accepted the label of 'madness'. At the very least one could say that their experiences seem to have informed their views on the madness of their fictional characters. They both presented critiques of reason and developed new styles of writing which reflect those critiques.

Virginia Woolf

Woolf was regarded as mad by her biographer, Quentin Bell, and her husband Leonard. Bell says that Woolf went mad at 13 and that this was always a sword above her head, which was so unendurable that, 'when the voices of insanity spoke to her in 1941, she took . . . the cure of death'.[30] Bell cites the following in support of his belief: she thought that people laughed at her in the street, she had an undue fear of being run down in the street, periodically she refused to eat, she behaved unreasonably towards her husband, sister and nurses, and she suffered hallucinations. Stephen Trombley, in the book '*All that Summer She was Mad': Virginia Woolf and her Doctors*, succeeds fairly well in explaining away these symptoms.[31] He points out that her husband said that people did laugh at her in the street. She had witnessed fatal accidents. She behaved unreasonably towards others because they behaved unreasonably towards her. They were reactions of a sane person who felt she was being manipulated and forced.[32] Yet Trombley still writes of her breakdowns and the fact that during these 'she had a peculiar relationship to her body. She felt that it was sordid; she found eating repulsive; she felt as if her body was not the centre of her "self" – that she somehow existed at odds with it, or divorced from it.'[33] Also it is hard to explain away hallucinations, even if they can be made meaningful. She thought that she heard birds singing in Greek. Woolf has written about her early and later childhood experiences of sexual abuse by her two half brothers, Gerald and George Duckworth, which began at the age of six and continued for 16 years.[34] Trombley points out that these molestations sometimes took place during her private Greek classes. To rationalize the hallucinations in this way seems a denial of the impact of these experiences. Speaking of George, Woolf says: 'one felt like an unfortunate minnow shut up in the same tank with an unwieldy and turbulent whale',[35] and elsewhere she says that her life 'contained a large proportion of . . . cotton wool, this non-being'.[36] These words express the importance of the experiences but they are not necessarily an admission of madness. It depends on how one conceives it, and we gain some insight on Woolf's conception from her novel *Mrs Dalloway*.

In *Mrs Dalloway* the exploration of the consciousness of one person interweaves gently with that of another, a soft intermingling, with very little actual conversation. Thus, without their ever meeting, a link is made between Mrs Clarissa Dalloway and Mr Septimus Smith. Septimus had witnessed the death of a friend in the war and thought that he was a criminal because he couldn't feel the death. He wrote prolifically, he had hallucinations, and he committed suicide on the night of Clarissa's party, causing his psychiatrist, Sir William Bradshaw, to be a little late. Septimus is a tragic figure, not because of his hallucinations but because he cannot forgive himself his lack of feeling for his friend's death. Nor is this ameliorated by understanding. Rezia, his wife, is loving and kind but does not understand. He sees Dr Holmes before Bradshaw, Holmes is a bully who pushes Rezia aside to see Septimus against the will of both. Holmes is completely unhelpful – perhaps even a murderer. It is in trying to avoid one of these visits that Septimus jumps from the window to his death. Holmes, not exactly willing to see his own culpability, calls out 'the coward!'.

Bradshaw gets the full weight of Woolf's venom. Encouraging repression, he says that he wants Septimus to 'try to think as little about yourself as possible'. Furthermore he urged Septimus to rest and definitely not to write or to read books, which leads Woolf into a general reflection on the psychiatrist:

> Worshipping proportion [which he called sanity], Sir William not only prospered himself but made England prosper, secluded her lunatics, forbade childbirth, penalised despair, made it impossible for the unfit to propagate their views until they, too, shared his sense of proportion . . . the friends and relations of his patients felt for him the keenest gratitude for insisting that these prophetic Christs and Christesses . . . should drink milk in bed, as Sir William ordered; Sir William with his thirty years' experience of these kinds of cases, and his infallible instinct, this is madness, this sense.[37]

Under the names of love, duty and self-sacrifice is a desire for power, a desire to beat the human will into submission. Lady Bradshaw had submitted: 'it was nothing you could put your finger on; there had been no scene, no snap; only the slow sinking, waterlogged, of her will into his',[38] a woman who had once caught salmon freely, 'now, quick to minister to the craving which lit her husband's eye so oilily for dominion.'[39]

If patients didn't submit to his treatment regimes, Bradshaw knew he had the police to back him and 'the good of society'. He was in a strong position to override opposition: 'he swooped; he devoured. He shut people up.'[40]

Towards the end of the novel, the two people to whom Clarissa has been closest, who do not include her husband, pick Bradshaw for a humbug without even hearing him speak, and Clarissa muses about his obscure evil and indescribable outrage – 'forcing your soul'. She understands how a psychiatrist like this might make life intolerable. She feels somehow like Septimus – the young man who had killed himself. 'She felt glad that he had done it; thrown it away.'[41]

Why? Because he escapes the tyranny of Bradshaw? Because life doesn't have any meaning if one is not allowed to write? Either answer is possible, but Woolf is not expressing the view that madness involves so much suffering that suicide is preferable. We can see in the story about Bradshaw that she does not accept conventional definitions, that Bradshaw's prescriptions on how to live were insane, that Septimus, though caught in a moral bind, had a better understanding of meaningful values. Septimus's distress can be understood in terms of oppression, the oppression of war, the wide-scale tyranny of one group over another, and the oppression of psychiatry in aiming 'to shut him up'. Alienation from one's role is relevant too. Septimus is portrayed as 'feminine', living a life in the emotional realm, and 'feminine' in his suicide. Clarissa, identifying with Septimus, is oppressed and alienated, but the causes are different. She is oppressed by married life. Comparing Clarissa with her husband, Woolf writes: 'with twice his wits, she had to see things through his eyes – one of the tragedies of married life.'[42] Mr Dalloway exercises a quiet but insidious domination over Clarissa. There is a scene which portrays this well. He orders her gently to rest after lunch. He brings a pillow and quilt. 'She would do it, of course, as he wished it. Since he had brought the pillow, she would lie down . . . But – but – why did she suddenly feel, for no reason that she could discover, desperately unhappy?'[43]

Repression is also an important aspect of Clarissa's life. At 52 she is still with her husband but sleeping alone, thinking she is at the end of her sexual life, yet acknowledging fleeting attractions to women and treasuring the kiss that Sally gave her in her youth as the most exquisite moment in her life. When Sally turns up unexpectedly at Clarissa's party, Clarissa longs to speak with her but avoids it, thinking, 'life was like that – humiliation, renunciation'. In the intervening years Sally has married a man with cotton mills in Manchester.

Drawing together the ideas about mental distress that emerge from *Mrs Dalloway*, it is unimportant whether one is labelled insane or not; there are states of despair and these states can be understood in terms of oppression and repression.

There is no reason to doubt that Woolf would have seen her own life also in this way, oppressed by the many years of sexual abuse and doctors' orders not to write but to rest, repressed in her sexuality. She had an intense and long friendship with Vita Sackville-West, to whom she dedicated the novel *Orlando*. Writing to her sister about her feelings for Vita, she says, 'you will never succumb to the charms of any of your sex – what an arid garden the world must be for you! What avenues of stone pavements and iron railings!'[44] Yet both Woolf and Sackville-West married. Woolf was physically distant from her husband and did not have children. She committed suicide in 1941, drowning in the River Ouse.

To turn now to the second group of questions concerning reason, madness and creativity: Woolf reflects on what it means to have a creative life as a woman. She stresses that in order to be creative a woman must break out of her female role and that this will be viewed as irrational by men. If a woman novelist is productive, 'she has thought of something, something about the body, about the passions which it was unfitting for her as a woman to say. Men, her reason told her, would be shocked. The consciousness of what men will say of a woman who speaks the truth about her passions had roused her from her artist's state of unconsciousness. She could write no more. . . . Her imagination could work no longer.'[45] It is not that she thinks that the male shock has a good basis. She provides an extensive critique of 'masculine intelligence' and the life of reason in her novels and essays. Mr Ramsey, in *To the Lighthouse*, is a good example. He is a philosopher who writes about abstract metaphysics and is outstandingly oblivious to the emotional needs of his children and wife. His son wants to kill him. His daughter in young adulthood reflects on his 'crass blindness and tyranny . . . which had poisoned her childhood and raised bitter storms, so that even now she woke in the night trembling with rage and remembered some command of his; some insolence: 'Do this,' 'do that,' his dominance: his "Submit to me." '[46] Woolf writes that Mr Ramsey 'never tampered with a fact, never altered a disagreeable word to suit the pleasure or convenience of any mortal being.'[47] In one scene, Mrs

Ramsey remarks optimistically on the weather, which is relevant to a proposed family outing to the lighthouse. Mr Ramsey, thinking she has unrealistically raised hopes, stamps his foot and says, 'Damn you.' The text continues: 'to pursue truth with such astounding lack of consideration for other people's feelings, . . . was to [Mrs Ramsey] so horrible an outrage of human decency. . . . There was nothing to be said'.[48]

In the essay *Women and Fiction* Woolf writes that 'both in life and in art the values of a woman are not the values of a man.'[49] When women write novels they alter established values, making serious what appears trivial to men and trivial what is important to men. Also, at the end of *Orlando*, Woolf says that, 'when we write of a woman, everything is out of place – culminations and perorations; the accent never falls where it does with a man.'[50] Yet earlier Orlando scoffs at the 'glories' of his noble male ancestors: 'but of all that killing and campaigning, that drinking and love-making, that spending and hunting and riding and eating, what remained? A skull, a finger.'[51]

Woolf grants that there are obstacles to exploring one's own sex as a woman. Lily, the female painter in *To the Lighthouse*, spurning the 'degradation of marriage', struggles to express herself in art but muses that 'life [is] like a wave which bore one up with it and threw one down with it, there, with a dash on the beach.'[52] She imagines someone whispering in her ear, 'women can't paint, women can't write.' Woolf mentions the 'Angel in the House', her phrase for what came between her and her writing: 'it was she who bothered me and wasted my time and so tormented me that at last I killed her.'[53] The Angel is the conventional woman who never had a mind or wish of her own but preferred to sympathize always with the minds and wishes of others.

Woolf's writings do then suggest an answer to the question: can we understand creativity as a violation of reason and hence close to madness? At least for women, if they begin to explore their own sex, if they do write of women as women, then they are likely to be viewed as irrational. She is also helpful in answering the question: is reason so phallocentric that the only way women can be true to their nature is by irrationality? In fact Mrs Ramsey answers this in *To the Lighthouse*. She lived in the world of feelings, but 'her simplicity fathomed what clever people falsified.' Being true to her nature, others see her as irrational. Woolf makes some direct comments about language and the need to subvert it to write as a woman:

The urgency of the moment always missed its mark. Words fluttered sideways and struck the object inches too low. Then one gave it up; then the idea sunk back again; then one became like most middle-aged people, cautious, furtive, with wrinkles between the eyes and a look of perpetual apprehension. For how could one express in words these emotions of the body? . . . It was one's body feeling, not one's mind.[54]

Elsewhere, speaking about sentences, she says that the form of a sentence does not fit women:

It is a sentence made by men; it is too loose, too heavy, too pompous for a woman's use. Yet in a novel, . . . an ordinary and usual type of sentence has to be found to carry the reader on easily and naturally from one end of the book to the other. And this a woman must make for herself, altering and adapting the current sentence until she writes one that takes the natural shape of her thought without crushing or distorting it.[55]

Woolf engages in limited experimentation with different sentence structures, violating normal punctuation and shifting easily from one thought to another – for example, in the beginning of *Mrs Dalloway* and in *Orlando*.[56] However, in the middle of one such experiment in *Orlando*, she comments accurately on the 'unwieldy length of this sentence'. There is a much more successful and brilliant exploration of innovative style in her novel *The Waves*. It is written in the form of waves, with the internal reveries of different people coming in, building up and drifting away. The voice is initially directed outwards and practical. By the end of the paragraph the voice turns inward and invites reflection. Such paragraphs, and there are many in the novel, are marked by a beginning quotation mark which has no complementary closing mark, reinforcing the reflective theme and the idea of a wave slowly disappearing. The following is illustrative:

'It is the first day of the summer holidays,' said Rhoda. 'And now, as the train passes by these red rocks, by this blue sea, the term, done with, forms itself into one shape behind me. I see its colour. June was white. I see the fields white with daisies, and white with dresses; and tennis courts marked with white. Then there was wind and violent thunder. There was a star riding through clouds one night, and I said to the star, "Consume me." . . . Wind and storm coloured July. Also, in the middle, cadaverous, awful lay the grey puddle in the courtyard, when, holding an envelope in my hand, I carried a message. I came to the puddle. I could not cross it. Identity failed me. We are nothing, I said, and fell. I was blown like a feather, I was wafted down tunnels. Then very gingerly, I pushed my foot across. I laid my hand against a brick wall. I returned very painfully, drawing myself back into my body over the grey, cadaverous space of the puddle. This is life then to which I am committed.[57]

For Woolf, it is reason that is embodied in the current phallocentric language which works against women expressing their being, and it is this reason which needs to be subverted. Women must have the courage to surmount oppositions and be true to themselves.

Woolf says that she flattered herself that she had killed the Angel, and indeed Kate Millett criticizes her for portraying the glorification of housewives.[58] This greatly undervalues her work, as I hope to have shown above. However, her prescriptions for breaking with a phallocentric style, which foreshadows Irigaray's ideas, are not consistently followed through in her writing. It is probably not until Janet Frame's novel *Owls Do Cry* that we see the beginning of a sustained break with conventional style in the attempt by a woman to express her self. It is possible that Frame is acknowledging her debt to Woolf in the choice of two of her titles: *To the Is-land* and *An Angel at my Table*.

Janet Frame

There are curious links between Woolf and Frame. I don't know what significance, if any, to attach to them. Both comment that they were given a narcissus. Woolf received hers from Freud, Frame hers from a Chinese friend. Contemplating the death of one of her sisters, Frame says, 'I had known and experienced the rhythm and feeling of Virginia Woolf's Waves.'[59] In a letter to another sister she quoted from Woolf, describing the gorse as having a 'peanut-buttery smell'. This description was used by a doctor to exemplify her apparent 'schizophrenia'.[60] The title of the first volume of Frame's autobiography is *To the Is-land*. 'Is-land' contrasts with 'Was-land' and means something like 'the present', but the title also relates back to a childhood story called *To the Island*, which made a deep impression on the young Frame. It was about children going to an island, the surface theme of Woolf's novel *To the Lighthouse*. In the latter the lighthouse is a metaphor for isolation, and it is towards isolation that Janet Frame moves in the years of the first volume of her autobiography.

The second volume of Frame's autobiography is called *An Angel at my Table*, perhaps from the Rilke poem quoted under the title, but perhaps also linking back to Woolf's *Angel in the House*? It is certainly not important to reach an answer. Frame is a natural successor to Woolf in reflections on creativity, reason and madness. She has provided us with a three-volume autobiography and two novels which explore these themes, but, as with Woolf, her writing goes into other areas as well.

Although Janet Frame was diagnosed with 'schizophrenia' and spent many years in mental hospitals in her native New Zealand and then had briefer stays in London institutions, she rejected this diagnosis from the first time it was made. She writes that the idea of her suffering from schizophrenia seemed unreal but her confusion increased when she learned that one of the symptoms was 'things seeming unreal'. She thought then that there was no escape.[61] Hounded by the diagnosis for over a decade she eventually submitted herself for tests at the Maudsley Hospital in London. The psychiatrists decided that she had been incorrectly diagnosed as schizophrenic in the past, that she should never have been admitted to hospital but that she was now suffering from her stay in hospitals and needed more hospitalization to get over that. Shortly after, she entered the Maudsley Hospital and stayed for many months. This sounds like more of the same but in fact it wasn't. She had the good fortune to meet Dr Cawley, who recognized the importance to her of her writing, probably the first psychiatrist to do so. He gave her permission to write. He gave her permission to design her life around writing. A New Zealand writer, Frank Sargeson, had tried to steer her in this direction some years previously but his misogyny got in the way. He encouraged her to write but colluded with her in the repression of her female self. He had kindly given her a place to stay where she could write, a humble hut at the end of his garden. They lived closely together for over a year. In one respect he was the angel at her table, but Frame reflects:

> In all his conversation there was a vein of distrust, at times of hatred of women as a species distinct from men, and when he was in the mood for exploring that vein, I listened uneasily, unhappily, for I was a woman and he was speaking of my kind. I was sexually naive, unaware, and only half awake, and I was ignorant of such subjects as homosexuality, but I felt constantly hurt by his implied negation of a woman's body. My life with Frank Sargeson was for me a celibate life, a priestly life devoted to writing, in which I flourished but because my make-up is not entirely priestly I felt the sadness of having moved from hospital where it had been thought necessary to alter the make-up of my mind, to another asylum where the desire was that my body should be of another gender.

The price I paid for the stay in the army hut was the realization of the nothingness of my body.[62]

With Dr Cawley she found someone who not only encouraged her writing but encouraged her to be herself: 'Dr. Cawley convinced me that I was myself, I was an adult, I need not explain myself to others. The "you should" days were over, he said. *You go here, go there, be this, be that, do this, do that – you should you know – it would be good for you!* Lifelong, largely because of my own makeup I had been a target for the *You should*-ers, with a long interval of *You must Or Else*: It was time to begin again.'[63] Why did she need a psychiatrist to tell her this? Pehaps that was another consequence of the institutionalization.

Leaving aside the label of 'schizophrenia', there were long periods in Janet Frame's life when she suffered from mental distress. After the death of her sister Myrtle when Janet was eight years old, she fell into a great depression, a 'world of misery'. She became very anxious and developed 'twitches and tics'. Probably as a result of her intelligence and originality, she came to be perceived by teachers and classmates as 'different'. In her world of school, 'to be different was to be peculiar, a little 'mad''.[64] Frame embraced this difference, partly because of her lack of success in trying to be the same, partly because she was starting to have writing ambitions and in her family 'there was a continued association between disability and proven ability'.[65] The latter idea was motivated by the desperation of trying to live with her brother Bruddie, who suffered from violent epileptic convulsions. Towards the end of her school years, she consulted a gypsy in a fun fair who 'warned me what I already knew, that my "personality" was in trouble, that I was too shy, too self conscious.'[66] She says that she saw herself as a 'background person'. She had many tearful outbursts. Leaving school, she feared madness. Thinking of the poverty and desolation of other poets, she remembers the lines:

> We poets in our youth begin in gladness; But thereof comes in the end despondency and madness.[67]

At the age of 21 she tried to kill herself. Happy that she didn't succeed, she threw herself into tertiary studies and writing. A psychology tutor encouraged her to show him her autobiography, where she had included the suicide bid. He arranged for her to be committed to a mental hospital, where she had a 'concentrated course in the horrors of insanity and the dwelling place of those judged insane'. It is here that she first received the label of 'schizophrenia', which she rejected, saying that she was just shy and fearful. However, she did play out some of the supposed symptoms of 'schizophrenia' to keep the interest of the tutor: 'I was an ordinary grey-feathered bird that spent its life flashing one or two crimson feathers at the world, adapting the feathers to suit the time of life. In my childhood I had displayed number riddles, memorizing long passages of verse and prose, mathematical answers; now, to *suit* the occasion, I wore my schizophrenic fancy dress.'[68] A dangerous game.

She visited another psychologist and 'turned on my "schizophrenia" at full flow: it had become my only way of arousing interest in those whose help I believed that I needed.'[69] This psychologist encouraged her to go into a mental hospital and have electro-convulsive therapy. Surprisingly she agreed, and her whole life was 'thrown out of focus'. The horrors of this procedure are depicted in her book *Faces in the Water*. Years of confinement followed, filled with fear and unhappiness. She says that she would not have survived had it not been for the sadness and courage of the other patients and her desire to 'speak' for them.[70]

In speaking for mental patients in *Owls Do Cry* and *Faces in the Water*, she documents the deplorable state of mental institutions in New Zealand in the 1940s and 1950s, the barbarity of electro-convulsive therapy and the ignorance and inhumanity of psychiatrists. We find out little about the antecedents of mental distress in these works. Daphne in *Owls Do Cry* is institutionalized for many years. It is not clear why. She is presented as rebellious and isolated. She is described as 'strange'. Her sister is accidentally killed while they are playing together. Her brother suffers from epilepsy. Her father is a miserable man, oppressive to the other family members, and the mother is constantly trying to make the peace and the pikelets. A psychiatrist recommends psychosurgery, claiming, 'this brain operation was the only chance of making Daphne into a normal human being, a useful citizen, able to vote and take part in normal life, without getting any of these strange fancies that she has now.'[71] We are left with the feeling that it is normality, not madness, that is thrown into question.

It is isolation that seems to be behind Istina Mavet's hospitalization in *Faces in the Water*, along with a desire to 'give up'. Frame gives Istina these words:

I will write about the season of peril. I was put in hospital because a great gap opened in the ice floe between myself and the other people whom I watched, with their world, drifting away through a violet-colored sea where hammer-head sharks in tropical ease swam side by side with the seals and the polar bears. I was alone on the ice. A blizzard came and I grew numb and wanted to lie down and sleep and I would have done so had not the strangers arrived with scissors and cloth bags filled with lice and red-labeled bottles of poison, and other dangers which I had not realized before – mirrors, cloaks, corridors, furniture, square inches, bolted lengths of silence – plain and patterned free samples of voices. And the strangers, without speaking, put up circular calico tents and camped with me, surrounding me with their merchandize of peril.[72]

Life in Istina's hospital reflected life for women on the outside. They were treated as children, unpaid domestic workers, and forced into submission and dependency: ' "For your own good" is a persuasive argument that will eventually make man agree to his own destruction.'[73] There is a strong suggestion that it is the oppressive nature of life in mental institutions that gives rise to extreme resentment, unhappiness and abandonment of the will to live.

In these two novels there are two central figures both diagnosed as mad and both experiencing long periods in mental hospitals. Frame is asking us to consider whether they were really mad or simply responding in a perfectly understandable way to oppression either on the outside or the inside of the mental hospital. Frame denies that either of these novels are autobiographical, but in her own life story it is precisely this consideration that is highlighted. The mental distress alluded to above was a problem for her, but was it madness?

Perhaps this distress too can be understood in terms of the inordinate amount of oppression that existed in her life. It would not be inaccurate to say that she was oppressed by life circumstances, living with a mother tied to household duties, whose 'real self washed away'. Frame writes of her in sadness:

I couldn't help thinking of the lifetime of words that mother never spoke: I saw them marching in single or double file (as words do) to the tip of her tongue, then being turned away because the time was not right or there was no-one to receive them . . . If only she had been able to *speak for herself*![74]

She describes her father as dour, with a strong sense of formal behaviour and 'an inability to accept that funny events happened in real life'. Bruddie's convulsions caused fear and arguments in the household. Frame reflects that before these convulsions began 'there had usually been somewhere within the family to find a "place" however cramped; now there seemed to be no place; a cloud of unreality and disbelief filled our home, and some of the resulting penetrating rain had the composition of real tears. Bruddie became stupefied by drugs and fits . . . while we girls . . . could not cope with the horror of it.'[75] Two of her sisters drowned in different incidents; one when Janet was eight and one when she was 22. She experienced the death of three grandparents and her aunt before the age of nine. Her dogs which she loved were deliberately drowned when a welfare inspector decided the house was unclean. The family was extremely poor and the father played on the children's fears about poverty. This led to further specific oppressions, for example, concerning clothes. She had to wear the same school tunic years after she had outgrown it. It caused her embarrassment and discomfort over her developing breasts. Because of this tunic she spoke of herself as being 'powerlessly in harness'. Her young life was full of 'disasters and nightmares' and she related closely to the words of the song:

> Thou holy art in many hours of sadness when life's hard toil my spirit hath oppressed . . .[76]

Janet Frame's love of writing from an early age fired ambitions to make it a life-long pursuit and to not be caught in domestic life. This put her at odds with what was expected of girls and women in the New Zealand of the mid-twentieth century. It may well have been the case that the oppression she experienced led indirectly to this alienation from the female role, as she found such solace in writing. Later in life she wonders in which world she might have lived 'had not the world of literature been given to me by my mother and by the school syllabus, and even by the death of Myrtle', her sister.[77]

Repression also seems to have played a key role in the distress that Frame felt in her early adulthood. She writes of leading a monastic life, a life devoted to learning and writing, and of being unaware of any sexual feelings in her early twenties. After the years of hospitalization, when she stayed with Frank Sargeson, she speaks of just emerging from 'a state of intimidation', but Frank's hatred of female bodies did nothing to lift her sexual repression. At the age of 32, living in Ibiza, a Spanish island, she decided that she was sick of being 'good' sexually and threw herself into an affair with a poet called Bernard. She abandoned her writing but gave him up when he reacted with horror at the idea of her having a baby. She did become pregnant but miscarried. Facing this, she says,

> I knew a feeling that was stronger than regret but not as intense as bereavement, a no-woman's land of feeling where a marvellous sense of freedom sprang up beside hate for myself, longing for Bernard and what he had given me and never knew, sadness for a lost path, vanishings, with the sense of freedom and the prospect of living a new life in Mirror City [city of the imagination], triumphing like the rankest, strongest, most pungent weeds that yet carry exquisite flowers, outgrowing the accepted flowers in no-woman's land.[78]

Moving to Andorra, she became involved in another serious relationship with an Italian, but resisted his offer of marriage. She returned to England and, thinking about her productivity on the Continent, says, 'living is slightly the opposite of expressing'[79] (echoing Woolf's ironic remark in *Orlando* that 'thought and life are as the poles asunder').[80] Repression is no longer an issue for Janet Frame. She is free to explore her sexuality in art or in life.

This is the time where she lost her psychiatric qualifications; she recommenced her career as a writer, and reviewers compared her with Virginia Woolf. Frame, like Woolf, provokes us into questioning fixed notions of madness or insanity. In her determination to throw off the label of 'schizophrenia', however, there is an implicit acceptance that this is genuine madness, a view that is very much in line with Chesler's. Both Frame and Woolf seem to come down to the belief that other states of mental distress may be very debilitating and unwanted, but not 'mad', because they are capable of explanation in terms of oppression or repression.

Returning to the second set of questions posed at the beginning of this chapter, Frame is against the view that her 'insanity' is a reason and explanation for her writing,[81] but she does acknowledge that her writing helped her to cope with loss and death. She would most likely not want to say that we can understand creativity as a violation of reason and hence as being close to madness. Yet her writing doesn't follow the dictates of reason. She makes extensive use of poetry and song lines in the autobiography and the novels, sometimes interspersing the prose with three poems on a page. The prose is sometimes close to poetry, as exemplified above. She speaks of 'the Ophelia syndrome . . . [as] a poetic fiction that nevertheless usefully allows a writer to explore varieties of otherwise unspoken or unacceptable feelings, thoughts, and language.'[82] Unacceptable by what or whose standard? Unacceptable because they are in the realm of the irrational? Unacceptable because they present a critique of psychiatry, the standard-bearer of reason? Unacceptable because they are up-wellings of femininity? All the answers are positive.

8 Beyond Psychiatry

Dandelion: *Taraxacum officinale*
A most valuable herb. Recommended for liver and gall problems. Excellent, safe diuretic. Rich in vitamins and minerals. (Waters, *Growing and Use of Herbs*)

Patterson's curse: *Echium plantagineum*
When in flower, the plants provide a useful nectar source for bees. (Gelfoldi, *Identifying the Weeds Around You*)
   A valuable plant for honey bees who make delicious honey from it.

Common Australian weeds: Dandelion, Patterson's curse.

Weed: wild herb springing where it is not wanted (says the dictionary).

Weed: a nuisance (says a friend).

The first distinction which I remember as troubling as a young child was that between a weed and other plants. Seduced by their prettiness, I was never persuaded that they were undesirable life forms which should be killed.

As an adult the distinction that has concerned me the most is that between sanity and madness, and I came to think that there were rough parallels with the first distinction: the mad as devalued individuals who were in the wrong place and a nuisance, yet often more sensitive and more creative than the sane. The resulting scepticism about the grounding of the distinction has not been dissipated by explorations into biological psychiatry. It has increased. As I have tried to show in chapters 3 and 4, the more one probes into the diagnosis of depression, premenstrual syndrome, anorexia and bulimia, the more difficult it is to agree that these are labels for definite conditions which mark a break with normality.

'Schizophrenia' stands out as the condition which is central to psychiatry's function from both inside and outside the discipline. Even writers such as Phyllis Chesler and Janet Frame, who are otherwise very critical of the sanity/madness distinction, accept that schizophrenia is genuine madness. However, as I indicated in Chapter 4, there have been critics of this construct, and the biological evidence to support the notion that schizophrenia is an illness is simply not there.

It is undeniable that in Western culture when someone hears voices that others do not hear, or doggedly holds onto beliefs which others reject, then something unusual is happening. We commonly call the first phenomenon 'having hallucinations' and the second 'having delusions'. As I indicated in Chapter 4, there have been variable definitions of 'schizophrenia'. Even the DSM notes that 'no single feature is invariably present or seen only in Schizophrenia.'[1] Nevertheless, definitions have often included hallucinations and delusions. A point that is usually ignored in these discussions is that, within some cultures and even within some religious groups in Western culture, to hear voices that others do not hear is a special ability that is valued by the group. Also to doggedly hold on to beliefs which others reject is often taken as a mark of faith and something to be valued. Sometimes the hearing of voices is understood as possession by a spirit who may empower the human to accomplish feats that would not otherwise be possible – for example, climbing down tree trunks head first, holding hot irons, chewing broken glass or walking barefoot on hot coals.[2] Spiritual possession has also been thought to be behind the ability of some people to prophesy the future. The oracle of Delphi was regarded in this light and held in high esteem. The shamans of some Indian cultures would often endure great physical hardship to try to achieve a state of trance which would give them powers of prediction and healing. Ruth Benedict has documented an account given by an old Zulu from South Africa concerning the trials that an aspiring shaman must go through to get the spirit to enter his body, so that he can hear voices which others do not hear and which will give him the power to heal.[3] Kiev describes the path to shamanism in Japan, where meditation, prayer, fasting and exercises produced emotional tranquillity and eventually the hearing of voices.[4]

Clastres writes about the Mbya Guarani Indians in Paraguay who valued the shamans in their society as mediators between other humans and gods.[5] What these and many other accounts say to me is that hearing voices that others don't hear, believing things that others don't believe, are human traits which may be devalued or valued depending on one's culture. If they are valued then they may bring about certain benefits to the individual – for example, high social status – or the group – for example, healing. If they are devalued then they may jetison the person into certain ceremonies of degradation, including forced hospitalization. These traits are very dangerous ones to admit to in Western culture so they are not usually intentionally adopted here. However, given that they mean something quite different in other cultures, perhaps we should be questioning whether it is appropriate to view them as signs of a mental illness. Perhaps they do have some adaptive function for the individual which is obscured by viewing them through the medical model.

Biological psychiatry promised a lot from its beginnings in the eighteenth century. But it hasn't met its promises – it has the nature of a degenerating research programme. To understand what this means, it is helpful to recall Popper's attack on *ad hoc* modifications, mentioned in Chapter 4. The central point is that it is illegitimate to hold on to and modify a theory in the face of falsifications if the modifications don't have any independent support. A theory might continually be saved in this way but only at the cost of becoming more and more empty. I agree with Lakatos that it is 'methodological cruelty' to reject a theory in its early stages when it doesn't square with observations,[6] but I do think it is a problem if there is no independent evidence in the long term. However, it is probably desirable to take a broader perspective and agree with Lakatos (and Kuhn) that it is better to consider theories within disciplines as constituting whole research programmes. More importance is then put on the evaluation of research programmes than particular theories. For Lakatos, programmes may be judged as progressive or degenerating – progressive when 'each new theory has some excess empirical content over its predecessor, that is, if it predicts some novel, hitherto unexpected fact.'[7] The emphasis is not so much on 'agreement with the observed facts' but rather the production of new facts. Corroboration does not fall out of the picture entirely but it is acknowledged that it may take a while to be achieved. Theories that look unpromising in the beginning may turn out to constitute a 'resounding success story'. Programmes are said to be degenerating when they aren't predicting anything new and are not turning out to be consistent with the facts in the long term.[8] This is a development of Popper's idea. It acknowledges that you can continually modify theories so that they square with 'the facts', but that is pretty useless unless the theories allow us to explain new facts. Even a degenerating research programme may be retained – for instance, when there is no alternative to take over the field. The degeneration is, however, certainly a sign that a fresh start is needed.

For Lakatos, two crucial elements of a research programme are the 'hard core' and the 'auxiliary hypotheses'. The hard core is made up from the principles on which the programme is based, which cannot change without moving to a different programme. The hard core is 'irrefutable' by the methodological decision of its protagonists. The auxiliary hypotheses are specific theories which may be adjusted or even completely replaced. They bear the brunt of testing, forming a protective belt around the hard core.

This is a useful framework with which to look at biological psychiatry, even though Lakatos did not make this extension. It is likely that, if he were alive today, he would brand psychiatry as an 'immature science' consisting of a mere patched-up pattern of trial and error and lacking the structure of research programmes. I suggest that biological psychiatry does constitute a science in his terms, but it is a science in a degenerating phase.

The hard core of this science consists of two basic assumptions: 1) that mental illness or disorders are separable conditions from sanity, and 2) the causes of mental illness or disorder are biological. Some of the auxiliary hypotheses that I have examined above are as follows: a) hysteria is a mental illness or type of insanity; b) depression is a mental illness or disorder; c) premenstrual syndrome is a psychiatric disease; d) schizophrenia is a psychiatric disease; and e) anorexia and bulimia are psychiatric disorders. All these particular hypotheses or theories give content to the methodological decision expressed in the hard core as (1). In various ways they capture the idea that on the one side there are the sane and on the other the insane.

There have been challenges to these theories. I have mentioned some throughout the first four chapters and immediately above, where I argue that this distinction is not nearly so clear-cut as commonly believed. Also we now have hindsight in the sense that (1) has been around since the eighteenth century. The theories have had time to develop, to respond to criticism, to move forward in a novel way. There have been small, piecemeal changes in the auxiliary hypotheses relating to (1) – for example, homosexuality has ceased to be on the 'insane' side and developmental disorders have come to be seen as psychiatric disorders. There has been an attempt to weaken the central concept from 'mental illness' to 'mental disorder'. However, there has been no progress in the development of a conceptual rationale for the distinction in (1) and corroboration along those lines. This point was explored in Chapter 2 and again indirectly in Chapter 3 in the discussion of depression and premenstrual syndrome. There is no consensus even among mental health professionals concerning the notions of mental illness or mental disorder. The DSM definition is imbued with hidden values and capable of different interpretation. Looking at the lack of the development that these auxiliary theories have provided for the research programme over two centuries makes it appear as though the programme is in a degenerating phase. Are there other auxiliary hypotheses that fare better?

A range of auxiliary hypotheses have been presented to fill out the content of the second part of the hard core. Some which I have mentioned are: a) hysteria is caused by the action of the reproductive organs on an unstable nervous system; b) insanity is inherited from the mother; c) removal of the ovaries and amputation of the cerivix will cure hysteria; d) hysteria develops upon a morbid constitutional base and there is defective heredity in 70 to 80 per cent of cases; e) endogenous depression is caused by a malfunction of neurotransmitters; f) depression is genetically inherited; g) the premenstrual syndrome is 'the world's commonest disease' affecting most women; h) schizophrenia is genetically inherited; i) schizophrenia is caused by a defect in the dopamine neurotransmitter system; j) there is a genetic disposition to develop anorexia or bulimia; and k) anorexia and bulimia are disorders of the neuroendocrine system.

The hypotheses among this list which are still actively researched were discussed in chapters 1 to 4 with the common result that the evidence is non-existent or very weak. Rival positions offer strong challenges. It is also the case that these auxiliary hypotheses don't move the programme forward but rather offer a succession of theories which do not build on earlier work. We cannot talk of the later theories having *excess* empirical contest over earlier ones. The new theories have to start from scratch as it becomes clear that the older theories need to be rejected. It has often happened that when one of these theories is first put up it seems to be corroborated, but in retrospect the corroboration is seen to be a result of methodological slackness rather than empirical fit. The studies into the genetics of schizophrenia illustrate this well.

Biological psychiatry has had 200 years to develop a progressive research programme. It has not done so, yet paradoxically it seems to be very successful and increasing its sphere of influence. Lakatos thought that degenerating programmes could stay around in the absence of strong rival programmes. Has biological psychiatry any strong rivals? If so, why haven't they succeeded in mounting a challenge? There is not space to canvass adequately all the answers here but, briefly, there are rivals but they have problems of their own. Psychoanalysis, for instance, appeared as though it might be a strong rival for some decades, but it lacks the forward-reaching ability to predict novel phenomena that characterizes progressive programmes. In the 1990s we are witnessing sudden and very obvious signs of its demise. This is not true of Irigaray's views, but they diverge a great deal from mainstream psychoanalysis and encompass much that could not be given that label.

Other psychiatries and psychologies, including the eclectic varieties, vie with each other for part or all of the domain of 'mental disorder' or 'mental illness', but they do not constitute a strong threat because of the lack of consensus in direction. They usually also accept part of the hard core of biological psychiatry, namely, a belief in the possibility of a distinction between sanity and madness. Perhaps a successful rival needs to reject (1) as well as (2).

Before looking into that, it should be pointed out that it is naïve to assume that scientific research programmes flourish or crumble solely by the rules of reason, a point that Feyerabend constantly makes in criticizing Lakatos.[9] Are there any non-rational factors that are propping up the research programme in question? I believe that there is a strong material factor and a powerful ideological one.

The material factor which is important in understanding the success of biological psychiatry is the enormous power of the pharmaceutical industry. Since 1955 the industry has ranked first or second in terms of profitability, with researchers in different parts of the world consistently finding that the recorded profits are far in excess of manufacturing industry averages.[10] In particular there are enormous profits made on psychiatric drugs. Richard Burack has documented the history of Valium and how it has been worth more than gold to the Roche company. In fact the wholesale price was 25 times the price of gold. The selling price was 140 times the original cost of materials and 20 times the total production cost.[11]

John Braithwaite, in *Corporate Crime in the Pharmaceutical Industry*, shows how strong the push is to expand markets, for example, by inventing new psychiatric disorders for use in advertisements in medical journals to promote new drugs. He notes that this is a creative response to the company's directive 'here's the cure, find the disease.'[12] Other psychiatric categories are made applicable to almost everyone so that wider drug use will be encouraged. A videotape produced by the Pfizer company for distribution to hospitals spoke of 'depression' as 'absence of joy' and claimed that it was 'everywhere and being under-diagnosed'.[13] The drug Librium has also been promoted very broadly for 'almost every psychological state which falls short of total serenity'.[14] Yet these drugs have potentially harmful side-effects and have been widely involved in abuse and addiction.[15] Other very powerful drugs have been promoted in some countries for extremely minor problems without publication of the side-effects. This occurs in countries where there is no realistic possibility of a legal challenge against a multinational company.[16]

The pharmaceutical companies spend an enormous amount of money and effort on promotion. The FDA estimated in the early 1980s that pharmaceutical companies in the United States were spending between $6,000 and $8,000 each year for every doctor in the country on prescription drug promotion.[17] There is no reason to think that this trend has reversed. Braithwaite's research revealed that doctors normally find out about drugs from the drug company representatives. These representatives are often very poorly trained and the research that the companies depend on is often deeply flawed, sometimes from negligence, but also from fraud.[18]

The picture that emerges is one of an extremely powerful industry which has definite interests in the flourishing of biological psychiatry and enormous funding to pour in that direction. It is vulnerable, however. Usually it is consumers who need to buy and take the drugs.

The ideological factor which keeps biological psychiatry in position is that it is very good at doing what it was in fact set up to do, namely, to act as a moral guardian. Psychiatry turns women's discontent with patriarchy and protests against the social order into mental symptoms of underlying physical pathology. The interests of patriarchy are then served very well. Complicity is encouraged, sometimes with the offer of a specific immediate gain – as in the legal defence of premenstrual syndrome – sometimes with the message 'regard yourself as mentally ill and we won't expect too much of you', obscuring the political content of women's discontent and protest.

What would we be left with if we dropped the hard core of biological psychiatry? Instead of 'mad' experiences and behaviours crying out for explanation, we would have human experiences and behaviours. It is undeniable that many people are unhappy, some extremely so; some have unusual imaginings, some eat too little, some exercise or smoke too much, some are social rebels, some are violent, some take on different personalities, some live lives of boredom, some are extremely conformist, some are selfish, and so on. Rejecting the sane/mad distinction does not mean that all problems disappear. Looked at from the position of the subject, the experiences and behaviours listed above may be undesired. So change may be sought. If biological causation is not assumed then it will be appropriate to look beyond alterations in biology – but where should we look?

The feminist theorists and novelists discussed in Chapters 6 and 7 highlight the notions of oppression and repression in understanding states which have been called 'mad', but they also challenge the appropriateness of that label and suggest that these notions are useful in understanding the normal states of women. Oppression and repression are relational. Perhaps the undesired states, then, can be understood as problems in relations. So another shift in thinking could be suggested. Instead of focusing on individuals and whether they are of this type or that, we could focus on relations. Questions that might be investigated are: how are relations structured within a particular social group? and then, more generally in a culture, which relations are damaging? which promote human flourishing? how are relations changed? and so on. As a starting point in answering the question about damage we could look at oppression and repression, which have been understood in various ways by the authors discussed above. For the purposes of developing an alternative account to biological psychiatry it might be useful to conceive of the notions in the following way: both are constraining and impinge on freedom. Oppression could be understood as a relation in which negative force is used by one party on another, causing harm of different sorts ranging from mild injustice to murder. 'Party' needs a broad interpretation. The oppressed could be a person or a group or a culture, etc. The oppressor could be a person or an institution or a set of ideas or practices, etc. When considering oppression it would be important to detail the different types, with abuse either in childhood or adulthood figuring very prominently. Some other types of oppression are threats, warnings, intimidation and enticements. The last is odd as 'enticements' seem so positive, but enticements can coerce just as effectively as threats – though of course not all enticements are oppressive. Similarly, not all threats and warnings are oppressive. The oppression that a woman feels tied up with the female role often involves a relation between her and a man but also a relation between her and a set of expectations and practices. Virginia Woolf and Janet Frame provide rich sources for thinking about these claims.

Repression, I suggest, is to be understood very broadly as a lack of freedom to do or to be. It isn't restricted to the lack of freedom to develop one's sexuality independent of patriarchal constraints; it also includes the lack of freedom to paint, to perform, to explore in nature and in mind. It could include the lack of freedom to develop in all areas of human endeavour.

In an attempt to foreshadow a rival explanatory programme to biological psychiatry, how can the ideas of oppression be developed further? Acknowledging that oppression can have many undesirable effects, for example, girls and women react in diverse ways to child abuse, the emphasis would not be on compartmentalizing those effects but rather on detailing the diverse types of oppression, expanding on the different forms of this relation. Just as the focus is not on the oppressed, on one side of the relation, so it is not on the oppressor, the other side of the relation. Rather, to focus on relations is to focus on structures, complex networks which people are caught up in often unawares. What happens between two people in the privacy of a home or in a dark street at night is not unrelated to a web of beliefs and practices existing outside those situations. At least part of this web will have a role in understanding the relations between the two people. Of course there have to be limits, as the web could expand out indefinitely, but placing limits is still consistent with some explanations being satisfactory.

An approach which focused on relations could still have something to say about individuals, but individuals and individuals' problems are now conceptualized relationally. We are what we are, with whatever problems we have, because of our connectedness to others. Take depression, for example. We saw in Chapter 3 that this could be understood as extreme unhappiness stemming from oppressive features of the female role, somehow related to abuse or simply the frustrations of trying to accommodate to the unfulfilling nature of the role, which has not been decided by the woman for herself. The account I am suggesting would not ignore the woman's unhappiness. However, it would direct us to the oppressive relationships in which the woman is immersed. Sometimes help will be needed in controlling the oppressor. If abuse is an issue then the criminal conviction could be appropriate. The woman may need help to overcome the feeling of being locked into the female role. She may need employment opportunities. She may need child care and so on. Thus, although the focus of this direction is outside the individual, individual problems and unsatisfactory ways of life can be addressed. The change is that they are not addressed by looking inside the person's head.

Theories, practical directions and new laws should also be developed to address human problems in the long term. High on the agenda should be answers to the question what is to be done about abuse? Firstly the enormity of the problem has to be recognized. As I mentioned in Chapter 2, a great deal of information is now available in the psychiatric journals on child abuse, yet there are various strategies of denial employed by the profession. There is no doubt that many outside of psychiatry, especially men, would also refuse to accept the reality of the findings, but they may not have been exposed to the information. In any case, their response is harder to document. This denial needs to be countered, partly from airing the research on independent validation, but also by making it easier for those who have been abused to speak out and not be 'punished'. This should apply at all age levels. Given that we know that very young children can be seriously affected by abuse, we should not deny them the right to tell their story.

One tactic that has been used in psychiatry when confronted by the reality of child abuse is to accept it but not relate it to psychiatric assessment, theorizing or therapy. The direction I would like to see develop would respond in a completely different way. It would make abuse a key *relation* of study in understanding human experiences and behaviour and abusive relationships would be the main targets for change.

In Chapter 2 I mentioned non-defensive reactions to the reality of child abuse put forward by some psychologists and psychiatrists, in particular the idea that reactions to abuse should be characterized by a single mental disorder. My objection to this was that the focus is still on the 'pathological individual'. Given the horror of abuse, the humiliation, the sense of violation, I'm not inclined to call even very extreme reactions pathological. Also the individual therapy approaches of the mental health workers are not going to have much sway in preventing abuse.

Once the reality of abuse is recognized and people are heard, what next? Effective responses to abuse should be available. Avenues should be opened up for girls and women who find themselves in an abusive relationship to get out of that relationship with the sympathetic and social/economic assistance of other people. Sharing experiences with other survivors is likely also to be useful in moving out of an abusive relationship. Children should be taught skills in the school curriculum to handle the threat of abuse or actual abuse. The laws relating to abuse need to be tough, well publicized and rigorously enforced.

These suggestions could be used to fill out some of the ideas about oppression canvassed in the last two chapters and to go towards developing an explanation of human experience and behaviour and directions for change which are alternatives to biological psychiatry.

The second starting point to the development of a new position suggested above was repression. The notion is harder to think about than oppression. By its very nature, it is more hidden. We won't know how much we are repressed and in what ways until the repression is lifted. Irigaray has detailed how repression operates on women's sexuality, language and identity and has offered a diverse range of avenues to pursue in order to end that repression. In Chapter 6 I discussed some of these: freeing up sexuality, allowing a female language to develop, re-evaluating the mother–daughter relationship, promoting respect for sexual difference and encoding more rights in law. While in general I applaud these directions, I am concerned that Irigaray is limiting the positive thrust of her approach by her anti-theoretical line: 'the issue is not one of elaborating a new theory of which woman would be the *subject* or the *object*, but of jamming the theoretical machinery itself . . .'[19] In the end, her great ideas look idealistic and impractical precisely because they are not embedded within a systematic theory. There are of course real dangers of confining women within male systems of representation by building such a theory, but without it there are worse dangers. I see these as centring around questions of acceptance of the ideas and their power to persuade. Take the suggestion about the legal encodification of virginity (or physical and moral integrity) as a component of female identity. As women, we can certainly *feel* this is on the right track. It strikes a sympathetic chord. However, it's difficult even to begin to think about how such a legal change could be promoted without developing a theory from which this flows as a recommendation. Theories have the power to help us organize our thinking and to help us to be persuasive. Perhaps these are masculine attributes, but they can be used to further feminist ends nevertheless.

A theory about women's repression would also be useful in providing directions for research. Some questions which are likely to emerge are: which relationships are repressive? Is some repression desirable and from whose point of view? How is it possible to change undesired repressive relationships? Traditionally studies of repression within psychiatry or psychology have focused on sexuality, but we need to get answers to questions about how women have been held back in all areas. In the 1990s many are starting to break through the constraints, but we still know very little about the harm that is done by the relationships which maintain women in repression or the potential that is there to be released. The releasing of women's potential is likely to be resisted by those who have an investment in the subordinate state of women grounded in inferiority. This was exemplified by the reactions reported in the media to the breakage of three women's world running records by Chinese women in 1993. The achievements were met with disbelief. According to *The Times*: 'Opinions polarise: something of this dimension is either magic or evil.'[20] There were (untested) confident assertions that they were on performance enhancing drugs. There was a suggestion that the feats were a political trick to assist the Chinese bid for the Olympic Games.[21] Even more tellingly, one correspondent claimed that 'the greatest believable margin of breakage of any selected record can be estimated by letting the men's to women's record ratio depart slightly but credibly from its established steady average',[22] and an Australian sports commentator reported the view of an unnamed expert that the athletes were really transsexuals![23] The sporting arena is not relevant to the concerns of this book, but this story illustrates what women are up against in general when they attempt to move out of their place.

Returning to the central line of argument: Irigaray's interest in psychiatry seems to be very marginal to her main concern, which is female sexuality broadly construed. However, her insights into aspects of female repression, I believe, could be usefully incorporated into a theory about human relations which could further our understanding of the experiences and behaviour of women and men. If relations are the focal point, then given that men and women are parties in these relations, they will both be objects of study. The behaviour and experiences of both sexes will be explained by reference to their positioning in the network of relations. Is this a paradoxical conclusion? I don't believe so. It was feminist insights which led to the emphasis on relations, and the crucial relations of oppression and repression are ones which disadvantage women more than men. However, part of learning about this disadvantage will be to discover the ways in which men are advantaged. Also, of course, not all relations work to the advantage of men.

However, the early focus of this new direction should be on the oppressive and repressive relationships that are particularly damaging to women. Firstly, because there is reason to believe from the above considerations that this will be fruitful. Secondly, more women than men are currently being treated by biological psychiatry, and there is an extremely urgent need for alternative thinking.

In the long term I envisage that a very broadly based research programme could develop. Some of the studies which have already been conducted into relationships of various kinds could be incorporated – for example, some of the studies on family interactions. To these should be added studies on all types of abusive relationships, on love relationships, friendship networks, interactions between peers and colleagues. Many of the past studies on relations of sex and class would also come in as important parts of the programme. Relationships between different cultural groups within one country and internationally, especially in times of war and economic conflict, would also need to form part of the broader picture.

I have attempted to suggest the lines along which an alternative explanatory framework to biological psychiatry might be developed. It could be linked with a new perspective on ethics and criminality. Currently the bad act or the criminal act are thought to be ways of behaving which emanate from individual agency. Given that the above relational account is proposed for all behaviour, immorality and illegality will be seen in these terms too. The 'badness' or the 'illegality' of an act will be explained by appeal to the set of relations in which the person is imbedded. Oppression again is likely to figure prominently. It is instructive here to note that many abusive people have themselves been abused. Also oppression surfaced in the discussion in Chapter 5 of women who kill their abusive partners, an act which immediately changes one's relations. In other instances of illegality or badness, individual attention might be desirable to change the person's positioning in the grid of relations. This is not a direction to kill the oppressor but rather to assist the oppressed. A theory of criminality could be developed where social change rather than individual correction would be taken as the best long-term strategy. The key issue would not be how to build better and bigger prisons to contain violence but how to develop a set of social relations such that violence is minimized.

In conclusion, there might be convincing theoretical grounds to make a fresh start in trying to come to grips with human distress. I have tried to expose the weaknesses within biological psychiatry by arguing more or less within its terms. I have drawn on feminist writers to suggest a new direction. This relational account would not fall within psychiatry or even psychology, as it collapses the distinction between sanity and madness, mental disorder and normality, and it also shies away from a focus on the individual. It is closer to a political account, but is not entirely at home there either as it contains explicit directions for empirical research which are different from traditional political theories – for example, research geared to answer the question: which relations promote human flourishing? Perhaps it could be said that it is not feminist either, as the focus is on relations rather than women. I hope this is not true for the reason outlined above.

The theoretical grounds don't stand aloof from values. I am coming from the position which says we are fed up with psychiatry as a moral guardian; we are fed up with the harm of chemical control. Let us investigate a direction which undermines psychiatry's prop to patriarchy.

Strolling through a garden nursery a few days before the completion of this book I discovered some dandelions for sale, encouraging the thought that change is possible.

Notes

Introduction

1 Peter Breggin, *Toxic Psychiatry* (Fontana, London, 1993).
2 Shelagh Supeene, *As for the Sky, Falling* (Second Story Press, Toronto, 1990).
3 Kate Millett, *The Loony-Bin Trip* (Simon & Schuster, New York, 1990).
4 Yannick Ripa, *Women and Madness: The Incarceration of Women in Nineteenth-Century France* (Polity Press, Cambridge, 1990).
5 Barbara Ehrenreich and Deirdre English, *For Her Own Good: 150 Years of the Experts' Advice to Women* (Anchor-Doubleday, New York, 1978).
6 Elaine Showalter, *The Female Malady: Women, Madness and English Culture, 1830–1980* (Virago, London, 1987).
7 Phyllis Chesler, *Women and Madness* (Avon, New York, 1972).
8 Jane Ussher, *Women's Madness* (Harvester Wheatsheaf, Hemel Hempstead, 1991).

Chapter 1   History of the Relationship between Women and Psychiatry

1 T. G. Graham, *Medieval Minds* (Allen & Unwin, London, 1967), p. 32.
2 See M. Foucault, *Madness and Civilization* (Vintage, New York, 1973), ch. 1.
3 Quoted in Graham, *Medieval Minds*, p. 34.
4 Ibid., p. 35.
5 Ibid., p. 38.
6 Ibid., p. 159.
7 D. Erasmus, *The Praise of Folly* (Hamilton Adams, London, 1887), pp. 28–9.
8 Foucault, *Madness and Civilization*, pp. 44–5.

9   Ibid., ch. 2.
10 Ibid., p. 229.
11 V. Skultans, *English Madness: Ideas on Insanity, 1580–1890* (Routledge & Kegan Paul, London, 1979), p. 4.
12 Foucault, *Madness and Civilization*, p. 223.
13 Ibid., ch. 7.
14 Barbara Ehrenreich and Deirdre English, *For Her Own Good: 150 Years of the Experts' Advice to Women* (Anchor-Doubleday, New York, 1978), p. 104.
15 Quoted in N. Parry and J. Parry, *The Rise of the Medical Profession* (Croom Helm, London, 1976), p. 131.
16 Ibid., p. 109.
17 B. Ehrenreich and D. English, *Complaints and Disorders* (Feminist Press, New York, 1973), p. 77.
18 A. Scull, *Museums of Madness* (Penguin, Harmondsworth, 1982), p. 160.
19 B. Rush, 'An enquiry into the influence of physical causes upon the moral faculty', in *Two Essays on the Mind* (Brunner/Mazel, New York, 1972), pp. 1–40.
20 Ibid., p. 20.
21 Ibid., p. 25.
22 H. Maudsley, *The Pathology of Mind* (1895; Friedman, London, 1979), p. 3.
23 Ibid., p. 4.
24 Ibid., p. 32.
25 Y. Ripa, *Women and Madness* (Polity Press, Cambridge, 1990), p. 119.
26 Elaine Showalter, *The Female Malady: Women, Madness and English Culture, 1830–1980* (Virago, London, 1987), p. 52.
27 See Ripa, *Women and Madness*.
28 Ehrenreich and English, *For Her Own Good*, p. 92; T. Morton, 'The Pennsylvania Hospital', in *The Age of Madness*, ed. T. Szasz (Anchor, New York, 1973), p. 12.
29 Scull, *Museums of Madness*, p. 29.
30 Ibid., p. 30.
31 Ripa, *Women and Madness*, p. 12.
32 R. Castel, F. Castell and A. Lovell, *The Psychiatric Society*, trans. A. Goldhammer (Columbia University Press, New York, 1982), pp. 6–7.
33 Ibid., p. 8.
34 Ripa, *Women and Madness*, p. 13.
35 Skultans, *English Madness*, p. 4.
36 Elaine Showalter, 'Victorian women and insanity', in *Madhouses, Mad-Doctors, and Madmen*, ed. Andrew Scull (University of Pennsylvania Press, Philadelphia, 1981), pp. 316–17.
37 Geoffrey Best, *Mid-Victorian Britain, 1851–75* (Panther, London, 1973), p. 161.
38 Showalter, 'Victorian women and insanity', p. 317.
39 Skultans, *English Madness*, p. 93.
40 Ripa, *Women and Madness*, p. 22.
41 Ehrenreich and English, *Complaints and Disorders*, p. 20.
42 Quoted in Ehrenreich and English, *For Her Own Good*, p. 108.

43 Quoted in Foucault, *Madness and Civilization*, p. 237.
44 Skultans, *English Madness*, p. 4.
45 Ripa, *Women and Madness*, p. 13.
46 Ibid., p. 17.
47 Ibid., p. 20.
48 Ibid., p. 22.
49 Ibid., p. 32.
50 Quoted in Foucault, *Madness and Civilization*, p. 237.
51 Dora Weiner, 'Philippe Pinel's "Memoir on Madness" of December 11, 1794: a fundamental text of modern psychiatry', *American Journal of Psychiatry*, 149 (1992), p. 725.
52 Ibid., p. 730.
53 Quoted in Skultans, *English Madness*, pp. 57–8.
54 Quoted in Foucault, *Madness and Civilization*, p. 249.
55 Weiner, 'Philippe Pinel's "Memoir on Madness"', p. 731.
56 Ibid., p. 732.
57 R. Castel, F. Castell and A. Lovell, *The Psychiatric Society*, p. 78.
58 P. Pinel, *A Treatise on Insanity*, trans. D. D. Davis (Hafner, New York, 1962), p. 221.
59 Ibid., p. 222.
60 Ibid., p. 69.
61 Weiner, 'Philippe Pinel's "Memoir on Madness"', p. 729.
62 Skultans, *English Madness*, p. 56.
63 Foucault, *Madness and Civilization*, pp. 260–7.
64 Quoted in Foucault, *Madness and Civilization*, p. 267.
65 Ibid., p. 268.
66 Ibid., p. 252.
67 Ripa, *Women and Madness*, p. 35.
68 Quoted in Skultans, *English Madness*, p. 57.
69 Quoted in Skultans, *English Madness*, p. 60.
70 Quoted in C. Zilboorg, *A History of Medical Psychology* (Norton, New York, 1941), p. 450.
71 See Chapter 2.
72 Zilboorg, *A History of Medical Psychology*, p. 303.
73 Rush, *Two Essays on the Mind*, p. 685.
74 Ibid., pp. 688–95.
75 Ibid., p. 20.
76 Quoted in R. Hunter and I. Macalpine (eds), *Three Hundred Years of Psychiatry, 1535–1860* (Oxford University Press, London, 1963), p. 1002.
77 Ibid., p. 1003.
78 H. Maudsley, *The Pathology of Mind*, p. 397.
79 Ibid., pp. 397–8.
80 H. Maudsley, *Body and Mind* (Macmillan, London, 1873), pp. 87–92.
81 Andrew Wynter, *The Borderland of Insanity* (Robert Hardwicke, London, 1875), pp. 52–3.
82 Gustav Braun, 'The amputation of the clitoris and labia minora: a contribution to the treatment of vaginismus', in *A Dark Science*, ed. and trans.

Jeffrey Masson (Noonday Press, New York, 1986), p. 131.
83   Skultans, *English Madness*, p. 63.
84   Masson, *A Dark Science*, pp. 128 and 187.
85   Elaine Showalter, *The Female Malady* (Virago, London, 1987), p. 75.
86   James Israel, 'Contribution to a discussion of the value of castration in hysterical women', in Masson, *A Dark Science*, pp. 139–45.
87   Alfred Hegar, 'On the sham castration performed by Dr Israel', in Masson, *A Dark Science*, p. 151.
88   Masson, *A Dark Science*, p. 151.
89   Paul Flechsig, 'On the gynecological treatment of hysteria', in Masson, *A Dark Science*, p. 53.
90   Ibid., pp. 54–6.
91   Masson, *A Dark Science*, pp. 173–4.
92   James Drife, 'Are breasts redundant organs?' *British Medical Journal*, 304 (1992), p. 1060.
83   Showalter, *The Female Malady*, p. 149.
94   Jean Martin Charcot, *Charcot the Clinician: The Tuesday Lessons*, trans. C. Goetz (Raven, New York, 1987), p. 107.
95   Ibid., pp. 104–22.
96   Ibid., p. 106.
97   Showalter, *The Female Malady*, p. 150.
98   Charcot, *Charcot the Clinician*, p. 107.
99   Sigmund Freud and J. Breuer, *Studies on Hysteria* (1895; Penguin, Harmondsworth, 1974), p. 54.
100 Jeffrey Masson (ed. and trans.), *The Complete Letters of Sigmund Freud to Wilhelm Fliess, 1887–1904* (Belknap Press, London, 1985), p. 144. The letter is dated 15 October 1895.
101 Freud, *Studies*, p. 53.
102 Ibid., p. 59.
103 Sigmund Freud, 'The aetiology of hysteria', in *The Assault on Truth*, ed. Jeffrey Masson (Harper Perennial, New York, 1992), p. 267.
104 Masson, *The Complete Letters of Sigmund Freud to Wilhelm Fliess*, pp. 264–6. The letter is dated 21 September 1897.
105 E. Kraepelin, *Clinical Psychiatry* (1907; Scholars' Facsimiles and Reprints, New York, 1981), p. 458.
106 Ibid., p. 147.
107 Ibid., p. 158.
108 Ibid., pp. 152–5.

Chapter 2   Modern Psychiatric Perspectives on Women

1   R. L. Spitzer and J. Williams (eds), *Diagnostic and Statistical Manual of Mental Disorders*, 3rd rev. edn (American Psychiatric Association, Washington, 1987).

2 The oppression of women is also tied to other areas of psychiatric theory and practice, but this is not to deny that the problems in the diagnostic area are important, contrary to the view expressed by Marjorie McC. Dachowski, 'DSM-III: sexism or social reality?' *American Psychologist*, 39 (1984), pp. 702–3.

3 In some of the descriptions attaching to certain diagnostic categories mention is made of 'illness'. There is no attempt to explain this usage. See, for instance, 'the diagnosis of Schizophrenia requires that continuous signs of the illness have been present for a least six months': Spitzer and Williams (eds), *Diagnostic and Statistical Manual of Mental Disorders*, p. 190.

4 For example, T. S. Szasz, *The Myth of Mental Illness* (Paladin, St Albans, 1972); R. D. Laing and A. Esterson, *Sanity, Madness and the Family* (Penguin, Harmondsworth, 1970).

5 Spitzer and Williams (eds), *Diagnostic and Statistical Manual of Mental Disorders*, p. xxii.

6 Ibid., p. 405.

7 Ibid., p. xxiii.

8 Ibid., p. xxii.

9 For example, Laing and Esterson, *Sanity, Madness and the Family*; Nancy Scheper-Hughes and Anne M. Lovell (eds), *Psychiatry Inside Out: Selected Writings of Franco Basaglia* (Columbia University Press, New York, 1987).

10 Spitzer and Williams (eds), *Diagnostic and Statistical Manual of Mental Disorders*, p. 331.

11 In Chapter 5 I discuss further the expansion of psychiatry into the field of criminology.

12 I. K. Broverman et al., 'Sex-role stereotypes and clinical judgements of mental health', *Journal of Consulting and Clinical Psychology*, 34 (1970), p. 4.

13 Ibid., p. 5.

14 Ibid., pp. 4–5.

15 Ibid., p. 4.

16 I. K. Broverman et al., 'Sex-role stereotypes: a current appraisal', *Journal of Social Issues*, 28 (1972), pp. 59–78.

17 G. Stricker, 'Implications of research for psychotherapeutic treatment of women', *American Psychologist*, 32 (1977), pp. 14–22.

18 S. Abramowitz et al., 'The politics of clinical judgment', *Journal of Consulting and Clinical Psychology*, 41 (1973), pp. 385–91; B. Fabrikant, 'The psychotherapist and the female patient: perceptions, misperceptions and change', in V. Franks and V. Burtle (eds), *Women in Therapy* (Brunner/Mazel, New York, 1974); A. Maslin and J. Davis, 'Sex-role stereotyping as a factor in mental health standards among counselors-in-training', *Journal of Counseling Psychology*, 22 (1975), pp. 87–91; C. Brown and M. Hellinger, 'Therapists' attitudes toward women', *Social Work*, 20 (1975), pp. 266–70; A. M. Brodsky and J. Holroyd, 'Report of the task force on sex bias and sex-role stereotyping in psychotherapeutic practice', *American Psychologist*, 30 (1975), pp. 1169–75; C. C. Nadelson, cited in P. Susan Penfold and G. A. Walker, *Women and the Psychiatric Paradox* (Eden Press, Montreal,

1983), p. 94; J. A. Sherman, 'Therapist attitudes and sex-role stereotyping', in A. M. Brodsky and R. T. Hare-Mustin (eds), *Women and Psychotherapy: An Assessment of Research and Practice* (Guilford Press, New York, 1980); P. S. Rosencrantz et al., 'One half a generation later: sex-role stereotypes revisited', Paper presented to the convention of the American Psychological Association, Los Angeles, August 1985.

19   L. J. Jordanova, 'Mental illness, mental health: changing norms and expectations', in Cambridge Women's Studies Group, *Women in Society* (Virago, London, 1981), p. 102.

20   M. Kaplan, 'A woman's view of DSM-III', *American Psychologist*, 38 (1983), p. 788.

21   S. Briar, 'Use of theory in studying effects of client social class on students' judgments', *Social Work*, 9 (1961), pp. 91–7.

22   P. Chesler, *Women and Madness* (Avon, New York, 1973), ch. 8.

23   B. Reiss, 'New viewpoints on the female homosexual', in *Women in Therapy*, ed. V. Franks and V. Burtle.

24   H. E. Lerner, 'Early origins of envy and devaluation of women: implications for sex-role stereotypes', in *Women and Mental Health*, ed. E. Howell and M. Bayes (Basic Books, New York, 1981), p. 34.

25   M. Bayes, 'Wife battering and the maintenance of gender roles: a sociopsychological perspective', in Howell and Bayes, *Women and Mental Health*, p. 442; P. Chodoff, 'The diagnosis of hysteria: an overview', *American Journal of Psychiatry*, 139, 5 (1982), pp. 545–51.

26   My italics.

27   Spitzer and Williams (eds), *Diagnostic and Statistical Manual of Mental Disorders*, p. 323.

28   Ibid., p. 326.

29   H. E. Lerner, 'The hysterical personality: a women's disease', *Comprehensive Psychiatry*, 15 (1974), pp. 157–64; H. Wolowitz, 'Hysterical character and feminine identity', in *Readings on the Psychology of Women*, ed. J. Bardwick (Harper & Row, New York, 1972), pp. 307–14; M. Hollender, 'The hysterical personality', *Comments on Contemporary Psychiatry*, 15 (1971), pp. 17–24; P. Chodoff, 'The diagnosis of hysteria: an overview', *American Journal of Psychiatry*, 131, 10 (1974), pp. 1073–8.

30   Kaplan, 'A woman's view of DSM-III', p. 789.

31   Brodsky and Holroyd, 'Report of the task force on sex bias and sex-role stereotyping in psychotherapeutic practice'.

32   Penfold and Walker, *Women and the Psychiatric Paradox*, pp. 108–11.

33   Broverman, 'Sex-role stereotypes: a current appraisal', p. 76.

34   Spitzer and Williams (eds), *Diagnostic and Statistical Manual of Mental Disorders*, p. xxii.

35   F. Kass et al., 'An empirical study of the issue of sex bias in the diagnostic criteria of DSM-III Axis II personality disorders', *American Psychologist*, 38 (1983), p. 800.

36   Spitzer and Williams (eds), *Diagnostic and Statistical Manual of Mental Disorders*, p. 347.

37 Ibid., p. 353.
38 Kaplan, 'A woman's view of DSM-III', pp. 789–90.
39 J. B. Williams and R. L. Spitzer, 'The issue of sex bias in DSM-III', *American Psychologist*, 38 (1983), p. 796.
40 Kass et al., 'An empirical study of the issue of sex bias in the diagnostic criteria of DSM-III Axis II personality disorders', p. 801.
41 Spitzer and Williams (eds), *Diagnostic and Statistical Manual of Mental Disorders*, p. 367.
42 U. Halbreich et al., 'The clinical diagnosis and classification of premenstrual changes', *Canadian Journal of Psychiatry*, 30 (1985), pp. 489–97.
43 J. Bardwick, 'The sex hormones, the central nervous system and affect variability in humans', in *Women in Therapy*, ed. V. Franks and V. Burtle, p. 32.
44 Spitzer and Williams (eds), *Diagnostic and Statistical Manual of Mental Disorders*, p. 369.
45 K. Dalton, *The Premenstrual Syndrome and Progesterone Therapy* (Heinemann Medical, London, 1977) p. 146.
46 Spitzer and Williams (eds), *Diagnostic and Statistical Manual of Mental Disorders*, p. 371.
47 K. Ritchie, 'The little woman meets son of DSM-III', *Journal of Medicine and Philosophy*, 14 (1989), pp. 696–7.
48 D. Franklin, 'The politics of masochism', *Psychology Today*, 1, 21 (1987), p. 56.
49 G. W. Brown and T. Harris, *Social Origins of Depression* (Tavistock, London, 1978); A. Miles, *Women and Mental Illness* (Wheatsheaf, Brighton, 1988).
50 Kaplan, 'A woman's view of DSM-III', p. 789.
51 Ibid., p. 790.
52 Williams and Spitzer, 'The issue of sex bias in DSM-III', p. 794.
53 M. H. Stone, 'Homosexuality in patients with borderline personality disorder', *American Journal of Psychiatry* 144 (1987), p. 1622.
54 M. R. Ford and T. Widiger, 'Sex bias in the diagnosis of histrionic and antisocial personality disorders', *Journal of Consulting and Clinical Psychology*, 57 (1989), pp. 301–5; R. Warner, 'The diagnosis of antisocial and hysterical personality disorders', *Journal of Nervous and Mental Disease*, 166 (1978), pp. 839–45.
55 Ford and Widiger, 'Sex bias in the diagnosis of histrionic and antisocial personality disorders', p. 305.
56 A. Ali, 'Borderline personality and multiple earrings', *American Journal of Psychiatry*, 147, 9 (1990), p. 1251.
57 Spitzer and Williams (eds), *Diagnostic and Statistical Manual of Mental Disorders*, p. 272.
58 Mentioned in S. D. Miller, 'Optical differences in cases of multiple personality disorder', *Journal of Nervous and Mental Disease*, 177, 8 (1989), p. 480.
59 G. N. Saxe et al., 'SPECT imaging and multiple personality disorder', *Journal of Nervous and Mental Disease*, 180, 10 (1992), p. 662.

60   M. Steiner et al., 'Biological markers in borderline personality disorders: an overview', *Canadian Journal of Psychiatry*, 33 (1988).

61   J. A. E. Fleming, 'Biological markers in borderline personality disorders: an overview', *Canadian Journal of Psychiatry*, 34, (1988), p. 873.

62   D. Gardner and R. Cowdry, 'Borderline personality disorder: a research challenge', *Biological Psychiatry*, 26 (1989), p. 657.

63   J. Paris and H. Zweig-Frank, 'A critical review of the role of childhood sexual abuse in the etiology of borderline personality disorder', *Canadian Journal of Psychiatry*, 37 (1992), p. 125.

64   B. van der Kolk, 'The compulsion to repeat the trauma', in The *Psychiatric Clinics of North America*, ed. R. P. Kluft (Philadelphia: Harcourt Brace Jovanovich, 1989), pp. 393–9.

65   Ibid., p. 393.

66   Quoted in C. Wilbur, 'Multiple personality and child abuse', in *The Psychiatric Clinics of North America*, ed. B. G. Braun (Philadelphia: Harcourt Brace Jovanovich, 1984), p. 3.

67   D. Speigel, 'Multiple personality as a post-traumatic stress disorder', in *The Psychiatric Clinics of North America*, ed. B. G. Braun, p. 101.

68   Wilbur, 'Multiple personality and child abuse'.

69   F. W. Putnam et al., 'The clinical phenomenology of multiple personality disorder: review of 100 recent cases', *Journal of Clinical Psychiatry*, 47, 6 (1986), p. 290.

70   Reported in C. A. Ross, 'Twelve cognitive errors about multiple personality disorder', *American Journal of Psychotherapy*, 44, 3 (1990), p. 353.

71   Reported in J. L. Herman et al., 'Childhood trauma in borderline personality disorder', *American Journal of Psychiatry*, 147, 4 (1989), p. 490.

72   Ibid., p. 490.

73   M. C. Zanarini et al., 'Childhood experiences of borderline patients', *Comprehensive Psychiatry*, 30, 1 (1989), p. 18.

74   S. N. Ogata et al., 'Childhood sexual and physical abuse in adult patients with borderline personality disorder', *American Journal of Psychiatry*, 147 (1990), p. 1008.

75   D. Westen et al., 'Physical and sexual abuse in adolescent girls with borderline personality disorder', *American Journal of Orthopsychiatry*, 60 (1990), pp. 55–66; P. S. Ludolph et al., 'The borderline diagnosis in adolescents: symptoms and developmental history', *American Journal of Psychiatry*, 147 (1990), pp. 470–6.

76   S. L. Shearer et al., 'Frequency and correlates of childhood sexual and physical abuse histories in adult female borderline inpatients', *American Journal of Psychiatry*, 147, 2 (1990), p. 214.

77   Spitzer and Williams (eds), *Diagnostic and Statistical Manual of Mental Disorders*, p. 374.

78   P. J. Caplan, *The Myth of Women's Masochism* (Methuen, London, 1985).

79   E. Carmen et al., 'Victims of violence and psychiatric illness', *American Journal of Psychiatry*, 141, 3 (1984), p. 378.

80   Caplan, *The Myth of Women's Masochism*.

81 J. Kinzl and W. Biebl, 'Sexual abuse of girls: aspects of the genesis of mental disorders and therapeutic implications, *Acta Psychiatrica Scandinavia*, 83 (1991), p. 429.

82 J. A. Bushnell et al., 'Long-term effects of intrafamilial sexual abuse in childhood', *Acta Psychiatrica Scandinavia*, 85 (1992), pp. 136–42.

83 Kinzl and Biebl, 'Sexual abuse of girls: aspects of the genesis of mental disorders and therapeutic implications'; J. Kinzl and W. Biebl, 'Long-term effects of incest', *American Journal of Psychiatry*, 149, 4 (1992), p. 578.

84 Carmen, 'Victims of violence and psychiatric illness'; P. M. Coons et al., 'Post-traumatic aspects of the treatment of victims of sexual abuse and incest', in *Psychiatric Clinics of North America*, ed. R. P. Kluft, p. 325; A. Jacobson and B. Richardson, 'Assault experiences of 100 psychiatric inpatients: evidence of the need for routine inquiry', *American Journal of Psychiatry*, 144, 7 (1987), pp. 908–12; J. Bryer et al., 'Childhood sexual and physical abuse as factors in adult psychiatric illness', *American Journal of Psychiatry*, 144, 11 (1987), p. 1426; J. C. Beck and B. van der Kolk, 'Reports of childhood incest and current behavior of chronically hospitalized psychotic women', *American Journal of Psychiatry*, 144, 11 (1987), p. 1474; G. M. Margo and E. M. McLees, 'Further evidence for the significance of a childhood abuse history in psychiatric inpatients', *Comprehensive Psychiatry*, 32, 4 (1991), p. 362; A. Husain and J. L. Chapel, 'History of incest in girls admitted to a psychiatric hospital', *American Journal of Psychiatry*, 140, 5 (1983), p. 591; G. J. Emslie and A. Rosenfeld, 'Incest reported by children and adolescents hospitalized for severe psychiatric problems', *American Journal of Psychiatry*, 140, 6 (1983), p. 708.

85 D. Whitwell, 'Childhood sexual abuse', *British Journal of Hospital Medicine*, 43 (1990), p. 350; L. McClelland et al., 'Sexual abuse, disordered personality and eating disorders', *British Journal of Psychiatry*, 158 (1991), p. 66; C. Sheldrick, 'Adult sequelae of child sexual abuse', *British Journal of Psychiatry*, 158 (1991), p. 55; R. L. Palmer et al., 'Childhood sexual experiences with adults reported by female psychiatric patients', *British Journal of Psychiatry*, 160 (1992), p. 261.

86 D. Russell, *The Secret Trauma* (Basic Books, New York, 1986), pp. 60–1.

87 Bushnell, 'Long-term effects of intrafamilial sexual abuse in childhood', p. 136.

88 J. M. Masson, *The Assault on Truth* (1985; Harper Perennial, New York, 1992).

89 C. L. Rich, 'Verifying patients' reports of childhood abuse', *American Journal of Psychiatry*, 146, 10 (1989), p. 1358; P. Dell, 'Professional skepticism about multiple personality', *Journal of Nervous and Mental Disease*, 176, 9 (1988), p. 528.

90 P. Dell, 'Not reasonable skepticism, but extreme skepticism', *Journal of Nervous and Mental Disease*, 176, 9 (1988), p. 537.

91 E. Bliss, 'Commentary: professional skepticism about multiple personality', *Journal of Nervous and Mental Disease*, 176, 9 (1988), p. 533.

92 Dell, 'Not reasonable skepticism, but extreme skepticism', p. 537.

93   J. Hoff, 'Multiple personality disorder?', *Journal of Clinical Psychiatry*, 48, 4 (1987), p. 174.
94   Husain and Chapel, 'History of incest in girls admitted to a psychiatric hospital', pp. 591–2.
95   Speigel, 'Multiple personality as a post-traumatic stress disorder', p. 101.
96   Mentioned in Sheldrick, 'Adult sequelae of child sexual abuse', p. 55.
97   Carmen, 'Victims of violence and psychiatric illness', p. 383.
98   J. Herman et al., 'Dr. Herman and associates reply', *American Journal of Psychiatry*, 146, 10 (1989), p. 1359.
99   P. M. Coons and V. Milstein, 'Psychosexual disturbances in multiple personality', *Journal of Clinical Psychiatry*, 47 (1986), pp. 106–10.
100   Bryer, 'Childhood sexual and physical abuse as factors in adult psychiatric illness', p. 1430; Kinzl and Biebl, 'Sexual abuse of girls', p. 430.
101   Spitzer and Williams (eds), *Diagnostic and Statistical Manual of Mental Disorders*, p. 247.
102   J. Briere, cited in McClelland, 'Sexual abuse, disordered personality and eating disorders', p. 63.
103   L. S. Brown, 'A feminist critique of personality disorders', in *Personality and Psychopathology* (Guilford Press, New York, 1992), pp. 223–4.

Chapter 3   Shifting Trends in Diagnosis

1   P. Pichot, 'Evaluation and typology of depressive states', in *New Advances in the Diagnosis and Treatment of Depressive Illness*, ed. J. Mendlewicz (Excerpta Medica, Amsterdam, 1980), p. 5.
2   R. L. Spitzer and J. Williams (eds), *Diagnostic and Statistical Manual of Mental Disorders*, 3rd rev. edn (American Psychiatric Association, Washington, 1987), pp. 218–22, 229.
3   Ibid., p. 323.
4   Pichot, 'Evaluation and typology of depressive states', p. 4.
5   Marilyn Scarf, *Body, Mind and Behaviour* (New Republic Book Co., Washington, 1976), p. 251.
6   M. Zimmerman, 'Why are we rushing to publish the DSM-IV?', *Archives of General Psychiatry*, 45 (1988), p. 1137.
7   Ibid., p. 1138.
8   Spitzer and Williams (eds), *Diagnostic and Statistical Manual of Mental Disorders*, pp. 229 and 231.
9   E. Kraepelin, *Clinical Psychiatry* (Scholars' Facsimiles and Reprints, New York, 1981).
10   M. R. Trimble, *Biological Psychiatry* (John Wiley & Sons, New York, 1988), p. 242.
11   Eugene E. Levitt, Bernard Lubin and James M. Brooks, *Depression: Concepts, Controversies and Some New Facts*, 2nd edn (Laurence Erlbaum Associates, Hillsdale, NJ, 1983), p. 33.
12   Ibid., pp. 24–7.

13 Ibid., p. 41.
14 Ibid., p. 43.
15 Trimble, *Biological Psychiatry*, p. 279.
16 Levitt et al., *Depression: Concepts, Controversies and Some New Facts*, p. 57.
17 Ibid., p. 59.
18 Ibid., p. 173.
19 H. M. van Praag, 'Central monoamines and the pathogenesis of depression', in Mendlewicz (ed.), *New Advances in the Diagnosis and Treatment of Depressive Illness*, pp. 34–5.
20 H. M. van Praag, 'The DSM-IV (depression) classification: to be or not to be?', *Journal of Nervous and Mental Disease*, 178, 3, (1990), p. 149.
21 Trimble, *Biological Psychiatry*, p. 243.
22 Kenneth S. Kendler et al., 'A population-based twin study of major depression in women', *Archives of General Psychiatry*, 49 (1992), p. 257.
23 Ibid., p. 263.
24 Trimble, *Biological Psychiatry*, p. 244.
25 G. Klerman et al., 'Increasing rates of depression', *Journal of the American Medical Association*, 261 (1989), p. 2233; Kendler, 'A population-based twin study of major depression in women', p. 257; E. S. Paykel, 'Depression in women', *British Journal of Psychiatry*, 158 (1991), p. 24.
26 Trimble, *Biological Psychiatry*, p. 246.
27 Ibid., p. 247.
28 Ibid., pp. 246–9.
29 B. Shopsin, 'Newer research strategies in depression', in Mendlewicz (ed.), *New Advances in the Diagnosis and Treatment of Depressive Illness*, p. 147.
30 Trimble, *Biological Psychiatry*, p. 249.
31 Shopsin, 'Newer research strategies in depression', p. 149; my italics.
32 Caroline McAdams et al., 'Alteration by a plasma factor of platelet aggregation and 5HT uptake in depression', *Biological Psychiatry*, 32 (1992), p. 298.
33 Trimble, Biological Psychiatry, p. 256.
34 B. J. Carroll et al., 'A specific laboratory test for the diagnosis of melancholia', *Archives of General Psychiatry*, 38 (1981), p. 15.
35 Trimble, *Biological Psychiatry*, p. 256.
36 M. M. Fichter et al., 'Depression, anorexia nervosa and nutrition: effects of starvation on endocrine function and mood', in *Psychiatry: The State of the Art*, ed. P. Pichot et al. (Plenum Press, New York, 1983), p. 721.
37 Ibid., p. 723.
38 Ibid., p. 726.
39 Paula Nicolson, 'Developing a feminist approach to depression following childbirth', in *Feminist Social Psychology*, ed. Sue Wilkinson (Open University Press, Milton Keynes, 1986).
40 Trimble, *Biological Psychiatry*, p. 273.
41 Ibid., p. 279.
42 M. Hamilton, 'Closing remarks', in Mendlewicz (ed.) *New Advances in the Diagnosis and Treatment of Depressive Illness*, p. 164.

43   Levitt et al., *Depression: Concepts, Controversies and Some New Facts*, p. 57.
44   Hamilton, 'Closing remarks', p. 165.
45   Ibid., p. 165.
46   R. L. Spitzer et al. (eds), *Diagnostic and Statistical Manual of Mental Disorders*, 3rd edn (American Psychiatric Association, Washington, 1980), p. 206.
47   Spitzer and Williams (eds), *Diagnostic and Statistical Manual of Mental Disorders*, pp. 218–24, 229–32.
48   G. W. Brown and Tirril Harris, *Social Origins of Depression* (Tavistock, London, 1978), pp. 235–6.
49   L. J. Jordanova, 'Mental illness, mental health: changing norms and expectations', in *Women in Society*, ed. Cambridge Women's Studies Group (Virago, London, 1981), p. 105.
50   Agnes Miles, *Women and Mental Illness* (Wheatsheaf, Brighton, 1988), p. 47.
51   Ibid., p. 57.
52   Ibid., p. 145.
53   Ibid., p. 151.
54   G. W. Brown et al., 'Social factors and recovery from anxiety and depressive disorders', *British Journal of Psychiatry*, 161 (1992), p. 52.
55   Jeffrey B. Bryer et al., 'Childhood sexual and physical abuse as factors in adult psychiatric illness', *American Journal of Psychiatry*, 144, 11 (1987), p. 1428.
56   J. A. Bushnell et al., 'Long-term effects of intrafamilial sexual abuse in childhood', *Acta Psychiatrica Scandinavia*, 85 (1992), p. 138.
57   Carol Sheldrick, 'Adult sequelae of child sexual abuse', *British Journal of Psychiatry*, 158 (1991), p. 57.
58   Idee Winfield et al., 'Sexual assault and psychiatric disorders among a community sample of women', *American Journal of Psychiatry*, 147, 3 (1990), p. 338.
59   Alison Corob, *Working with Depressed Women: A Feminist Approach* (Gower, Aldershot, 1987), p. 33.
60   J. M. Murphy, 'Trends in depression and anxiety: men and women', *Acta Psychiatrica Scandinavia*, 73 (1986), pp. 113–27; G. Klerman et al., 'Increasing rates of depression', *Journal of the American Medical Association*, 261 (1989), pp. 2229–35; P. R. Joyce et al., 'Birth cohort trends in major depression: increasing rates and earlier onset in New Zealand', *Journal of Affective Disorders*, 18 (1990), pp. 83–9.
61   Klerman, 'Increasing rates of depression', p. 2234; Murphy, 'Trends in depression and anxiety', p. 122.
62   Murphy, 'Trends in depression and anxiety', p. 124.
63   Katharina Dalton, *Once a Month: The Menstrual Syndrome, its Causes and Consequences* (Harvester, London, 1978), p. 206.
64   J. V. Ricci, *The Genealogy of Gynaecology* (Blakiston, Philadelphia, 1950).
65   S. Icard, *La femme pendant la periode menstruelle* (Felix Alan, Paris, 1890), p. 266.

66   A. Clare, 'Premenstrual syndrome: single or multiple causes?' *Canadian Journal of Psychiatry*, 30 (1985), p. 474.

67   Katharina Dalton, *The Premenstrual Syndrome and Progesterone Therapy* (Heinemann Medical, London, 1977), p. 3.

68   Ibid., p. 20.

69   Dalton, *Once a Month*, p. 11.

70   Ibid., p. 103.

71   Dalton, *The Premenstrual Syndrome*, p. 4.

72   Ibid., p. 13.

73   Judith Bardwick, 'The sex hormones, the central nervous system and affect variability in humans', in *Women in Therapy: New Psychotherapies for a Changing Society*, ed. Violet Franks and Vasanti Burtle (Brunner/Mazel, New York, 1974), p. 32.

74   U. Halbreich et al., 'The clinical diagnosis and classification of premenstrual changes', *Canadian Journal of Psychiatry*, 30 (1985), pp. 489–97.

75   D. Rubinow et al., 'Premenstrual syndromes: past and future research strategies', *Canadian Journal of Psychiatry*, 30 (1985), p. 470.

76   Dalton, *Once a Month*, p. 206.

77   F. Stewart et al., *Understanding your Body: Every Woman's Guide to Gynecology and Health* (Bantam, New York, 1987), p. 551.

78   Dalton, *The Premenstrual Syndrome and Progesterone Therapy*.

79   Rubinow et al., 'Premenstrual syndromes: past and future research strategies', p. 471.

80   W. S. Maxson, 'The use of progesterone in the treatment of PMS', *Clinical Obstetrics and Gynecology*, 30 (1987), pp. 465–77.

81   Bardwick, 'The sex hormones, the central nervous system and affect variability in humans', p. 29.

82   Clare, 'Premenstrual syndrome: single or multiple causes?', p. 476.

83   D. Rubinow and A. P. Roy-Byrne, 'Premenstrual syndromes: overview from a methodological perspective', *American Journal of Psychiatry*, 141 (1984), p. 166.

84   W. Price et al., 'Premenstrual tension syndrome in rapid-cycling bipolar affective disorder', *Journal of Clinical Psychiatry*, 47 (1986), p. 416; Clare, 'Premenstrual syndrome: single or multiple causes', p. 477.

85   Clare, 'Premenstrual syndrome: single or multiple causes', p. 477.

86   W. R. Keye, 'Medical treatment of premenstrual syndrome', *Canadian Journal of Psychiatry*, 30 (1985), p. 483; Rubinow and Roy-Byrne, 'Premenstrual syndromes: overview from a methodological perspective', p. 167.

87   Halbreich et al., 'The clinical diagnosis and classification of premenstrual changes', p. 495.

88   Rubinow and Roy-Byrne, 'Premenstrual syndromes': overview from a methodological perspective', p. 169.

89   *The Lancet*, Editorials, 19 December 1981, pp. 1393–4; 22 October 1983, pp. 950–1.

90   R. Spitzer et al., 'Late luteal phase dysphoric disorder and DSM-III-R', *American Journal of Psychiatry*, 146, 7 (1989), pp. 894–5.

91   Clare, 'Premenstrual syndrome: single or multiple causes?', p. 479.
92   R. K. Koeske and C. F. Koeske, 'An attributional approach to mood and the menstrual cycle', *Journal of Personality and Social Psychology*, 31 (1975), pp. 473–8.
93   P. Chandra et al., 'Cultural variations in attitudes toward menstruation', *Canadian Journal of Psychiatry*, 37 (1992), pp. 196–8.
94   O. Janiger et al., 'Cross cultural study of premenstrual symptoms', *Psychosomatics*, 13 (1972), pp. 226–35.
95   Rubinow et al., 'Premenstrual syndromes: past and future research strategies', p. 470.
96   Clare, 'Premenstrual syndrome: single or multiple causes?', p. 479.
97   Ana D. Rivera-Tovar and Ellen Frank, 'Late luteal phase dysphoric disorder in young women', *American Journal of Psychiatry*, 147, 12 (1990), p. 1634.
98   P. Englander-Golden et al., 'Menstrual cycle as focus of study and self-reports of moods and behaviors', *Motivation and Emotion*, 2 (1978), pp. 75–86.
99   P. G. AuBuchon and K. S. Calhoun, 'Menstrual cycle symptomatology: the role of social expectancy and experimental demand characteristics', *Psychosomatic Medicine*, 47 (1983), pp. 35–45.
100 Cited in S. Laws, V. Hey and R. Eagan, *Seeing Red: The Politics of Premenstrual Tension* (Hutchinson, London, 1985), p. 86.
101 Bardwick, 'The sex hormones, the central nervous system and affect variability in humans', p. 32.
102 Joan S. Tucker et al., 'Premenstrual syndrome', *International Journal of Psychiatry in Medicine*, 21, 4 (1991), pp. 319–24.
103 Dalton, *The Premenstrual Syndrome and Progesterone Therapy*, p. 146.
104 Ibid., p. 146.
105 Dalton, *Once a Month*, pp. 119–20.
106 A. J. DuBrin et al., 'Premenstrual changes and job performance: guidelines for individuals and organisations', *Human Resource Management Australia*, 26, 2 (1988), p. 84.
107 Jean A. Hamilton et al., 'Evidence for a menstrual-linked artifact in determining rates of depression', *Journal of Nervous and Mental Disease*, 177, 6 (1989), pp. 359–65.
108 Jacquelyn N. Zita, 'The premenstrual syndrome "dis-easing" the female cycle', *Hypatia*, 3, 1 (1988), p. 93.

Chapter 4   Epistemological Problems with the Dominant Medical Psychiatric Perspective

1   The term is placed in quotes here as I do not wish to assume that it refers to a unified entity. This applies to all my uses of the term, even though the quotes are sometimes deleted for ease of reading.

2   Mary Boyle, 'The non-discovery of schizophrenia', in *Reconstructing Schizophrenia*, ed. Richard P. Bentall (Routledge, London, 1990).

3   R. L. Spitzer and Janet Williams (eds), *Diagnostic and Statistical Manual of Mental Disorders*, 3rd rev. edn (American Psychiatric Association, Washington, 1987), p. 194.

4   Victor Peralta et al., 'Are there more than two syndromes in schizophrenia?', *British Journal of Psychiatry*, 161 (1992), pp. 335–43; Didi Goldman et al., 'Bizarre delusions and DSM-III-R schizophrenia', *American Journal of Psychiatry*, 149 (1992), pp. 494–9.

5   David Pickar, 'Neuroleptics, dopamine, and schizophrenia', in *Psychiatric Clinics of North America*, 9 (1986), p. 35.

6   Robin M. Murray et al., 'Genetic vulnerability to schizophrenia', in *Psychiatric Clinics of North America*, 9 (1986), p. 3.

7   Lyn E. DeLisi et al., 'Gender differences in the brain: are they relevant to the pathogenesis of schizophrenia?', *Comprehensive Psychiatry*, 30 (1989), p. 197; Jeffrey D. Klausner et al., 'Clinical correlates of cerebral ventricular enlargement in schizophrenia', *Journal of Nervous and Mental Disease*, 180 (1992), p. 411.

8   Soloman Snyder, *Madness and the Brain* (McGraw-Hill, New York, 1974), p. 126.

9   F. Kallman, *The Genetics of Schizophrenia* (Augustin, New York, 1938).

10 Snyder, *Madness and the Brain*, p. 85.

11 Quoted in R. C. Lewontin et al., *Not in our Genes* (Pantheon, New York, 1984), pp. 219–20.

12 Peter McGuffin et al., 'Twin concordance for operationally defined schizophrenia', *Archives of General Psychiatry*, 41 (1984), p. 544.

13 R. D. Laing, *The Politics of Experience and the Bird of Paradise* (Penguin, Harmondsworth, 1971), p. 95.

14 See especially P. H. Wender et al., 'A psychiatric assessment of the adoptive parents of schizophrenics'; S. S. Kety et al., 'The adoptive families of adopted schizophrenics'; and D. Rosenthal et al., 'Schizophrenics' offspring reared in adoptive homes', all in *The Transmission of Schizophrenia*, ed. David Rosenthal and Seymour Kety (Pergamon, Oxford, 1968).

15 Kety et al., 'The adoptive families of adopted schizophrenics', p. 361.

16 Snyder, *Madness and the Brain*, p. 88.

17 In the study undertaken by Kety et al., 'The adoptive families of adopted schizophrenics.'

18 S. S. Kety et al., 'Genetic relationship within the schizophrenic spectrum: evidence from adoption studies', in *Critical Issues in Psychiatric Diagnosis*, ed. Robert L. Spitzer and Donald F. Klein (Raven Press, New York, 1979), p. 214.

19 Robin Sherrington et al., 'Localization of a susceptibility locus for schizophrenia on chromosome 5', *Nature*, 336 (1998), pp. 164–7.

20 James L, Kennedy et al., 'Evidence against linkage of schizophrenia to markers on chromosome 5 in a northern Swedish pedigree', *Nature*, 336 (1988), pp. 167–70.

21 Raymond R. Crowe et al., 'Lack of linkage to chromosome 5q11–q13 markers in six schizophrenia pedigrees', *Archives of General Psychiatry*, 48 (1991), pp. 357–61.

22 Joachim Hallmayer, 'Exclusion of linkage between the serotonin$_2$ receptor and schizophrenia in a large Swedish kindred', *Archives of General Psychiatry*, 49 (1992), pp. 216–19; Hans W. Moises, 'No linkage between D$_2$ dopamine receptor gene region and schizophrenia', *Archives of General Psychiatry*, 48 (1991), pp. 643–7.

23 Snyder, *Madness and the Brain*, p. 15.

24 Ibid., p. 37.

25 Ibid., p. 201.

26 Ibid., p. 209.

27 Ibid., p. 111 and p. 158.

28 Ibid., pp. 210–14.

29 See, for example, S. H. Snyder et al., 'Drugs, neurotransmitters and schizophrenia', *Science*, 184 (1974); Snyder, *Madness and the Brain*, ch. 11.

30 L. L. Prilipko, 'Biological studies of schizophrenia in Europe', *Schizophrenia Bulletin*, 12 (1986), p. 87.

31 See T. R. Sarbin and J. C. Mancuso, *Schizophrenia: Medical Diagnosis or Moral Verdict?* (Pergamon, New York, 1980), pp. 145–6.

32 D. Horribin, 'A singular solution for schizophrenia', *New Scientist*, 28 Feb. 1980, p. 642.

33 Nicholas A. Bercel, 'A study of the influence of schizophrenic serum on the behavior of the spider: zilla-x-notata', in *The Etiology of Schizophrenia* (Basic Books, New York, 1960), pp. 159–74.

34 R. W. Cowdry and F. K. Goodwin, 'Amine neurotransmitter studies and psychiatric illness', in Spitzer and Klein, *Critical Issues in Psychiatric Diagnosis*, p. 290.

35 D. L. Murphy and M. S. Buchsbaum, 'Neurotransmitter-related enzymes and psychiatric diagnostic entities', in Spitzer and Klein, *Critical Issues in Psychiatric Diagnosis*, p. 306.

36 Ibid., p. 307.

37 Ibid., p. 308.

38 F. Owen et al., 'Platelet monamine oxidase in schizophrenia', *Archives of General Psychiatry*, 33 (1976).

39 Murphy and Buchsbaum, 'Neurotransmitter-related enzymes and psychiatric diagnostic entities', p. 308.

40 Ibid., p. 310.

41 Mary V. Seeman and Philip Seeman, 'Psychosis and positron tomography', *Canadian Journal of Psychiatry*, 33 (1988), p. 299.

42 J. Lieberman et al., 'Qualitative assessment of brain morphology in acute and chronic schizophrenia', *American Journal of Psychiatry*, 149 (1992), p. 790.

43 Ibid., p. 790; Peter Buckley et al., 'Schizophrenia research: the problem of controls', *Biological Psychiatry*, 32 (1992), p. 215.

44 For recent summaries of research, see Terry L. Jernigan et al., 'Magnetic resonance imaging abnormalities in venticular nuclei and cerebral cortex

in schizophrenia', *Archives of General Psychiatry*, 48 (1991), pp. 881–90; Peter F. Liddle, 'PET scanning and schizophrenia – what progress?' *Psychological Medicine*, 22 (1922), pp. 557–60.

45 Seeman and Seeman, 'Psychosis and positron tomography', p. 299.

46 Karl Popper, *The Logic of Scientific Discovery* (Hutchinson, London, 1968), sections 19 and 20.

47 Seeman and Seeman, 'Psychosis and positron tomography', p. 304.

48 R. D. Laing and A. Esterson, *Sanity, Madness and the Family* (Penguin, Harmondsworth, 1964).

49 Nancy Scheper-Hughes and Anne M. Lovell (eds), *Psychiatry Inside Out: Selected Writings of Franco Basaglia* (Columbia University Press, New York, 1987).

50 T. R. Sarbin, 'Toward the obsolescence of the schizophrenia hypothesis', *Journal of Mind and Behavior*, 11 (1990), pp. 259–84; R. P. Bentall et al., 'Abandoning the concept of "schizophrenia"', *British Journal of Clinical Psychology*, 27 (1988), pp. 303–24.

51 Sarbin, 'Toward the obsolescence of the schizophrenia hypothesis', p. 280.

52 Elaine Showalter, *The Female Malady* (Virago, London, 1987), p. 204.

53 Spitzer and Williams (eds), *Diagnostic and Statistical Manual of Mental Disorders*, p. 67.

54 Ibid., pp. 68–9.

55 E. Eckert, 'Characteristics of anorexia', in *Anorexia Nervosa and Bulimia: Diagnosis and Treatment*, ed. J. Mitchell (University of Minnesota Press, Minneapolis, 1985), pp. 4–8; D. J. Ben-Tovim et al., 'Bulimia: symptoms and syndromes in an urban population', *Australian and New Zealand Journal of Psychiatry*, 23 (1989), pp. 73–80.

56 E. J. Button et al., 'A reappraisal of body perception disturbance in anorexia nervosa', *Psychological Medicine*, 7 (1977), p. 235.

57 J. Treasure, 'Psychopharmacological approaches to anorexia and bulimia', in *Anorexia and Bulimia Nervosa*, ed. D. Scott (New York University Press, New York, 1988), p. 128.

58 Treasure, 'Psychopharmacological approaches to anorexia and bulimia', pp. 129–30.

59 Ibid., p. 130; B. T. Walsh et al., 'Phenelzine vs placebo in 50 patients with bulimia', *Archives of General Psychiatry*, 45 (1988), p. 474.

60 Michael Strober, 'Family-genetic studies of eating disorders', *Journal of Clinical Psychiatry*, 52 (1991), pp. 9–10.

61 R. L. Palmer, *Anorexia Nervosa*, 2nd edn (Penguin, Harmondsworth, 1988), p. 16.

62 Ibid., p. 71.

63 Eckert, 'Characteristics of anorexia', p. 14.

64 A. J. Holland et al., ' "Anorexia nervosa": a study of 34 twin pairs and one set of triplets', *British Journal of Psychiatry*, 145 (1984), pp. 414–19.

65 Palmer, *Anorexia Nervosa*, p. 63.

66 Ibid., p. 55.

67 Ibid., p. 57.

68 Ibid., p. 63.

69 Treasure, 'Psychopharmacological approaches to anorexia and bulimia', p. 126.
70 Palmer, *Anorexia Nervosa*, p. 57.
71 Ibid., p. 59.
72 A. Levy, 'Neuroendocrine profile of bulimia nervosa', *Biological Psychiatry*, 25 (1989), pp. 98–109.
73 Treasure, 'Psychopharmacological approaches to anorexia and bulimia', p. 126.
74 B. Walch, 'Eating behavior of women with bulimia', *Archives of General Psychiatry*, 46 (1989), pp. 54–8.
75 Treasure, 'Psychopharmacological approaches to anorexia and bulimia', pp. 126–7.
76 P. Garfinkel and D. Garner, *Anorexia Nervosa: A Multi-Dimensional Perspective* (Brunner/Mazel, New York, 1982), p. 91.
77 Mentioned in E. Button, 'Review of K. M. Pirke et al. (eds), The Psychobiology of Bulimia Nervosa, Springs-Verlag, Berlin, 1988', *British Journal of Psychiatry*, 154 (1989), p. 583.
78 Levy, 'Neuroendocrine profile of bulimia nervosa', pp. 105–6.
79 Garfinkel and Garner, *Anorexia Nervosa*, p. 91.
80 H. Pope and J. Hudson, *New Hope for Binge Eaters* (Harper & Row, New York, 1985), p. 39.
81 Mentioned in Button, 'Review', p. 583.
82 J. C. Krieg et al., 'Brain morphology and regional cerebral blood flow in anorexia nervosa', *Biological Psychiatry*, 25 (1989), p. 1041.
83 Ibid., p. 1042; G. W. Hoffman et al., 'Cerebral atrophy in bulimia', *Biological Psychiatry*, 25 (1989), p. 894.
84 James E. Mitchell et al., 'Comorbidity and medical complications of bulimia nervosa', *Journal of Clinical Psychiatry*, 52 (1991), pp. 13–20.
85 N. Caskey, 'Interpreting anorexia nervosa', in *The Female Body in Western Culture*, ed. S. R. Suleiman (Harvard University Press, Cambridge, MA, 1986), p. 175.
86 H. Bruch, *Eating Disorders* (Basic Books, New York, 1973), p. 4.
87 S. Bordo, 'Anorexia nervosa: psychopathology as the crystallization of culture', in *Feminism and Foucault*, ed. I. Diamond and L. Quinby (Northwestern University Press, Boston, 1988), p. 88.
88 Ben Tovim et al., 'Symptom and syndromes in an urban population', p. 38.
89 Pope and Hudson, *New Hope for Binge Eaters*, p. 38.
90 S. Lee et al., 'Anorexia nervosa in Hong Kong: why not more in Chinese?', *British Journal of Psychiatry*, 154 (1989), pp. 683–8.
91 R. Berkow (ed.), *The Merck Manual of Diagnosis and Therapy*, 14th edn (Merck, Sharp & Dohme, Rahway, NJ, 1982), p. 1904.
92 J. F. Waller et al., 'Anorexia nervosa: a psychosomatic entity', in *Evolution of Psychosomatic Concepts*, ed. R. M. Kaufman and M. Heilman (Hogarth Press, London, 1965).
93 K. Chernin, *The Hungry Self* (Harper & Row, New York, 1985), p. 197.

94 H. Bruch, *The Golden Cage* (Vintage, New York, 1979), p. 112.
95 Ibid., p. 36.
96 Caskey, 'Interpreting anorexia nervosa', pp. 185–7.
97 Karl Popper, *Conjectures and Refutations* (Routledge & Kegan Paul, London, 1963), pp. 34–6.
98 J. Sayers, 'Psychodynamic and feminist approaches to anorexia and bulimia nervosa', in Scott, *Anorexia and Bulimia Nervosa*, p. 92.
99 Ibid., p. 90.
100 Ibid., p. 92.
101 R. Palmer and R. Oppenheimer, 'Childhood sexual experiences with adults', *International Journal of Eating Disorders*, 12 (1992), pp. 359–64.
102 Bordo, 'Anorexia nervosa', p. 112.
103 Ibid., p. 89.
104 Ibid., p. 95.
105 ibid., p. 96.
106 Ibid., p. 102.
107 S. L. Bartky, 'Foucault, femininity and the modernization of patriarchal power', in Diamond and Quinby, *Feminism and Foucault*, pp. 61–86.
108 E. Székely, *Never Too Thin* (Women's Press, Toronto, 1988), p. 18.
109 Ibid., p. 182.
110 Ibid., p. 190.
111 Ibid., p. 191.
112 Claire V. Wiseman et al., 'Cultural expectations of thinness in women', *International Journal of Eating Disorders*, 11 (1992), p. 85.
113 Quoted in B. Luscombe, 'Return to slender', *Who*, 19 July 1993, p. 49.
114 Peter Breggin, *Toxic Psychiatry* (Fontana, London, 1993).

Chapter 5 Women, Psychiatry and Criminality

1 See Carol Smart, *Women, Crime and Criminology* (Routledge & Kegan Paul, London, 1976).
2 Quoted in Smart, *Women, Crime and Criminology*, p. 133.
3 Smart, *Women, Crime and Criminology*, p. 87.
4 R. L. Spitzer and J. Williams (eds), *Diagnostic and Statistical Manual of Mental Disorders*, 3rd rev. edn (American Psychiatric Association, Washington, 1987), p. 323.
5 M. Oberman, 'The control of pregnancy and the criminalization of female-ness', *Berkeley Women's Law Journal*, 7 (1992), p. 12.
6 P. T. d'Orban, 'Women who kill their children', *British Journal of Psychiatry*, 134 (1979), p. 562.
7 Ibid., p. 563.
8 A Wilczynski, 'Images of women who kill their infants: the mad and the bad', *Women & Criminal Justice*, 2 (1991), p. 76.
9 Ibid., p. 84.

10   J. Bryson, *Evil Angels* (Viking, Ringwood, 1985), p. 203.
11   L. Harvey et al., 'Gender differences in criminal justice', *British Journal of Criminology*, 32 (1992), p. 42.
12   See J. Braithwaite, *Corporate Crime in the Pharmaceutical Industry* (Routledge & Kegan Paul, London, 1984).
13   C. Lombroso and W. Ferrero, *The Female Offender* (1895; Appleton, New York, 1985), p. 152.
14   C. R. Cloninger and R. B. Guze, 'Psychiatric illnesses in the families of female criminals', *British Journal of Psychiatry*, 122 (1973), p. 697.
15   C. R. Cloninger et al., 'The multifactorial model of disease transmission', *British Journal of Psychiatry*, 127 (1975), pp. 11–12.
16   A. Freedman et al., *Modern Synopsis of Comprehensive Textbook of Psychiatry/ II*, 2nd edn (Williams & Wilkins, Baltimore, 1976), p. 1297.
17   K. O. Christiansen, 'A preliminary study of criminality among twins', in *Biosocial Bases of Criminal Behavior*, ed. S. A. Mednick and K. O. Christiansen (Wiley, New York, 1977).
18   S. A. Mednick et al., 'Genetic influence in criminal behavior', in *Prospective Studies of Crime and Delinquency*, ed. K. Van Dusan and S. A. Mednick (Kluwer-Nijhoff, Boston, 1983).
19   L. J. Kamin, Letter to the editor, *Science*, 227 (1985), p. 983.
20   T. C. N. Gibbons, 'Female offenders', *British Journal of Hospital Medicine*, 9 (1971), pp. 279–86.
21   S. S. Shanok and D. D. Lewis, 'Medical histories of female delinquents', *Archives of General Psychiatry*, 38 (1981), pp. 211–13.
22   G. H. Gudjonsson and J. C. Roberts, 'Psychological and physiological characteristics of personality-disordered patients', in *Aggression and Dangerousness*, ed. D. P. Farrington and J. Guss (Wiley, New York, 1985).
23   S. Icard, *La femme pendant la periode menstruelle* (Felix Alan, Paris, 1890).
24   O. Pollak, *The Criminality of Women* (University of Pennsylvania Press, Philadelphia, 1950), p. 129.
25   Cited in K. Dalton, *Once a Month: The Menstrual Syndrome, its Causes and Consequences* (Harvester, London, 1978), p. 39.
26   Ibid., pp. 45–6.
27   Ibid., p. 101.
28   Cited in S. Laws et al., *Seeing Red: The Politics of Premenstrual Tension* (Hutchinson, London, 1985), p. 22.
29   R. R. Kinch and G. E. Robinson, 'Symposium: premenstrual syndrome – current knowledge and new directions', *Canadian Journal of Psychiatry*, 30 (1985), p. 467.
30   E. Meehan and K. MacRae, 'Legal implications of premenstrual syndrome: a Canadian perspective', *Canadian Medical Association Journal*, 135 (1986), p. 606.
31   S. Edwards, *Women on Trial* (University of New Hampshire Press, Manchester, 1984), p. 85.
32   D. T. d'Orban and J. Dalton, 'Violent crime and the menstrual cycle', *Psychological Medicine*, 10 (1980), pp. 353–9.

33   Ibid., p. 358.
34   D. Ellis and P. Austin, 'Menstruation and aggressive behavior in a correctional center for women', *Journal of Criminal Law, Criminology and Police Science*, 62 (1971), p. 392.
35   R. C. D. Wilson, 'Why do women commit arson?', *Canadian Medical Association Journal*, 139 (1988), p. 104.
36   Meehan and MacRae, 'Legal implications of premenstrual syndrome', p. 605.
37   Spitzer and Williams (eds), *Diagnostic and Statistical Manual of Mental Disorders*, pp. 344–5, 53, 331. I have elaborated this point in 'Psychiatry: marking criminals mad', *Australian Left Review*, 92 (1985).
38   For more on this, see my article 'Murder and madness', *Australian Left Review*, 104 (1988).
39   R. D. Mackay, 'Post-Hinckley insanity in the USA', *Criminal Law Review*, Feb. (1988), p. 91.
40   Meehan and MacRae, 'Legal implications of premenstrual syndrome', p. 605.
41   P. A. Fairall, 'Voluntariness, automatism and insanity: reflections on Falconer', *Criminal Law Journal*, 17 (1993), p. 86.
42   Mentioned in D. Kochan, 'Beyond the battered woman syndrome', *Hastings Women's Law Journal*, 1 (1989), pp. 100–1.
43   A. M. Madden, 'Clemency for battered women who kill their abusers', *Hastings Women's Law Journal*, 4 (1993), pp. 6–7.
44   C. K. Gillespie, *Justifiable Homicide: Battered Women, Self-Defense, and the Law* (Ohio State University Press, Columbus, 1989), p. 5.
45   Kochan, 'Beyond the battered woman syndrome', p. 109.
46   S. Yeo, 'Battered women: in between syndrome and conviction', *Current Issues in Criminal Justice*, 4 (1992), p. 76.
47   N. Stoller Shaw, 'Female patients and the medical profession in jails and prisons', in *Judge, Lawyer, Victim, Thief*, ed. N. Rafter and E. Stanko (Northwestern University Press, Boston, 1982), pp. 261–76.
48   H. R. Lamb and R. W. Grant, 'Mentally ill women in a county jail', *Archives of General Psychiatry*, 40 (1983), pp. 367–8.

Chapter 6   Contrasting Feminist Philosophies of Women and Madness: Oppression and Repression

1   Phyllis Chesler, *Women and Madness* (Avon, New York, 1972).
2   See in particular Luce Irigaray, *Je, tu, nous: Towards a Culture of Difference* (Routledge, New York, 1993); Margaret Whitford (ed.), *The Irigaray Reader* (Blackwell, Oxford, 1991), esp. section 1.
3   Chesler, *Women and Madness*, ch. 2.
4   Ibid., p. 47.
5   Ibid., pp. 18–19.

6   Ibid., ch. 1, note 17.
7   Ibid., p. 22.
8   Ibid., p. 46.
9   Ibid., p. 47.
10   Ibid., pp. 49–52.
11   Ibid., p. 27.
12   Ibid., p. 28.
13   Ibid., p. 50.
14   Ibid., p. 52.
15   Ibid., p. 282.
16   Ibid., p. 288.
17   Luce Irigaray is a Belgian feminist, loosely called a French feminist, and currently working in Amsterdam.
18   Luce Irigaray, 'Psychoanalytic theory: another look', in *This Sex which is Not One*, trans. C. Porter (Cornell University Press, Ithaca, NY, 1985).
19   Luce Irigaray, 'This sex which is not one', in *This Sex which is Not One*, p. 28.
20   Ibid., pp. 28–9.
21   Ibid., pp. 25–6.
22   Kiki Amsberg and Aafke Steenhuis, 'An interview with Luce Irigaray', trans. R. Van Krieken, *Hecate*, 9 (1983), pp. 191–201.
23   Luce Irigaray, 'I won't get AIDS', in *Je, tu, nous*, p. 65.
24   Luce Irigaray, 'Women's exile', *Ideology and Consciousness*, 1 (1977), pp. 62–75.
25   Irigaray, 'This sex which is not one', p. 25.
26   Irigaray, 'Women's exile', p. 64.
27   Ibid., pp. 64–5.
28   Irigaray, 'This sex which is not one', p. 29.
29   Luce Irigaray, 'The bodily encounter with the mother', trans. D. Macey, in *The Irigaray Reader*, ed. Margaret Whitford (Blackwell, Oxford, 1991), pp. 36–40.
30   Ibid., p. 36.
31   Ibid., p. 40.
32   Luce Irigaray, *Speculum of the Other Woman*, trans. G. C. Gill (Cornell University Press, Ithaca, NY, 1985), p. 140.
33   Luce Irigaray, 'Women-mothers, the silent substratum of the social order', trans. D. Macey, in *The Irigaray Reader*, pp. 47–8.
34   Irigaray, 'Women's exile', p. 74.
35   Irigaray, 'Women-mothers', p. 48.
36   Luce Irigaray, 'The poverty of psychoanalysis', trans. D. Macey, in *The Irigaray Reader*, p. 99.
37   Ibid., p. 92.
38   Luce Irigaray, 'And the one doesn't stir without the other', trans. H. V. Wenzel, *Signs: Journal of Women in Culture and Society*, 1, 7 (1981), p. 62.
39   Luce Irigaray, 'Your health: what, or who, is it?', in *Je, tu, nous*, pp. 102–3.
40   Irigaray, 'This sex which is not one', pp. 25–6.

41 Irigaray, 'Women's exile', p. 71.
42 Ibid., p. 66.
43 Irigaray, 'Your health', p. 104.
44 See Luce Irigaray, 'Why define sexed rights', in *Je, tu, nous*, pp. 81–92.
45 Irigaray, 'The power of discourse', in *This Sex which is Not One*, p. 78.
46 Irigaray, 'Women's exile', p. 65.
47 Irigaray, 'The power of discourse', p. 78.
48 Luce Irigaray, 'Women's discourse and men's discourse', in *Je, tu, nous*, p. 29.
49 Luce Irigaray, 'The cost of words', in *Je, tu, nous*, p. 127.
50 Luce Irigaray, 'The neglect of female genealogies', in *Je, tu, nous*, p. 20.
51 Irigaray, 'The cost of words', p. 128.
52 Irigaray, 'Women's discourse and men's discourse', p. 33.
53 Irigaray, 'The neglect of female genealogies', p. 17.
54 Luce Irigaray, 'Writing as a woman', in *Je, tu, nous*, pp. 47–8.
55 Irigaray, 'Why define sexed rights', pp. 86–8.
56 Luce Irigaray, 'The limits of the transference', trans. D. Macey, in *The Irigaray Reader*, p. 112.
57 Luce Irigaray, 'Religious and civil myths', in *Je, tu, nous*, pp. 25–6.

Chapter 7 Women, Creativity, Reason and Madness

1 Quoted in Barbara Ehrenreich and Deirdre English, *For Her Own Good* (Anchor Press, New York, 1978), pp. 91–2.
2 Charlotte Perkins Gilman, 'The yellow wallpaper', in *Charlotte Perkins Gilman Reader* (Pantheon, New York, 1980).
3 Charlotte Perkins Gilman, *The Man-Made World* (Charlton, New York, 1911), p. 260.
4 Charlotte Perkins Gilman, *Herland* (Pantheon, London, 1979), p. 137.
5 Nancy Milford, *Zelda Fitzgerald* (Penguin, Harmondsworth, 1974), p. 300.
6 F. Scott Fitzgerald, 'The crack-up', in *The Bodley Head Scott Fitzgerald*, vol. III (Bodley Head, London, 1960).
7 Ibid., pp. 388–9.
8 Sylvia Plath, *Ariel* (Faber & Faber, London, 1965), pp. 54–6.
9 Ibid., p. 19.
10 Sylvia Plath, *Letters Home*, ed. Aurelia Schober Plath (Faber & Faber, London, 1975).
11 Ibid., p. 479.
12 Ibid., p. 488.
13 Ted Hughes, Foreword to *Journals of Sylvia Plath* (Dial Press, New York, 1982).
14 Ed Cohen, 'Bitter fame', *New York Times*, 8 Oct. 1989, p. 19.
15 Phyllis Chesler, *Women and Madness* (Avon, New York, 1972), p. 12.
16 See in particular, Antonia White, *Beyond the Glass* (Virago, London, 1979).

17 Margaret Coombs, *The Best Man for This Sort of Thing* (Black Swan, Sydney, 1990).

18 Frances Farmer, *Will There Really Be a Morning?* (Fontana, New York, 1983), p. 11.

19 Kate Millett, *The Loony-Bin Trip* (Simon & Schuster, New York, 1990), p. 61.

20 Ibid., p. 143.

21 Ibid., p. 242.

22 Shelagh Lynne Supeene, *As for the Sky, Falling* (Second Story Press, Toronto, 1990), p. 231.

23 Marie Cardinal, *The Words to Say It*, trans. Pat Goodheart (Picador, London, 1984), p. 121.

24 Ibid., p. 79.

25 Ibid., p. 159.

26 See, for example, Joyce Carol Oates, *Angel of Light* (Dutton, New York, 1981); *Wonderland* (Gollancz, London, 1972); *Do with Me What You Will* (Gollancz, London, 1974); *Them* (Vanguard, New York, 1969); and *The Garden of Earthly Delights* (Gollancz, London, 1970).

27 Joyce Carol Oates, *Solstice* (Pan, London, 1986), p. 154.

28 Persimmon Blackbridge, Sheila Gilhooly and Kiku Hawkes, *Still Sane* (Press Gang, Vancouver, 1985).

29 Andrea Dworkin, *Mercy* (Arrow Books, London, 1990), p. 324.

30 Quentin Bell, *Virginia Woolf: A Biography*, vol. 1: *Virginia Stephen, 1882–1911* (Triad/Paladin, St Albans, 1976), p. 44.

31 Stephen Trombley, *'All that Summer She was Mad': Virginia Woolf and her Doctors* (Junction Books, London, 1981).

32 Ibid., p. 150.

33 Ibid., p. 10.

34 Virginia Woolf, '22 Hyde Park Gate', in *Virginia Woolf: Moments of Being: Unpublished Autobiographical Writings*, ed. Jeanne Schulkind (Sussex University Press, Brighton, 1976); Virginia Woolf, *Letters*, 6: *1936–1941*, ed. N. Nicolson and J. Trautmann (Harcourt Brace, New York, 1980), p. 3678.

35 Woolf, '22 Hyde Park Gate', p. 147.

36 Virginia Woolf, 'A sketch of the past', in Schulkind, *Virginia Woolf: Moments of Being*, p. 71.

37 Virginia Woolf, *Mrs Dalloway* (Zodiac Press, London, 1947), p. 110.

38 Ibid., p. 111.

39 Ibid., p. 112.

40 Ibid., p. 113.

41 Ibid., p. 204.

42 Ibid., p. 86.

43 Ibid., p. 133.

44 Quoted in Victoria Glendinning, *Vita: The Life of V. Sackville-West* (Weidenfeld & Nicolson, London, 1983), p. 175.

45 Virginia Woolf, 'Professions for women', in *Virginia Woolf: Women and Writing*, ed. Michèle Barrett (Women's Press, London, 1979), pp. 61–2.

46 Virginia Woolf, *To the Lighthouse* (Harcourt, Brace & World, New York, 1927), p. 253.

47 Ibid., p. 11.
48 Ibid., p. 51.
49 Virginia Woolf, 'Women and fiction', in Barrett, *Virginia Woolf: Women and Writing*, p. 49.
50 Virginia Woolf, *Orlando* (Hogarth Press, London, 1928), pp. 280–1.
51 Ibid., p. 76.
52 Woolf, *To the Lighthouse*, p. 73.
53 Woolf, 'Professions for women', p. 58.
54 Woolf, *To the Lighthouse*, p. 265.
55 Woolf, 'Women and fiction', p. 48.
56 Woolf, *Orlando*, pp. 73 and 231.
57 Virginia Woolf, *The Waves* (Penguin, Harmondsworth, 1931), pp. 54–5.
58 Mentioned by Barrett, *Virginia Woolf: Women and Writing*, p. 38.
59 Janet Frame, *An Angel at my Table: Autobiography 2* (Paladin, London, 1987), p. 96.
60 Ibid., p. 96.
61 Ibid., p. 78.
62 Ibid., pp. 141–2.
63 Janet Frame, *The Envoy from Mirror City: Autobiography 3* (Women's Press, London, 1985), p. 114.
64 Janet Frame, *To the Is-land: Autobiography 1* (Paladin, London, 1987), p. 136.
65 Ibid., p. 97.
66 Ibid., p. 156.
67 Quoted in Frame, *An Angel at my Table*, p. 14.
68 Ibid., p. 81.
69 Ibid., p. 95.
70 Ibid., p. 105.
71 Janet Frame, *Owls Do Cry* (Women's Press, London, 1985), p. 157.
72 Janet Frame, *Faces in the Water* (Avon, New York, 1961), p. 14.
73 Ibid., p. 75.
74 Frame, *An Angel at my Table*, p. 179.
75 Frame, *To the Is-land*, pp. 48–9.
76 Quoted in Frame, *To the Is-land*, p. 115.
77 Frame, *To the Is-land*, p. 148.
78 Frame, *The Envoy from Mirror City*, p. 84.
79 Ibid., p. 89.
80 Woolf, *Orlando*, p. 240.
81 Ibid., p. 151.
82 Ibid., p. 93.

Chapter 8   Beyond Psychiatry

1 R. L. Spitzer and J. Williams (eds), *Diagnostic and Statistical Manual of Mental Disorders*, 3rd rev. edn (American Psychiatric Association, Washington, 1987), p. 188.
2 Ari Kiev, *Transcultural Psychiatry* (Penguin, Harmondsworth, 1972).

3   Ruth Benedict, *Patterns of Culture* (Routledge, London, 1935), p. 193.
4   Kiev, *Transcultural Psychiatry*, pp. 39–40.
5   P. Clastres, *Society Against the State* (Blackwell, Oxford, 1977), p. 134.
6   Imre Lakatos, 'Falsification and the methodology of scientific research programmes', in *Criticism and the Growth of Knowledge*, ed. Imre Lakatos and Alan Musgrave (Cambridge University Press, Cambridge, 1970), p. 151.
7   Ibid., p. 118.
8   Ibid., pp. 91–7.
9   See, for example, P. K. Feyerabend, 'Consolations for the specialist', in Lakatos and Musgrave, *Criticism and the Growth of Knowledge*, pp. 214–19.
10   John Braithwaite, *Corporate Crime in the Pharmaceutical Industry* (Routledge & Kegan Paul, London, 1984), pp. 160–1.
11   Quoted in Braithwaite, *Corporate Crime in the Pharmaceutical Industry*, p. 208.
12   Ibid., pp. 208–9.
13   Ibid., p. 209.
14   Ibid., p. 214.
15   Peter Breggin, *Toxic Psychiatry* (Fontana, London, 1993), ch. 11.
16   Braithwaite, *Corporate Crime in the Pharmaceutical Industry*, p. 249.
17   Ibid., p. 211.
18   Ibid., ch. 3.
19   Luce Irigaray, 'The power of discourse', in *This Sex which is Not One*, trans. C. Porter (Cornell University Press, Ithaca, NY, 1985), p. 78.
20   David Miller, 'China's feats demand explanation', *The Times*, quoted in *The Australian*, 15 Sept. 1993.
21   Editorial, 'Fast footwork out of China', *Sydney Morning Herald*, 16 Sept. 1993.
22   D. Jacobsen, 'Unbelievable records', Letter to the Editor, *Sydney Morning Herald*, 16 Sept. 1993.
23   Michael Cowley, 'Debate rages over record-breakers', *Sydney Morning Herald*, 18 Sept. 1993.

Index